Exit Capitalism

Exit Capitalism explores a new path for cultural studies and re-examines key moments of British cultural and literary history. Simon During argues that the long and liberating journey towards democratic state capitalism has led to an unhappy dead end from which there is no imaginable exit.

In this context, what do the humanities look like? What's alive and what's dead in the culture and its heritage?

It becomes clear that the contemporary world order remains imperfect not just because it is unjust but because it cannot meet ethical standards produced in a past that still knew genuine hope. Simon During emphasizes the need to rethink the position of Christianity and religion in the past and, at a more concrete level, also analyzes how the decline of the socialist ideal and the emergence of endgame capitalism helped to produce both modern theory and cultural studies as academic fields.

Simon During teaches in the English Department at Johns Hopkins University, Baltimore MD. He is also a Professorial Fellow of the School of Culture and Communications at the University of Melbourne. His most recent books are *Modern Enchantments: The Cultural Power of Secular Magic* (2002) and *Cultural Studies: A Critical Introduction* (2005). He is also the editor of the three editions of the *Cultural Studies Reader*.

Exit Capitalism

Literary culture, theory, and
post-secular modernity

Simon During

 Routledge
Taylor & Francis Group

LONDON AND NEW YORK

First published 2010
by Routledge
2 Park Square, Milton Park, Abingdon, Oxon. OX14 4RN

Simultaneously published in the USA and Canada
by Routledge
270 Madison Ave, New York, NY 10016

Routledge is an imprint of the Taylor & Francis Group, an informa business

Typeset in Garamond by
Taylor & Francis Books
Printed and bound in Great Britain by
CPI Antony Rowe, Chippenham, Wiltshire

British Library Cataloguing in Publication Data
A catalogue record for this book is available from the British Library

Library of Congress Cataloging in Publication Data
During, Simon, 1950–
Exit capitalism: literary culture, theory and post-secular modernity / Simon During.
    p. cm.
  Includes bibliographical references and index.
  1. Capitalism and literature. 2. Literature, Modern – History and criticism.
3. Capitalism – Social aspects – History. 4. Culture – Study and teaching. 5.
Great Britain – Intellectual life – Twentieth century. I. Title.
  PN51.D87 2009
  809'.933553 – dc22
                                2009005277

ISBN10: 0-415-24654-7 (hbk)
ISBN10: 0-415-24655-5 (pbk)
ISBN10: 0-203-87264-9 (ebk)

ISBN13: 978-0-415-24654-5 (hbk)
ISBN13: 978-0-415-24655-2 (pbk)
ISBN13: 978-0-203-87264-2 (ebk)

Contents

Introduction

Spring 2008. Out there where history happens, neo-liberalism is coming to an end while around the world, in fits and starts, disbelief slips into panic.

But not here, not yet – I'm lunching at the Sydney Museum of Modern Art's rather up-market restaurant, having just visited this year's Biennale exhibition. Under the punning rubric "Revolutions: Forms that Turn" it presents contemporary works alongside hallowed pieces from the European historic avant garde, all relating somehow or other to the concept "revolution." It's been a rewarding morning, an experience of contemporary tastefulness and reflection. And now my carefully prepared beetroot salad blends subtly with an Otago pinot noir. The sea, about fifty feet away, is a lavish blue: on a sparkling morning it civilizes the city.

Quite suddenly, looking up, I see the Biennale's publicity sign. It is positioned exactly between the Opera House – that icon of Sydney's Pacific glamor – and an elegant Mediterranean-style apartment building on the harbor's far shore. It reads "Is this freedom?"

Is this freedom? Whatever it is, it's pretty damn good. And the sign only makes it better. The question it poses is so right because, as its apparent dumbness unfurls into an interesting complexity, it's directed flatteringly precisely at *me*, that is, at *us*, at the relatively small group who will attend to and realize its irony, who will appreciate its subtle knotting of the connections between (1) the institutionally sanctioned art that I have just been visiting, and which is, at least for the moment, preserved from economic fear, (2) the now merely historical will to political revolution which the exhibition, fashionably acknowledging capitalism's crippling failures, treats with ironized nostalgia, and (3) the relative if somewhat fragile privilege which allows me to spend a morning at the gallery completed by an expensive lunch on a sunny morning among Sydney's civic beauty. Here, as finance capital runs to the state for protection, I'm near the centre of contemporary Australia's vortex of prosperous cosmopolitanism and democratic energy out of which the art show, down to its signage, delivers all its sensory and intellectual pleasures, especially to those whom the education system has cared for most.

If that knotting and the reminder of revolutionary desire, muted as it is, also ignites a flicker of loathing for and within the experience itself; if it sparks a flash of hatred for capitalism's capacity to spill forth so much misery alongside so much happiness, so much stupidity alongside so much intelligence, so much that is ugly alongside so much that is beautiful, so much cynicism alongside so much belief; if it sparks a flash of hatred for bourgeois radicalism's complacency (mine included) as well as for the art world's complicit cunning and mere suggestiveness – then, once more, all the better. Since about 1760 (when Edmund Burke wrote his treatise on the sublime and the beautiful) it has been recognized that aesthetic experiences are only intensified by smudges of darkness.

I'd like to think that this book is written as a way out of – *against* – that generic experience. Written from within the somewhat protected citadel of the academic humanities, it seeks out exits from a social and cultural order I will call "democratic state capitalism."[1] By my lights, that order has become unsupportable at the same time as, and in part because, its crucial structures have become unassailable and its replacement unimaginable. Democratic state capitalism is now, as Marcel Gauchet has said of democracy, a horizon which cannot be passed ("l'horizon indépassable," Gauchet 2007: 16). It is important to protect ourselves against an easy misunderstanding of what this proposition here entails: my claim is that we find ourselves not at the sanctioned "end of history" but at something like its opposite. Capitalism without hope, hopeless capitalism, endgame capitalism.

Much of this book, placed in no-exit indirection, explores, from a literary-historical point of view, certain paths through which we have arrived at where we now are. But I hope that my readers don't have difficulty seeing that a path out of endgame capitalism is nonetheless where I am pointed.

Part I consists of three scholarly literary-historical essays which examine the mid-eighteenth-century moment in England when market-orientated culture gradually displaced the old oligarchic order dominated by the Anglican Church and the (still largely rural) landed classes. The first chapter describes a lost world of gentlemanly intellectual production and thinks about what our relation to this exotic, if sometimes strangely modern, domain of life and writing can now be. The second concentrates on market-orientated culture at a moment of fast and transformative expansion: it explores certain structures of feelings that were produced in the intimacy that bound the book trade to patent medicine vendors in the mid-eighteenth century. The third analyzes how the category "interesting" became a key term of praise around the same time. The tribute that we continue to pay to being interesting (in full display at the Sydney Biennale) has, I argue, helped displace the sympathetic imagination's political usefulness.

The book's second part is more obviously contemporary in scope. Its first essay contends that the Australian-born novelist Christina Stead, a committed Stalinist, deployed her communism to write wonderful yet underappreciated fictions which present a profoundly disabused account of capitalist subjectivity, but that her political affiliation, along with her refusal of cultural nationalism and identity politics, has prevented her from becoming sufficiently canonized within the contemporary structures of world literature. Two of the next essays are more self-inspecting: they make a case that British cultural studies (a discipline or post-discipline to which this book still just belongs) is a product of the 1960s new left's failure to renovate socialism, and that cultural studies' relation to theory (and today to Alain Badiou's post-Maoism in particular) needs to be assessed in that light. They show that today theory and cultural studies are two halves of a broken whole that do not add up, and that other, perhaps more "conservative," theo-political positions may be more effective in the difficult task of distancing oneself from endgame capitalism. Chapter 7 deals explicitly with what has been an intermittent theme throughout, namely the notion of Latin Christianity as capitalism's lost other, at least in certain of its institutions. Written in response to Charles Taylor's *A Secular Age*, it turns away from Taylor's spiritual anthropology to consider how the mundane might provide an outside to the division between the religious and the secular.

It will be apparent even from these brief remarks that this is not a book that easily fits disciplinary compartments. I take no pride in that, since I believe that the disciplined academic humanities need all the help they can get just because in the end they don't fit particularly comfortably into the contemporary social order. The humanities disciplines are worthwhile in part just because they can't overcome a certain obsolescence.

Given that my disciplinary ecumenicalism may be a little disorientating, it might help to note in advance two further broad stakes for these essays. While I do think of this as a British cultural studies book, it is both more historical and more literary than most cultural studies now is. In fact the book's model is Raymond Williams, although it shares nothing with him politically, and its historical cases adhere to a very different understanding of British cultural history from his. I believe that the focus on the contemporary which has been more or less definitive of cultural studies since Williams's time is now a crippling limit, not because, as a historicist might say, to understand the present you need to understand the past, but because the past is where other presents than the one we inhabit can be engaged and imagined. That's become especially important since 1968. And cultural studies' habitual suspicion of literary studies (which is less apparent today than it was ten years ago) makes (or made) sense in terms of academic self-assertion (the new field had to detach itself from English's domination) but makes no sense intellectually or – outside the university – politically.[2] Literary criticism, which contemporary cultural studies rarely gets the point of, is too important to be left either to the narrow methods and purposes of professionalized literary criticism or to the superficiality and pieties of the commercial media.

Second, the book explores a non-disciplinary theme that it never treats directly at length, namely the narrowing of the distinction between radical conservatism and radical leftism as a result of the disappearance of practical alternatives to democratic state capitalism. Today strange convergences along these lines are everywhere to be found, especially in relation to religion: for instance, that between postcolonial anti-secularists and rightist defenders of theocracy; that between green asceticism and orthodox Christian anti-accumulation thought; that between various modes of anti-progressivism, since the refusal of the concept of progress and thence of all "progressivism" has become a base note of advanced political theory, whether from the left or from the right. Let us put it like this: in endgame capitalism the old pro-mises of secular modernity begin to falter at the point at which they are being thought of as realized. As a result, although revealed religion cannot be revived in any intellectually respectable way, new post-secular occasions for leaps of faith appear along with a (skeptical) attention to the history of (defenses of) faith and Church institutions.

These chapters have been written during a period when I moved from one academic system to another, and their topics, disciplinary connections, and arguments were formed in the move from Australia to the United States. The book could not have been written outside the stimulation I found and the help I was given at both the Melbourne and the Hopkins English departments: I'd mention in particular David Bennett, John Frow, Amanda Anderson, Michael Moon and Frances Ferguson. Many chapters were written for particular events: "Quackery and the emergence of the modern literary marketplace" (2004) was first given at Prato, Italy, where I was invited by Peter Cryle and CHED; "Interesting" (2001) was first given in Adelaide for a conference at the Humanities Research Centre, to which I was invited by Paul James; the Christina Stead chapter was originally written to be given at an ASAL conference in Brisbane to which I was invited by Rob Dixon; "Socialist ends" (2005) was first given at Brisbane for a CHED seminar on the "History of Theory" under Ian Hunter's invitation; "Completing secu-larism" (2008) was first given at Yale at a seminar on Charles Taylor's book to which I was invited by Michael Warner and Craig Calhoun (and Michael Warner's response to my presentation led me to revise the paper); "Against capitalism" was first given at the Asia Research Institute at the National University of Singapore, to which I was invited by Ryan Bishop, John Phillips, Alan Chun and Chua Beng Huat and then in more developed form for Justin Clemens and the theory group at the University of Melbourne. Justin's comments on a draft version of this chapter meant, again, that I radically revised my summary of Badiou's thought. (Its errors remain mine, though.) Peter Holbrook's very perceptive critique of that chapter was no less useful to me. All the chapters have been presented more than once at various institutions, I can't mention them all but in almost all cases my thoughts were revised in the light of discussion. I thank my colleagues for that. In the end, academic work, even where it is most marked by individualism, is institutionally collective: that's one of the things I love about it.

S.D.

Part I

Modernizing the English literary field

Chapter 1

Church, state, and modernization
Literature as gentlemanly knowledge after 1688

Methodologically, this chapter belongs neither to literary criticism, nor to literary history as conventionally understood, nor to cultural studies, even in its historical modes. It is, instead, a form of historical sociology, which considers literature as a social institution with specifiable material interests, organizational structures and social functions rather than simply as a body of writing. But a caveat needs to be entered at once. The moment I am concerned with, the long eighteenth century, is, of course, when the term "literature" came to cover not written knowledge available to the literate in general but the kind of writing produced specifically by men and women of letters – and, in particular, imaginative writing.

From the sociological perspective, this change of "literature's" denotation is a consequence of a mutation of social function that the literary field underwent across the century.[1] To put a familiar case succinctly: literature became less centered on polite learning, including classical scholarship, and more centered on sympathetic imagination and the suspension of disbelief. At the same stroke, it also claimed a greater role in moral education. As it thereby extended its capacity for social agency and engagement, new readerships, particularly among women, were created alongside new genres and hierarchies of genres. By the time of Walter Scott's death in 1832, realist prose fiction had become dominant.[2]

This restructuring of the literary world is usually understood through categories like commercialization, political liberalization, secularization, domestification, the emergence of the Habermasian public sphere, and the feminization of literary life – categories that can be grouped together under the head of "modernization."[3] While the modernization model cannot be discounted (in fact the relation between liberty, commerce, and the increase of the "trade of writing" was often adduced at the time), I want to argue that it is inadequate to describe the conditions under which the literary world underwent transformation.[4] Indeed, over the past twenty or so years a rather different account of eighteenth-century social and intellectual history has appeared in the scholarship of historians like J. C. D. Clark and J. G. A. Pocock.[5] Here the period is not analyzed as anticipating a modernized future but as imbricated in its pasts. In Clark's case particularly, eighteenth-century England becomes a "confessional state" in which political differences remain primarily expressions of religious differences, and church–state relations are key to social, cultural, and intellectual formations.[6] A secular polity cannot be assumed. In a similar spirit, a series of recent studies have made the case that the Anglican religion played a more significant role in public life and attracted wider support and participation than had been recognized by earlier historians, undercutting accounts which present the period as primarily governed by the modernizing forces just mentioned.[7]

These revisionist accounts, whose impulse has indubitably been conservative but whose insights need not be contained within conservativism, have only been spottily absorbed by literary historians, and when they have been so absorbed, have often lapsed into only partly persuasive arguments that particular writers were more closely connected to Jacobitism than previous scholarship had supposed.[8] Yet they do allow us to inquire into the degree to which the transformation of literature's social function and status in England can be understood as an – admittedly highly mediated – effect of the shift of relations between church, market, and state after 1688. More particularly they can provide the terms through which we can understand how a new literary formation came into being from within the older, only partly secularized concepts and institutional structures of polite learning. Such a revisionist account can also help us understand how older forms of literary production and knowledge responded to mutations in the literary field, since the "modernization" of the literary field cannot effectively be understood macrologically as the smooth transformation from one set of structures and conditions into another but rather as the outcome of continual local frictions and exchanges between older and newer formations, both themselves under constant transformation. This chapter presents itself as an account of two moments in which newer, secular formations energetically brushed against older, non-secular ones – and vice versa.

Church–state relations

To this end it is necessary to point to the church–state relations that are most relevant to the locations where old and new literary formations interacted with particular intensity. The 1688 English revolution put in place a quasi-confessional (*pace* Clark) state in which the established church retained important privileges but which tolerated other confessions, despite severe formal (if consistently obviated) civil penalties against those outside the Anglican fold.[9] At a more abstract level, once the church was detached from and subordinated to the state under the terms of the 1689 settlement, sovereignty was no longer securely legitimated by religion. These new state–church relations were passionately experienced as, and through, division, oppression, and efforts at reconciliation.[10] A series of negotiations between the established church and the state in the period immediately after the deposition of the Stuart regime led both to a structural connection between the rural clergy and the oppositional "country" groupings as well as widespread sympathy for the small breakaway group of clergy, the so-called nonjurors, who could not accept the terms of the revolutionary settlement (the breaching of apostolic succession and the overthrow of the divine right of kings) and who later refused to sign oaths of allegiance to new monarchs in 1701 and 1715 (Bennett 1975; Mather 1992: chapter 1). A slow reconnection of the church hierarchy to state administration during the post-1714 period of Whig hegemony, although threatened by anticlerical acts like the Quaker tithe and Mortmain Bills of 1736, reached its apogee under the last years of the Walpole and Pelham administrations. This was a remarkable feat, since the Whig hegemony was also consistently supported by the Dissenting churches largely in response to the continuing threat of Jacobitism and the High Church interest.

During this period the Anglican clergy became increasingly professionalized, increasingly absorbed into state politics, as I say, and increasingly drawn from filiative chains within the elite (in the latter half of the century about half of all clergymen were the sons of clergymen, Holmes 1982) In many rural parishes, clergymen were uncontested intellectual leaders, not least through their sermons (which became a routine element of their professional duties after about 1710) and their role as educators. They held considerable control over channels for the dissemination of political and ethical discourse. The church's strong presence within the education system, not least through its influence in the universities, allowed it to select and recruit talented youth. Edmund Gibson, Richard Hurd and Thomas Percy's careers stand as examples: all became bishops though they were born into plebeian families.[11]

The American Revolutionary War marked a break within this structure, since it effectively shunted the Dissenters along with the Anglican Low Church into political opposition. The founding of the republican state in North America enabled a certain transference of the dissident spirit from religious Nonconformity to secular political radicalism at home (Bonwick 1977: 199–215; Bradley 1990: 121–58). And from the 1780s, the Hanoverian church–state alliance began to dissolve, in part because the church was no longer a central organ of social control; in part because the promise of toleration was reneged upon (the elder Pitt's rejection of the repeal of the Test and Corporation Acts in 1787 was a pivotal event in this regard); and in part because the church had become less and less connected, affectively and discursively, to large segments of the population, riven as it was by competition from evangelical "new birth" Christianity on the one side and skepticisms and deisms on the other.[12] By the second decade of the nineteenth century, conservative intellectuals, all Anglicans, facing various resistances both to the old oligarchic, paraconfessional state structures and to the newer industrial capitalism, echoed old ecclesiastical social theory by calling for a new stronger church–state alliance to resist democratization and industrialization, with Coleridge's *Constitution of Church and State* (1830), written against Irish Catholic emancipation, leading the way. Quickly too, the Tractarians revived the old theo-politics of the nonjurors with their calls for Anglicanism to separate itself from the state, and to reinvent itself as an autonomous and solely legitimate ethical institution.

Literature, thought of as written polite learning, was largely if decreasingly shaped within the structures that comprise this history, mainly because the Anglican church remained the largest and richest single institution engaged in intellectual production over the period.[13] For heuristic purposes, it is possible to divide literary production over the period into two blocs. The first, aimed at the marketplace, disseminated practical information, discipline, and various kinds of readerly excitement. In the mid-century, this bloc was dominated by market-attuned book-trade businessmen who turned away from collaborative enterprises, and concentrated on distribution (export) marketing, periodicals, and the development of new formats (especially periodicals), primarily pitching their wares towards discretionary consumers from the middling ranks.[14] The second was produced from within the gentlemanly world at whose intellectual and material center lay the established church: it was Burke who was to say that "European civilization" was formed by two forces, "the spirit of a gentleman and the spirit of religion," and, like many of his genteel contemporaries, Burke did not think of these two spirits as separable (Burke 2003: 67). The English universities are to be included in this second bloc, since they effectively formed part of the established ecclesiastical apparatus.[15] Like market-orientated writing, gentlemanly, churchly literature was internally various, although it was often produced for selection mechanisms that intermittently governed professional entry and advancement within the church. It was characteristically aimed at maintaining the episcopate's intellectual legitimacy and social power despite schisms within the church itself (and was, for instance, made available in church-owned libraries for that reason). Theological, devotional, scholarly and pedagogic writing poured from the presses, with sermons being a staple of the publishing industry through the period (although admittedly collections of sermons from both the established church and Dissent were often published by Dissenting ministers).[16] This bloc also covered more discretionary forms of learning as produced by writers supported by the Anglican church and in particular by relatively leisured and intellectually trained members of the country clergy. Local antiquarianism and natural philosophy were at the forefront here.

Alongside these two main blocs we can add two more: print primarily of professional interest to lawyers and medical practitioners; and the printed intellectual production of those groups outside or on the margins of the established church, namely republicans, Dissenters and, especially in the period

from about 1689 to about 1740, and from the other side of the political
spectrum, the nonjurors.[17] These groups have occupied recent scholarly
attention to a degree that is incommensurate with their significance at the
time, not least because women had more license to participate in print culture among Dissenters and republicans than among Anglicans (although key
women intellectuals in the immediate Restoration period were Tory royalists,
such as Aphra Behn and Mary Astell), and also because rational Dissent, in
particular, figures so prominently in the genealogy of secular radicalism, not
least through the sponsorship of the Dissenting academies.[18] This is not at
all to deny that these minor blocs were also important to eighteenth-century
literary culture, nor to claim that they were wholly isolated from the two
main streams.

In the end, commercial literature possessed most energy, and certainly that
was where the genres that would come to dominate the literary world were
developed, in part because it too provided a relatively welcoming environment for women to participate.[19] But we should not think of the gentlemanly literature of the orthodox as undynamic over the period, nor, indeed,
as outside of commercial play, given that a significant proportion of the
capital which supported intellectual life over the period was channeled
through the church and those associated with it. For instance, Jan Fergus,
drawing on information from two provincial booksellers' archives in the
period 1744–1807, argues that "almanacs, school texts, Bibles, common
prayer books, divinity, sermons, history and belles letters were all much
more popular than novels" (Fergus 2006: 7). Indeed, it would be an error to
think of the market-orientated and gentlemanly-ecclesiastical blocs except as
engaged in constant, often mutually supportive interaction and exchange.
Commercially-minded booksellers like John Newbery published periodicals
aimed at the theological market such as *The Religious Magazine*. A successful
market enterprise like Edmund Cave's *Gentleman's Magazine* could come to
prominence by promoting a competition (first prize £50) for the best poem
on a religious topic, as it did in 1734 (Carlson 1938: 214 ff.). The two blocs
also often combined forces in educational writing in which both the church
and the market had an interest. Moreover, the gentlemanly bloc routinely
called upon the market bloc just to get its writing into print, even where it
sought to subvent the booksellers through subscription or self-publishing
(hence the key role of intellectually engaged printers like William Bowyer,
Samuel Buckley, Samuel Richardson, John Nichols, and William Sandby).
Several of the most prominent authors in the market for imaginative writing
were clergymen: Laurence Sterne, Edward Young, Richard Graves, and Charles
Churchill, to name just four of the more popular. Ecclesiastical careers could
also be built on market-orientated scholarship, as in the case of Thomas
Newton, Bishop of Bristol, onetime fashionable London preacher, and editor
of the bestselling, standard edition of Milton. And, more important still,
clergymen were crucial to the characterology of a purely market-orientated

genre – the sentimental-realist novel. Parson Adams, Yorick, the Vicar of Wakefield, Elizabeth Inchbald's Catholic priest Dorriford in *A Simple Story* and Jane Austen's Edmund Bertram in *Mansfield Park* come immediately to mind.

At this point we can turn to two particularly revealing intersections of the market and the gentlemanly-ecclesiastical literary blocs. The first is John Nichols's prodigies of labor and print output from the middle of the 1770s to the 1820s, of which the finest fruit was his monumental nine-volume *Literary Anecdotes* with its eight-volume sequel, *Illustrations of Eighteenth Century Literary History*, the last volumes of which were, admittedly, edited by Nichols's son (Duitz 1968). These books provide a significant amount of the information that allows us to map the period's literary history to this day, even though they can be understood as a rebuke to the transformations within the print culture of their time. The second, from the heart of the gentlemanly-ecclesiastical bloc, is the writing of a group of authors closely associated with William Warburton, Bishop of Gloucester, sometimes known as the Warburtonians. As we shall see, this group developed some of the concepts that would become central to secular art literature.

John Nichols and *Literary Anecdotes*

Nichols was primarily a printer. He had been apprenticed in the 1750s to the Bowyer firm, whose then proprietor, William Bowyer the younger, was a nonjuror who played a significant part in bringing Tory and nonjuring scholarship and polemic into print from the 1720s, but who also had lucrative contracts with the Whig-dominated House of Commons.[20] We can take the 1721 two-volume folio edition of Charles Leslie's self-published *Theological Works* (a source of much subsequent anti-liberal political theology) and the fine 1732 illustrated edition of Theodore Bathurst's Latin translation of Edmund Spenser's *The Shphearde's Calender* as prestigious expressions of the firm's interests at that time.[21] But those interests ranged widely, and included important books in Welsh and monuments of book production such as William Cheselden's astonishing osteological atlas, *Osteographia*, whose illustrations of pathological skeletal anatomy seem (in this context) to belong not just to medical science but to ideology, invoking as they do the human "mortification" that so underpins contemporary absolutist theories of sovereignty. Finally, and tellingly, the printshop produced a number of books on the history of printing and typography, an expression of a cult of the book which seems to have been particularly intense in this political-religious grouping.[22]

In 1766 Nichols became Bowyer's partner and controlled the shop from the mid-1770s when he purchased a share of the *Gentleman's Magazine*, whose editor he became. In addition to his work as a printer and magazine editor, he compiled a series of books mainly aimed at keeping the literary culture of the first half of the century in circulation. Many of these transposed into print manuscripts, letters, and papers that he had personally acquired. Indeed, many relied on information solicited by him either via the correspondence columns of the *Gentleman's Magazine* or privately. Such books included an edition of Swift's minor works, Steele's letters, Benjamin Hoadly's sermons and pamphlets, Francis Atterbury's writings and papers, documents around Hogarth's life, and of course the *Literary Anecdotes* and *Literary History*. The "anecdote" genre was well established in the later eighteenth century, examples being William Seward's *Anecdotes of some Distinguished Persons* (1795–97), Richard Gough's *Anecdotes of British Topography* (1768), and the more widely known *Anecdotes of English Painting* (1762–71) by Horace Walpole. In effect, the genre consisted of works that collected together fragments of information or recollection, whether transmitted orally, in manuscript, or in print, without organizing them either as history or as biography. Certainly it possessed little of the essayistic and reflective quality later ascribed to it by Isaac Disraeli (Disraeli 1849).

Nichols's contribution to the genre began as a record of the books printed by the Bowyer firm – it was first published under the title *Anecdotes of William Bowyer*. Nichols listed Bowyer's publications in chronological order and added biographical information about their authors in footnotes that could stretch across pages, drowning the body of the text. Later volumes of the *Anecdotes* and the *Literary History* extended the range of this feat of memorialization by elaborating on what had become a key feature of the *Gentleman's Magazine* – the obituary. They are effectively collections of extended death notices and literary remains addressed to an uncertain posterity.[23] It was as if Nichols were trying to ensure that the lived world of post-1688 gentlemanly polite learning would be transmitted into a future in which it was being displaced by the modern literary institution. Indeed, although quite successful as a book-trade entrepreneur, Nichols was entrenched in the fading literary bloc: his firm failed to keep pace with contemporary developments such as the separation of retail, distribution, publishing, and printing arms, or the emphasis on fiction.[24] The paucity of fiction printed by the Bowyer firm is striking: leaving aside exceptional cases such as the second edition of *Robinson Crusoe* (demand for that book was so strong that much of the London trade become involved in printing it), only one novel is listed in its ledgers until the 1740s, the little-known *Rosalinda: A Novel* (1733).

Nichols himself was probably not politically partisan – perhaps he even began as a Whig – and he is on record as an admirer of Richard Steele. But his publishing enterprises are unambiguously Tory in their interests and range: thus one of his partners in producing the *Literary Anecdotes*, and more especially its sequel, was the Tory politician and lawyer George Hardinge, Queen Charlotte's attorney, and the notorious defender of those charged with property damage in the 1791 Birmingham "king and country" riots against Joseph Priestley. Nichols's Tory inclination was encouraged by the Bowyer firm being so entrenched in the nonjuring networks during his halcyon period from about 1720 to 1740, but he shared it with his readership (both for the *Gentleman's Magazine* and for his various document compilations) who largely belonged to the country gentry and particularly the country clergy, which began the century linked to the country interest and especially the Tory country interest and ended it as evangelicals or as Burkean conservatives awaiting the Anglo-Catholicism to come, as we shall see in regard to the Warburtonians.[25] Furthermore Nichols's feats of memorialization and retrieval can be twinned with the radical sentimentalism of novelized clergymen like Yorick and Parson Adams, since both are expressions of the slow ecclesiastical displacement from the emergent social sectors of the time – urban commerce and secular professionalism – as well as political interests bound to these sectors.

At any rate what Nichols retrieves from the Bowyer archive in the first volumes of his magnum opus *Literary Anecdotes* is a literary institution very different from that organized by successful book-trade contemporaries such as the Robinsons, John Murray, James Lackington, Henry Coburn, and William Lane. He recovers a world dominated by learned, productive clergymen, clustered in families, and often suspicious or contemptuous of the Whig hegemony as well as (in the early period) nonjuror scholars who remained outside the state-sanctioned church. For him, their contribution constitutes what the period's literature *was*. The resonant names include Hilkiah Bedford, Joseph Bingham, Thomas Brett, Thomas Carte, Edmund Chishull, William Cole, Jeremy Collier, Thomas Deacon, Henry Dodwell, Elizabeth Elstob, Zachary Grey, George Hickes, Samuel Jebb, William Law, Thomas Smith, John Urry, and Thomas Wagstaffe, most of whom have been forgotten by literary history, despite Nichols's efforts, as has, indeed, the literary field of which they were ornaments.[26]

In addition to the ordinary classical fare of polite learning, the writers memorialized by Nichols produced pioneering research on oriental languages and Hebrew, whether in extension of an interest in "primitive Christianity" and patristic history, dating back at least to Archbishop Laud's time, or (in the case of the Hutchinsonians) in the interests of anti-Newtonianism. (See Miller 2001 for the emergence of this scholarship.) They also made important inroads into knowledge of what would later come to be called the Anglo-Saxon dialect, although not so much to recover a tradition of English liberty but of a religious England not yet divided by the Reformation.[27] The Bowyer shop authors also printed masses of sermons and pamphlets combating arianism, socinianism and latitudinarianism. And they put into print a vast array of topographical and local historical information (sometimes original, sometimes transcribed from records and manuscript archives, sometimes reprinted), occasionally out of self-interest, since rural clergymen could increase their income from tithes and glebes by retrieving lost and ancient rights from parish records. As Jeremy Gregory puts it, "parochial income could only be properly collected if the incumbent had a good grasp of local history."[28] Finally the firm printed some of the natural philosophy that was flowing from the church through this period, although, given the political nature of its networks, less than many of its competitors.

This literary production, like Nichols's own, was allied to the accelerated institutionalization of literary knowledge across a number of spheres. That is to say, Nichols was involved in preservation and recollection but he was also participating in a process by which writing of all kinds joined the public sphere in an organized fashion so as to attract new forms of sociability and display. The gentlemanly-ecclesiastical bloc here helps to create polite learning as a public institution and utility. Examples of this process include the donation of large collections of printed and manuscript materials to libraries, with the Tory politician Robert Harley making the most ostentatious contribution. The professionalization of librarianship and record keeping was important, too, with Andrew Ducarel, the Lambeth librarian under Secker's patronage, playing a particularly important role, along with Thomas Astle, indexer of the Harley manuscripts and rationalizer of state record keeping. At the same time formal associations of antiquarians were developed, with the prestigious Society of Antiquaries (1717) at their head. Semiformal scholarly clubs such as the Spalding Gentlemen's Society also helped archives find their way into the public sphere – for instance, one of its members, the clergyman and antiquarian Samuel Pegg, appointed Nichols his literary executor, thereby transmitting another trove of dialect and Anglo-Saxon remains into print.[29] Less formally still, this gentlemanly, Tory institutionalization of public knowledge spread into the expanding popularity of book collecting itself, since collecting, at the time at least, was a semi-public activity entwined in the formal and semi-formal gentlemanly associations of scholarship and librarianship as well as the market, and was exposed to notice through widely advertised sales and book auctions. We can say, then, that the gentlemanly-ecclesiastical literary bloc helped develop the modern institution of literature despite its (qualified) opposition to that institution's means and purposes, and despite its products' failure to survive in cultural memory.

At the level of cultural politics, the Tory ethic that sounds through Nichol's enterprises can now be seen to resonate with later *dissident* intellectual groupings that helped constitute the modern literary institution. Although the intense scholarly activity of Nichols and the Bowyer printshop drew upon the productive labors of rural parsons, although it helped create literature as a public resource and helped secure the genealogy of eighteenth-century literary history, it nonetheless operated at a remove from full participation in sanctioned citizenship. It expresses a social alienation which, in its more radical forms, respected the supernaturally legitimated sovereignty that the 1688 revolution had overthrown. Once the 1689 constitution and its principles became all but unassailable, those grounding principles of Anglican and nonjuring politics – "passive obedience" and "non-resistance" –

can be understood as early theorizations of elite internal exile that finds little hope even in the politics of "patriot" identity and recognition, let alone in commercialized culture.[30] Later, these habits of retreat from the apparatuses of state and commerce would be shared by many alienated literary intellectuals as they produced avant-gardes within literary worlds in which, however, the remnants of the old gentlemanly-ecclesiastical bloc played no important role.

The Warburtonians

From a certain point of view it may seem that the nonjuring and Tory networks that provide the bulk of the material in the first two volumes of Nichols's *Literary Anecdotes* stand at the opposite end of the spectrum of ecclesiastical-gentlemanly learning from that occupied by the "Warburtonians." After all, William Warburton himself is an ornament of J. G. A. Pocock's "conservative enlightenment," and, as a self-ascribed "religious deist," he was a chief spokesman of the established church's Whiggish and rationalist wing.[31] He came to prominence after the publication of the first edition of his *Alliance of Church and State* in 1736 (augmented edition in 1766), in which he offered a legitimation for the actually existing English church–state relation on pseudo-Lockean philosophical grounds. There he argued that relations between the English church and English state were implicitly based on a contract with similar philosophical force to the pre-historical social contract between a sovereign and his people. The church and state were conceived of as two separate sovereign "societies," each possessing distinct corporate personalities and wills, which must necessarily enter into contractual agreement with one another, since only the church can provide sufficient sanction for state law (through its promise of immortal life), while only the state can provide the force and legal structure that assures the church's survival. By this account, the state has no right to interfere with religious belief yet must insist upon the fundamental principles of natural religion. Only these principles can sanction the oaths which provide, so Warburton supposes, the necessary foundation of civil society.

In the end, Warburton's argument was a functionalist one that emphasizes the church's use to the state more than the inverse.[32] Indeed, in the context of 1736 – the year *The Alliance* was written – its policy implications were those of conservative Whiggism. After all 1736 was an important year for church–state relations. The repeal of the Test and Corporation Acts was discussed in Parliament (and was decisively rejected in 1739, being put off the political agenda for almost half a century as a result); the Mortmain Bill passed that year made it harder to bequeath property to the church and thus liberated capital for the market; Lord Chancellor Hardwicke (one of Warburton's patrons) delivered a judgment in the case of Middleton v. Croft, "which effectively exempted laymen from the jurisdiction of the Church, thus definitively asserting the supremacy of statute over canon law," and the

Tithe Bill made it easier for Quakers to avoid paying tithes. (Langford 1998: 92). Warburton's book was an intervention into this welter of legal and governmental activity, which can be seen as rejecting Walpole's Mortmain and Quaker's Tithe Bills while buttressing Whiggish political theory. In these terms it paved the way for future Pittite and post-1760 Tory governments, under which Warburton's career was secured.

Warburton's position within the gentlemanly-ecclesiastical intellectual bloc is characterized by the authority that he personally achieved and by the particular balance between what we, from within the current cultural organization, can recognize as its literary as well as its theological elements. In regard to the first, there is no doubt that despite a reputation for arrogance, Warburton was widely acknowledged as having achieved a pre-eminent position on the mid-century British intellectual scene.[33] Warburton's work was translated and discussed on the Continent, including by Lessing, Herder, Mendelssohn, Voltaire and Rousseau. At home, he gathered a circle of younger clergymen disciples/dependants, among whom the most notable were Richard Hurd, John Brown (of *Estimate of the Manners and Principles of the Times*), Thomas Balguy, William Mason, and, in the next generation and at one remove, Thomas Percy (of the *Reliques of Ancient English Poetry*). These members of the Warburton connection were aligned more loosely and occasionally to a wider, mainly Cambridge-based circle, many of them clerics, including Thomas Gray, Conyers Middleton, William Whitehead, Thomas Warton, and Richard Farmer.

Warburton attained this position through a particularly complex set of achievements and alliances which involved theological, social, literary, and political engagements largely aimed at securing patronage. To put this in slightly different, but still summary, terms, Warburton's position was a complex, composite construction, drawn together from disparate (indeed, *opposing*) elements which, probably by a mix of strategy and luck, enabled him to connect to the central cultural political logics of the period between the fall of the court Whigs (1756) and the American Revolutionary War. It was a position that enabled his followers to occupy (or turn down) positions of authority in the first decades of George III's reign. And (at least from the perspective of the inner Warburton circle) one of its implicit objectives was to defend the Anglican church's privileged status in relation to the state: see for instance the debate between rational Dissent and Thomas Balguy after the latter had offered a very tight version of the Warburtonian line on church authority in 1769 ("it is the duty of a churchman, as well as a citizen, to submit to the powers that be," he wrote) and once again in response to the 1772 Feathers Tavern petition.[34] The church's privileged relation to the state could, so Warburtonians hoped, support the transference of religious/political institutional and intellectual hegemony on to a wider cultural authority over public opinion, especially in the domains of taste and morals. This latter aim becomes apparent, for instance, in the letters sparked by Hurd's reading

Francis Atterbury's *The Rights, Powers and Privileges, of an English Convocation* (1700) in 1760, in which Hurd and Warburton discussed the possibility of resuscitating Convocation, and in which it becomes clear that they conceived of Convocation as a censoring body, allied to the state, against free thought and licentiousness.[35] Or, to take another instance, in his *Dissertation on the Rise of Poetry and Music* (1763) John Brown called for a revivication of the old role of the bard, as a "useful servant of the State" with a role in setting norms for manners and customs.[36]

At the heart of Warburton's position lay his institutional power: he was himself a minor patron (he established, for instance, the Warburton Lectures, designed to bring young divines to London notice) and, more to the point, was a conduit through whom others could find more important patrons. But he was also bound to his allies by complex codes of friendship and honor, partly derived from idealized courtly-militaristic norms of gentlemanly conduct in lieu of strong patterns of solidarity among the Anglican clergy. This code lies behind the intense personal loyalty among this group as well as the bitterness with which supposed insults and slights were attacked. It's given ironical expression in Richard Hurd's reply to a critique by the learned clergyman John Jortin of Warburton's interpretation of Virgil in a 1755 pamphlet entitled "On the Delicacy of Friendship," and its negative side is shown in Warburton's falling out with Samuel Richardson following a slight against Pope in *Clarissa*.[37]

The Warburtonians also held an identifiable if reactive intellectual position, whose core elements can be listed quite simply. They deployed Lockean rationalism to defend the quasi-confessional state against seven main formations: Dissent especially in its Calvinist varieties; evangelicalism; High Church Toryism; Low Church Arianism; Shaftesburyian moral naturalism and its associated aestheticism; neoclassicism and the predominance of the classical over the Christian heritage; and free thought. We can concentrate on the last of these: if Warburton's career began with his tract on church–state relations, it was consolidated by the publication of the first volume of a long theological treatise, *Divine Legation of Moses demonstrated on the Principles of a Religious Deist* (1737–41), which established his reputation, at least among centrist Anglicans, as the victorious champion of orthodoxy against freethinking deism. Indeed, the book's argument is persuasive only within conceptual structures within which Enlightenment rationalist deism met Protestant Christianity.

Warburton argues that both the Jews' special protection by divine providence and the truth of Christian revelation can be ascertained by the Jews having a strong social morality without any doctrine of future rewards or punishments, and by Moses' having failed to disseminate the concept of eternal life among his people. Today that seems a stunningly counter-intuitive claim. What made it seductive at the time was its turning two of the free-thinking deists' main historicist arguments against them: that the Old

Testament did not mention the afterlife, and that pagan priestcraft was
"accommodating" or esoteric – that is, that pagan priests did not publicly
reveal their personal skepticism so that they might maintain their power
over the superstitious populace. Hence Warburton is able to claim that
Moses did not play the priestcraft game precisely because he was a genuine
"prophet" granted genuine revelations from God. He did not have to pro-
mulgate "mysteries" because he knew that God was actively intervening in
the world on behalf of the Jewish peoples. He could remain confident in his
(typological) dissemination of religious truth if not fully cognizant of Christ's
capacity to redeem mankind. The tortured argumentation here is a sign of
the problem that post-Lockean/Newtonian divines faced as they attempted to
balance rationalism and revelation basically by mapping out the borders
between those moments in history in which God appeared and those in
which He was absent and where "natural" processes were maintained.

On one side of this position, Hume lay in wait, whose *History of England*
Warburton thought spelled "the end of all pretence of religion." (Warburton
1808: 207.) On the other stood those who resolutely rejected reason as a
buttress for religion like William Law (who wrote the most cogent attack on
Divine Legation from the High Church side). For the Warburtonians, God's
presence (through prophecy and miracles) was mainly confined to the era
before Christ's death (Richard Hurd in his sermons confined it more narrowly still to the period of the Gospels themselves) although God continued
to use nature to warn and reward mankind. But God was also present in
certain Established Church rites: Warburton, for instance, joined the
pamphlet war against Benjamin Hoadly (to whom he was nonetheless in
many ways bound), and who in his *Plain Account of the Lord's Supper* (1735)
had famously argued that the eucharist was merely an edifying act of
remembrance of Christ's redemptive suffering without efficacy for future
salvation.[38]

Warburton's project, however, fell outside certain of the political interests
and values connected to the Whig cause, not least when it approached the
border between polite letters and theological dispute. Warburton had forged
a literary career for himself from the beginning. He had begun it attached to
the circle around Lewis Theobald under the patronage of the shady Whig
financier Sir Robert Sutton.[39] But in 1738 he formed a friendship with Pope
after jumping to the poet's defense against Jean-Pierre de Crousaz's *Examen
de l'Essai de Monsieur Pope sur l'Homme* which accused the *Essay on Man* of
Leibnitzean deism. It was an apposite moment, since 1738 was, in Christine
Gerrard's words, "'the *annus mirabilis*' of Pope's opposition career."[40] Warburton's defense of Pope, though no doubt attuned to political nuances and
certainly distancing him from Walpole's policies, was primarily literary-
theological, and probably in part motivated by Warburton himself having
come under attack for deism after the publication of *Divine Legation's*
first volume, most vociferously by William Webster, a High Church

Anglican clergyman and editor of *The Weekly Miscellany*, part owned by William Bowyer.

After Warburton's pamphlet came to his notice, Pope seems to have welcomed Warburton warmly into his life because he felt the need of ecclesiastical support to buttress his claims to Christian orthodoxy, from which, as was posthumously publicly to be revealed, his friend and patron, Henry St John, Lord Bolingbroke, had lapsed. Warburton quickly took advantage of his warm welcome: Pope introduced him to the rich and philanthropic Ralph Allen (Warburton married his niece, and Allen's house, Prior Park, became Warburton's home) as well as to William Murray (later Lord Mansfield), a lawyer with a Whig power base but persistently linked to Jacobitism. Warburton's new connections also led him to the court Whigs, and at last to William Pitt, who promoted Warburton to a lucrative bishopric in 1760. During Pope's lifetime Warburton had influenced him in choosing targets for the last version of *The Dunciad*, and upon Pope's death Warburton was named Pope's literary executor and bequeathed Pope's copyrights.

Warburton assiduously promoted his Pope connection: he went on to produce a posthumous edition of Pope's works that controversially pushed their sense into Warburtonian channels. Warburton's official portrait (now in London's National Portrait Gallery) depicts him with a medallion of Pope in the background, as if Pope were the inspiring genius of his life and work (Wimsatt 1965: 339–40). He formed a bond with Pope's publisher, John Knapton, and through him with Knapton's printer, none other than William Bowyer, whose London office served as Warburton's London postal address for many years, despite a sometimes difficult relation between the two men. The Bowyer connection led to Warburton's own literary remains becoming an archive drawn upon for later volumes of John Nichols's *Literary Anecdotes*.[41] And on occasion Warburton transferred Pope's mantle on to his own disciples, as when he encouraged John Brown to write a critique of Shaftesbury's deism, a project that Pope had earlier recommended to Warburton himself; when he introduced his own disciples/dependants to patrons met through the Pope–Allen circle; and when he recommended William Bowyer to Richard Hurd (and vice versa), so that Bowyer came to print one of Hurd's early self-published works. Through that connection John Nichols was to be employed by Hurd and was able to collect materials for Hurd's biography, published first in Nichols's *History of Leicestershire* and then in *Literary Anecdotes*.[42]

The Pope–Warburton alliance also produced its own intellectual energy. In particular, Warburton and his disciples took up the republican/Popean/patriot critique of luxury and the leveling, vulgarizing, feminizing effect of commercial interests on national taste and energy, and channeled them into the new social settings and discursive channels of the Seven Years' War period, with John Brown's 1757 *Estimate* being the key text in this move.[43] Indeed, Brown's book might be regarded as a point at which a conventional classical *topos* is transmuted into a new discourse of modern anti-commercialism and anti-capitalism. But the Warburtonian position contained two limiting internal tensions, each played out both on institutional and intellectual terrains: that between politics and the church; and that between literature and religion.

The tension between politics and religion can be quite quickly passed over for our purposes. Warburton and later Hurd were involved in politics since they were called upon to offer weakly Providential spiritual legitimations of the administrations to which their patrons were linked. It is this particular binding of religion to politics that marks the Warburtonians out from Hoadly and Thomas Herring, the dominant Whig ecclesiastical intellectuals of the previous generation. Thus as a young divine in 1745, Warburton delivered a series of sermons which deemed the Jacobite invasion "unnatural," and on November 29, 1759, the day appointed for public thanksgiving for British victories against the French, he preached a sermon at Bristol, which (in line with Warburtonian limited Providentialism) made the claim that God knew that Britain was the "sole remaining Trustee of Civil Freedom, and so of the great Bulwark of Gospel Truth," as Robert Ingram puts it.[44] Somewhat similarly, Richard Hurd delivered a series of sermons between 1776 and 1786 on the occasion of national events in which George's policies were identified with the will of God. (See Bradley 1989 for a slightly different take on Hurd's position in the wider context of late Georgian sermonizing on behalf of the Crown.) In his "Sermon before the House of Lords on the General Fast Day in 1776 on Account of the American Rebellion" the American revolt is seen as a criminal outrage against a "law and order" sanctioned by both God and George III; as the result also of a fanatical attachment to "theory" against morality (in terms that pre-empt Burke on the French Revolution) and, finally, as divine retribution for the growth of irreligious rationalism and Luxury.[45] A similar logic is at work in Hurd's invocation of George III's sacral presence in his 1786 sermon to the House of Lords on the anniversary of Charles I's execution/"martyrdom":

> Have we that reverence of just authority, not only as lodged in the persons of inferior magistrates, or in the sacred person of the supreme Magistrate, but as residing in the LAW itself (in which the public will, that is, the whole collective authority of the State is, as it were, concentrated) – Have we, I say, that ingenuous and submissive respect for this authority, which not only reason and religion, but true policy, and every man's proper interest requires?
>
> (Hurd 1811 VIII: 50)

Here, in a characteristic mix of appeals to supernature, reason, and interest, it is as if the old doctrine of divine right has been transferred from the monarch (as in traditional Toryism) or the constitution (as in traditional

Anglican Whiggism) to the state itself, in a move which belongs to the emergence of a new Toryism from out of the intermingled ashes of Jacobitism and court Whiggism.

In this context, it is barely surprising that the Warburtonians set themselves against the push for parliamentary and administrative reform. Warburton (along with his patrons William Murray and Charles Yorke) was one of the leading agents in having John Wilkes removed from Parliament – the excuse being Wilkes's role in writing a pornographic parody of Warburton's own edition of Pope's *Essay on Man*. By contrast, there were rare occasions on which Warburton's understanding of the church's authority over souls had political implications at odds with certain strong interests of the ruling caste. In 1766 he gave an influential sermon to the Society for the Propagation of the Gospel in Foreign Parts on the relation between colonialism and Christianity, which may well have influenced the famous (if reluctant) judgment against the legality of slave-owning in England by his patron and friend, Lord Mansfield, a few years later, since both came down against the notion that a slave could be deemed simply *property* (Warburton 1808: 125).

Yet Warburton was also tempted to dismiss the political scene in its entirety on very different terms, as in this letter written privately to Hurd in 1759:

> This as you truly say, is an age of real darkness: or, at least, of *false lights*. For what else are all the national advantages gained by spreading slaughter and desolation round the world. However it is much better to *win*, by this bad means, than, as in former bad administrations, to lose. I will venture therefore to congratulate you, even as a philosopher, on these late *glorious successes* in this annus mirabilis. And though I begin to think with Bolingbroke, *this earth may be the bedlam of the universe*, yet I think the great genius who presides in our counsels, may be called the sage master of this mad-house, who directs their unmeaning extravagances to useful and salutary purposes.
>
> (Warburton 1808: 220)

The "Sage Genius" presiding over the secular madhouse is the elder Pitt, who was about to appoint Warburton to a bishopric, but the drive to repudiate the whole social-political scene stands out from a passage like this. It is an esoteric message, intended for elect intimates only. In his younger disciples, however, the will to social non-participation and the blanket condemnation of the public worlds of politics and commerce become more open, fervent, and consequential. It is clearly expressed in Hurd's "Dialogue on Retirement" (where Hurd's spokesman for the choice of opting out of public life is the seventeenth-century royalist Abraham Cowley), and in Hurd's interest in the pastoral as a literary genre at the beginning of his career as he reconciled himself to taking up an isolated rural parish in Thurcaston,

Leicestershire. It also appears in the everyday retreat from public life through the musical aestheticism cultivated by the younger Warburtonians, especially by William Mason, who was one of the first to import a pianoforte (in 1755) into Britain (Draper 1924: 288–89). This turn away from the public world, slowly to reconnoiter a new kind of bourgeois private life, can also be recognized in Hurd's more pastoral (in the ecclesiastical sense) sermons, which, striking a very different note from that of Hurd's public-occasion sermons, present critiques of the passions that drive hegemonic sociability (emulation, the love of fame, honor) while preaching humility, interior spirituality, and retreat from the rewards of the world. Reading these sermons, tinged as they are by quietism, it is possible to see how Hurd and Warburton became such ardent fans of Rousseau's *Julie* on its publication in 1760: there's a real flow across from their esoteric spiritualizing and privatizing Christian ethic, dismissive and fearful of the public world, to a Rousseauian domestic sentimental primitivism – Fénelon no doubt being their common ancestor (Hurd 1995: 368 ff.).

Now to the second internal tension in the Warbutonians' intellectual project: that between literature and religion, which can be more concretely described as a tension in the alliance between polite taste/learning on the one side and the clerical profession on the other. Warburton was on record as discouraging, indeed attempting to forbid, his clerical protégés from pursuing creative writing on the ground that, as Hurd put it, the profession was a "sacred one" and that its business "lay elsewhere" than literature (Hurd 1995: 300). Warburton also admonished clergymen outside his sphere of direct influence for their literary writings, most famously Laurence Sterne, and he could put his case very forthrightly. In his report to Hurd about his discussions with Mason when Mason was pondering a clerical career in 1754, Warburton presents his reasoning as a functionalist revision of a traditional High Church program (in this instance, that of his antagonist, William Law):

> I found him [i.e., Mason] yet unresolved whether he should take the Living. I said, was the question about a mere secular employment, I should blame him without reserve if he refused the offer. But as I regarded going into orders in another light, I frankly owned to him he ought not to go, unless he had a *call*: by which I meant, I told him, nothing fanatical or superstitious; but an inclination, and, on that, a resolution, to dedicate all his studies to the service of religion, and totally to abandon his poetry. This sacrifice, I said, I thought was required at any time, but more indispensable so in this, when we are fighting with infidelity *pro aris et focis*.[46]

Despite this admonition, Mason did take orders without jettisoning poetry. And, in general, the younger generation of Warburtonians were more involved in secular literature than Warburton himself. It is true that Hurd gave up writing poetry as he gained preferment (though he still cultivated serious literary interests and passions and published editions of Addison and Cowley), but John Brown, for instance, the most literary (in the modern sense) member of the group, wrote plays for the London stage, attracting both Warburton's and Hurd's disapproval as a result. Brown's poems were published in Dodsley's *A Collection of Poems by Several Hands*, and his astonishing (but neglected) written response to visiting the Lake District, published in 1753, was a key moment in the development of the concept both of the sublime and of the romanticized picturesque, as worked out in practice by his pupil William Gilpin. That is to say, John Brown is a conduit from a theologically motivated admiration of, and attention to, the natural landscape as articulated by that wing of the Anglican church that accommodated Newton's findings to the more purely secular, aestheticized and commercializable notion of the picturesque. (See Eddy 1976 for Brown in this context; see Mayhew 2000 for the Latitudinarian underpinnings of Gilpin's picturesque.)

The institutional reason for encouraging the laying aside of literary/ aesthetic interests was that, given the pressures both of free thought and evangelicalism, the orthodox Anglican clerical profession required its members' full attention. Yet, somewhat ironically, it was partly in response to these pressures on the clergy that Richard Hurd sketched out an innovative theory of literature in a series of essays written between 1755 and 1765, "On the Idea of Universal Poetry," "On the Provinces of the Drama", "A Discourse on Poetical Imitation" and "Letters on Chivalry and Romance." They present few, if any, wholly original concepts and they are not as fully worked out or coherent as, for instance, Edmund Burke's 1757 essay on the sublime (which Brown and Hurd would seem to have influenced), but as a whole, and in relation to the institutional position from which they were written, they articulate a critical theory that helped ground the modern idea of literature.

Thus, in one of the earliest of his literary-theoretical contributions, "On the Idea of Universal Poetry" (1755), Hurd's basic move is to define poetry's main purpose as the giving of pleasure.[47] This was a radicalization of the definition of literature formulated in John Brown's *Essays on the Characteristics* (1751), which creates the category "pure poetry" to describe that form of writing wholly in the service of imagination unlicensed by reason (and, according to Brown, for that reason primarily committed to "simplicity"). Brown develops this concept in a critique of Shaftesbury's aestheticizing of virtue, which also led him to articulate an early argument for what became the Benthamite "greatest happiness" principle, if one that itself draws upon theological utilitarian political theory (Tillotson, Hoadly and Joseph Butler's), since, for him, utilitarianism requires religious backing to be effectively transmitted, i.e., the greatest happiness principle has to be calculated with immortal life in mind (Brown 1751: 19; Draper 1924: 139).[48] It is because religion and reason each involve calculation of utilities that poetry can be freed from both.

In Hurd's essay, certain consequences of Brown's move are explored in more detail. The deceptively simple claim that poetry primarily involves pleasure now decisively breaks with the rhetorical and ethical models of literature that dominated Renaissance humanism and neoclassicism. It also breaks with the critical problematic of figures like John Dryden and John Dennis, as well as that sketched out by Warburton himself in his preface to Volumes III and IV of Samuel Richardson's *Clarissa*. At the same time – and this is once again its basic point – this definition hardens the division between religion and poetry. ("Poetry" here means, to all intents and purposes, literature as we moderns categorize it, in contradistinction to polite learning.) We can state this conceptual structure in its simplest terms: poetry as defined as productive of pleasure is being removed from the public world of professional Anglican practice, which now needs stronger weapons of defense and stronger principles of authority. But defining poetry as primarily aimed at pleasure is also extraordinarily liberating: it frees literature from moral duties as well as from responsibilities to rhetorical precedent. Indeed, it enables literature to become something like autonomous. Thus in "On the Idea of Universal Poetry" Hurd begins to sanction what he calls a "licence of representation, which we call *fiction*" as well as a liberation of style itself: "The *style* is, as it were, the body of poetry; *fiction* is its soul" (Hurd 1811 II: 11). Literature becomes the expression of "something in the mind of man, sublime and elevated, which prompts it to overlook all obvious and familiar appearances, and to feign to itself other and more extraordinary; such as correspond to the extent of its own powers, and fill out all the faculties and capacities of our souls." It is in the service of restless imaginative drives that literature is drawn to "pagan fable" and "gothic romance." At the same time, literature's search for pleasure means that poetry aligns itself with rhythm, rhyme and music (a theme which will be taken up by John Brown in his *Dissertation on the Rise of Poetry and Music*). Indeed, for Hurd the most recent mode of imaginative literature – realist prose fiction – which detaches the music of language from that imaginative liberation whose vehicle is romance, is a sign of the contemporary vitiated taste that was condemned most forcefully by Pope and Brown.

Of course this account of "poetry" as primarily imaginatively liberating and pleasurable stands against the project I described above: the transference of authority from the state and church to the domain of taste as a whole. This contradiction was lived out in a number of ways. For instance, while the Warburtonians discouraged literary pursuits by clergy, they also encouraged churchmen to maintain and extend their secular scholarship and command of polite learning, once again the better to resist deistic and evangelical currents and (esoterically) to shore up their social status. And individual Warburtonians struggled to avoid the responsibilities of the higher ranks of church office in order to protect that leisure in which they could be literary according to their own lights. Hurd turned down the archbishopric of Canterbury and Balguy the bishopric of Gloucester. The terms of this struggle were spelled out in Mason's sonnet to Hurd on his taking up a less onerous bishopric earlier in his career (Lichfield and Coventry in 1775):

> Still let my HURD a smile of candour lend
> To scenes that dar'd on Grecian pinions tow'r,
> When "in low Thurcaston's sequester'd bower"
> He prais'd the strain, because he lov'd the friend:
> There golden leisure did his steps attend,
> Nor had the rare, the well-weigh'd call of Power,
> To those high cares decreed his watchful hour,
> On which fair Albion's future hopes depend.
> A fate unlook'd-for waits my friend and me;
> He pays to duty what is Learning's claim,
> Resigning classic ease – for dignity;
> I yield my Muse to Fashion's praise or blame.[49]

Mason thinks of leisure as golden, and power as an oppressive weight. He hopes that Hurd, as a bishop, will continue to attend to and enjoy Mason's own experiments in revivifying Ancient Greek dramatic forms for the modern stage while necessarily submitting to fashion's control of contemporary taste. But at the same time, in a then instantly recognizable reminiscence of Cicero's move in the other direction, he applauds Hurd's giving up learning and classical *otium* for dignity, which Hurd does to protect "fair Albion's future hopes," a choice directed at the nation-state's ecclesiastical, cultural, and political well-being. The sonnet form that Mason chooses is already coded in this situation: despite the publicity given to it through Richardson's *Sir Charles Grandison* (1753), it is something of a coterie taste, emblematic of the imaginative freedom (and love of Italian Renaissance poetry) allowed to these gentlemanly clergymen scholars only as a problem, a tension, in what is not quite yet in the modern sense their "private" time.

This chapter has argued that key sectors of the eighteenth-century literary field can be understood in terms of triangulated relations among the Anglican church, the state, and the market during a period when literature underwent profound changes as an institution. It makes this case to demur from those who believe that the period is most intelligible through narratives of modernization, on the one side, or of the privatization of religious belief on the other. Here the gradual modernization of literature is not conceived as a smooth process of transformation in which the old polite learning gave way to new forms of market-orientated imaginative writing. Rather it is presented as an uneven mutation of a segmented field, in which some innovations (like the Warburtonian theory of literature) first appear in non-secular resistance to forces of transformation and secularization themselves.

But in conclusion I want to break with historical sociology for a moment to ask a more classically humanist question: what value do literary projects like those of the Warburtonians and the Nichols printshop have today, belonging as they do to a world and structure of literary/intellectual life that has vanished and which retains only slight continuities with our own? Are projects like these now culturally inert? And I think that the argument outlined above does help us answer a hesitant "no" to that. To take the first of my two cases here: as I have argued, Nichols's enormous labors of memorization, retrieval, and preservation can be conceived of as reaching back to the nonjuring intellectual world in which the Bowyer firm first made its mark — that is, to a theo-political collectivity that refused to sign on to a Whiggish, liberal order. That refusal (and the Tory/Anglican/Lutheran political ethics of non-resistance and passive obedience to which it problematically adhered) retains a force today for those of us in the humanities who are often in the business of trying to breathe life into cultural/literary remnants whose public interest and value are disappearing into oblivion. But in the end the value of Nichols's literary labors, like that of the Warburtonians' anticipation of a literature wholly given up to an autonomous imagination, is not to be found in what we share with them or what use-value they retain for us, including their use as evidence for renarrativizations of literary history such as in this chapter. Rather it's to be found precisely in their otherness, their strangeness, which historical sociology can also help us specify and recognize. It is the mute chill of death and mortification that emanates from them that makes them dangerous (if easy) to forget.

Chapter 2

Quackery, selfhood, and the emergence of the modern cultural marketplace

We know that British literary production became increasingly commercialized across the eighteenth century, and that shifts in literary genre, address, and mood over the period need to be considered in that light. In this chapter, I want to move away from ecclesiastic writing to address two quite specific structures within mid-eighteenth-century commercial literature which can, indeed, be regarded as the gentlemanly bloc's dangerous others. The first of these structures is the close relationship between commercial writing and charlatanism or quackery. The second structure, which I will attend to more briefly, is the slow emergence among writers of what will later come to be called *ressentiment* from out of that old Satanic vice, envy. Setting these very different events side by side may seem perverse, but, by focusing on a cluster of commercial book-trade participants – John Newbery, Oliver Goldsmith, and Christopher Smart – I want to make the case that, in the narrow period between about 1750 and 1780, they are in fact linked and in ways that help us make sense of the romanticism to come.

In brief, my argument is that literary production in the period was "charlatanized" in three related ways: first, the book trade was materially connected to the patent medicine trade, which was often regarded as a diluted and rationalized form of quackery; second, the literary world itself was often engaged in practices of charlatanism; and third, the difficulties of escaping the contingencies of commerce and politics led to a widely accepted diagnosis of charlatanism as infecting the society and culture quite broadly. In this environment, I further contend, cultural affects were unstable – a situation that fostered not just sentimentalism but a particular nexus between feeling and print in which certain writers were dominated by resentments that they could not transparently express in their writings – Goldsmith and Smart being my examples.

Definitions

When Hester Piozzi discussed in her *British Synonymy* (1794) the terms "charlatans," "quacks," and "mountebanks" – words which had become familiar in the early modern period and which, with their demystifying force, had helped carry out enlightenment's work – she declared her personal preference for the first, but nonetheless claimed that they shared a single meaning (Piozzi 1794 II: 174–75). In fact, however, these terms do seem quite quickly to have acquired somewhat different senses. Who was a quack or a charlatan? Not just mountebanks who earned their bread in the medicine trade by making grandiose claims about nostrums but any self-advertiser pretending to more knowledge or power than they possessed. That extension of reference arrived early, perhaps most famously in Johann Burkhardt Menke's polemic *De Charlatanerie Eruditorium* (1715). And there is a sense in which, across the eighteenth century, while the craft of the mountebank declines, charlatans of a vaguer and more figurative kind become more prevalent. It is telling that Samuel Butler's *Characters*, written in the late 1670s, describes mountebanks but no charlatans, and that by the time Butler's manuscript was first published in 1759 the old mountebank, the nomadic trader working fairs, public houses, and village greens had, on the one hand, been marginalized by nationally distributed patent medicines and, on the other, been subsumed by charlatans of a very different ilk with prominent cultural profiles – such as John Henley, the unorthodox preacher, lecturer, and political journalist, or John Hill, the journalist, botanist, novelist, reviewer, and patent-medicine proprietor.

Yet these terms, charlatanism and quackery, are hedged by ambiguities. As Roy Porter notes, no one calls themselves a charlatan or quack – and this in itself exposes the terms to dispute (Porter 2000: 15). More than that: the fraud or pretension that at one level defines them cannot easily be dismissed as valueless, for the simple reason that non-truthful, non-rational marketing claims helped extend commercial activity over the period (and, of course, since). Indeed eighteenth-century charlatanism can be regarded as an avant-garde of the modern consumer marketplace. We can put it like this: charlatanism, thought neutrally or analytically, becomes diffused through the market economy as more and more services and commodities derive their value primarily from the seductive force of their sales pitch rather than from any post-purchase use value, and, hence, when attracting custom is sufficient justification for production. At the same time, the critique of charlatanism turns away from its enlightenment targets – superstition, credulity and ignorance – towards the empty promises and valorized nullities of a culture organized around the market.

Books, newspapers, and patent medicines

And so to turn to the connections between the patent medicine trade and literature which helped underpin the era's charlatanism.[1] What form did they take? To begin with: many booksellers were involved in retailing and in some cases preparing, patent medicines. Given that medicines seem to have been more profitable than books (it was estimated that profits of 25 percent were possible in the pharmaceutical business), one might suppose that, at least for some booksellers, they subsidized the book trade, although there is little good evidence on this matter, and according to Jan Fergus, patent medicines were marginally less important to total sales (but not necessarily to profits), which in turn were less important than stationery and other items, especially as the century went on (Fergus and Portner 1987; Ferdinand 1997: 24).[2] Newspapers could add complexity to these relations, since larger booksellers were also sometimes involved in the production or distribution of newspapers (Harris 1981: 71 ff.). This tied them to patent medicines, since newspaper profits depended on advertising, and patent-medicine proprietors were heavy advertisers. Once newspapers were being circulated across most of Britain, patent-medicine brand name recognition could become national, indeed they seem to have constituted the first national brands.

This interdependence of print and proprietary medicines was further structured around certain similarities between the two commodities. Both could be more or less mass-produced. Both could be identified by legally protected proper names. Both were normally retailed at fixed prices which, still rare through retailing as a whole, was a prerequisite of the modern market. Both could be easily transported. Both could be stored without decaying, and easily sold alongside one another (Mui and Mui 1988: 229–30). And finally, both had a value largely dependent on commentary, marketing and reputation, but which was not necessarily acknowledged as such.

Patent medicines themselves were so saleable for two main reasons. There were relatively few physicians per head of population, and the non-patent medicines that they prepared were often prohibitively expensive.[3] Furthermore patients routinely self-diagnosed: the modern structure of authority by which doctors provide the sick with binding expertise after physical examination was not yet in place. Patent medicines operated under a different philosophy than that underpinning university-legitimated medicine. In one direction they sometimes claimed that their powers derived from analogical relations that referred back to older "magical" cosmic ontologies in which the world was bound by esoteric sympathies. In another direction, they worked simply because they worked ("empiric" was another name for a quack, after all), which was why testimonials were so important to their profitability (and one mode of modern medical research begins in the testing of quack medicine's claims – such work made the philosopher David Hartley's name, for instance). It was because patent medicines were testimonial and brand-name driven that they required massive publicity – which the book trade could provide.

John Newbery

Let me now turn to a particular case within these exchanges between patent medicine and print – John Newbery, who stands near the center of the charlatanized literary world. Newbery began his career in Reading but in 1744 transferred his business to London, where he purchased distribution rights to Dr James's Fever Powder, which was to become the era's most widely used patent medicine.[4] One of the reasons for the Powder's success was that Robert James, its inventor, was a well known authority on the basis of his *Medicinal Dictionary*, whose preface, for instance, had been written by Samuel Johnson. Dr James's reputation underpinned a sustained sales blitz on behalf of his Powder, incorporating not just advertisements, handbills, testimonials from famous figures like Lord Chesterfield, Colley Cibber, and the playwright Richard Cumberland, but mentions in fictions mainly published by Newbery and his associates.[5] For example, John Shebbeare's *The Marriage Act* (1754) included a chapter heading attesting to the medicine's efficacy; Dodsley's *The World* inserted a puff in a widely reprinted essay-fiction; and, most famously, the children's tale *Little Goody Two-shoes* has its heroine's father deposed from his land, dying because he was "seized with a violent Fever in a place where Dr James's Powder was not to be had."[6] From a different ideological position, when Christopher Smart recovered from a nervous breakdown in 1756, he published his *Hymn to the Supreme Being* to which he attached a letter to Dr James which began:

> Having made an humble offering to HIM, without whose blessing your skill, admirable as it is, would have been to no purpose: I think myself bound by all the ties of gratitude, to render my next acknowledgments to you, who, under God, restored me to health from as violent and dangerous a disorder, as perhaps ever man survived. And my many thanks become more particularly your just tribute, since this was the third time, that your judgement and medicines rescued me from the grave, permit me to say, in a manner almost miraculous.
>
> (Smart 1991: 67)

This may have been a response to an anti-powder advertisement inserted into Fielding's *Amelia*, but, whatever its immediate intent, here Dr James acquires a quasi-magical power deriving from divinity itself, which is all the more ironical since it is possible that his Powder was actually causing Smart's mental illness. Certainly there is a body of respectable medical opinion today suggesting that George III's madness may have been caused by the arsenic that he absorbed through the Powder.[7]

The Powder was not without its contemporary critics. In 1748, Dr James wrote another book, *A Dissertation on Fevers*, in order to support faltering sales, and to shore the product up against its earliest critics, notably the anonymous author of *Quackery Unmask'd* (1748; Hambridge 1982: 80–82). The Powder soon sustained a number of more damaging attacks, including in 1751 a claim by the printer and pharmacist William Baker that its patent had been granted on false grounds, since its formula had been first developed in Germany (Baker 1754). In the early 1750s the Admiralty, desperate to find a cure for scurvy, instructed James Lind to undertake trials of supposed therapies against fevers, especially James's Powder. His results, remarkably carefully obtained for the time, and guided by a suspicion of medicines that claimed effectiveness over a wide range of complaints, were negative. But Lind's work was to have little impact for at least twenty years.

Perhaps most damaging of all was the scandal surrounding Oliver Goldsmith's death in 1774, which produced a minor paper war. Goldsmith turned to the Powder when he fell victim to kidney disease, insisting on taking it in large doses against the recommendation of his medical advisor, William Haynes. After Goldsmith's death Haynes published a pamphlet declaring that James's Powder was responsible for the fatality. This was rebutted in a campaign organized by the Newberys, contending that the medicine which Goldsmith had taken had not been produced by the correct formula.[8]

In 1783 new government charges were laid on the patent-medicine trade and this, along with a gradual increase in the availability of medical practitioners, the formal professionalization of medical practice (particularly as implemented in the 1815 Apothecaries Act), and the increasing credibility of critiques of proprietary medicines, very slowly reduced the medicines' economic value in Britain, although, despite its formula having been publicized, James's Powder remained profitable well into the next century.[9] For a while, none other than Byron's publisher, the gentlemanly John Murray, held a share in it (Zachs 1998: 46). But the book trade's interconnection with the pharmaceutical business was also in decline by the 1780s because the print market was becoming increasingly self-sustaining, mainly as a consequence of increased affluence and opportunities to buy books but also because of the 1774 reform of copyright (which led, at least in the short term, to a flood of cheap books), and the development of more sophisticated business techniques, such as, for instance, wholesaling, remaindering, and the prominent display of new books in bookshops. In sum: as books became an increasingly autonomous commodity within the market, their dependence on pharmaceuticals declined.

John Newbery was also a key player in these developments. He was one of the publishers of the era who clearly recognized the opportunities opened up by the print market's extension. He reached into new readerships by multiplying the opportunities for reading in everyday life: developing new consumer-friendly binding formats; investing heavily in the children's and schoolroom markets; and publishing how-to and reference works, many in the increasingly popular pocket format, as well as periodicals and daily newspapers.

As a result of this commercial activity he became a widely recognized public figure, famous for his energy, multitasking and, more dubiously, for his benevolence via a suite of representations which carry a whiff of charlatanism, since once more they tended to appear in his own publications. He figures as Jack Whirler in *The Idler* (1758), where he is presented as the type of the modern businessman, too active to live life except through substitutes. He also makes an entry in Goldsmith's *The Vicar of Wakefield* (1766), where he is referred to, less obliquely, as the "philanthropic bookseller in St. Paul's Church-yard" (Goldsmith 1974 [1766]: 91). A more contemptuous sketch was published by George Colman, whose account of an uneducated, boastful, money-grubbing bookseller under the name of Mr Folio was taken to refer to him (Townsend 1994: 117–27). And indeed, Newbery was capable of charlatanism on his own account. To help sell his edition of Walter Raleigh's *The Interest of England*, he claimed that a copy of the original MS could be viewed at his shop, although no such manuscript existed – a trick that was later to be tried by another literary figure who was regularly to be described as a charlatan, James Macpherson of Ossian fame.

Literary charlatanism

We are beginning to see that the relations between patent medicines and publishing that I have been describing underpinned a series of looser or more discursive intersections of literature and charlatanism. In turning to examine these relations more closely we should briefly note the old practice of comparing literature positively to a "pill" (to cure melancholy, for instance) or as "purge" – as if writing could itself be medicinal. But, of course, such tropes could not create a functional equivalence between writing and patent medicine, and cannot themselves be aligned to charlatanism. More to our point in thinking about forms of literary charlatanism: books were often over-advertised. Typeface could be surrounded by a sea of white paper in order to fill books out, a charge James Ralph brings against the Warburtonians in *The Case of Authors* (Ralph 1762: 18 ff.). Book titles routinely promised much more than the text finally provided, in a practice which John Nichols called "titulary puffing" (Nichols 1812 III: 508). (Laurence Sterne's *Tristram Shandy*, with its creative use of the white page for much more than print, would seem to be simultaneously a joke on, and a case of, this kind of puffing – it's no accident that Sterne himself was portrayed in a popular satirical print as a mountebank, and *Tristram Shandy* does claim that enjoying it is of medicinal value.)[10] Publishers also routinely exaggerated edition numbers to hype the popularity of their books. The common practice of advertising for subscription could also lapse into charlatanism, as Henry Fielding remarks at some length in *Joseph Andrews* (Fielding 2001 [1742]: 269–70). Sometimes outright fraud was involved: in the 1760s a self-ascribed French aristocrat canvassed for subscriptions for a luxury book (a fifteen-volume history of England in French) which was probably never intended to appear (Wardle 1957: 168). Later in life, Christopher Smart turned to subscription publishing as a form of begging, producing one slight book after another so that his friends might support him, although he was ashamed of the practice (Sherbo

1967: 222–23). Something like charlatanism is at work here, at least to the degree that promise exceeds performance.

Book-trade debates could also be tinged with charlatanism. One thinks in particular of what we can call false paper wars in which authors and publishers conspired to create controversies so as to gain publicity. These were quite common in the mid-eighteenth century, and John Newbery organized several. No less important, during this period writing and entrepreneuralism systematically overlapped. Authors themselves were often entrepreneurs, and drawn into charlatanism in this way. In many cases, books can be regarded as business projects managed by authors – Johnson's *Dictionary* being one example, and Macpherson's collection of the Ossian poems another. Not even Johnson escapes charlatanism, at least to the degree that his project – the authoritative fixing of meanings to words – can be regarded as making overweening claims for commercial gain. Writers were also regularly involved in dubious non- or quasi-literary businesses. For instance, Smollett projected an Academy of Belles Lettres in terms which were at least criticized as quackery. One critic dismissed the project in these terms: "in the close of the Year 1755, a certain *Caledonian* Quack, by the Curtesy of *England*, call'd a *Doctor of Physick*, whose real, or assum'd Name was FERDINANDO MAC FATHOMLESS, form'd a Project for initiating and perfecting the Male-Inhabitants of this Island, in the Use and Mangaement of the *linguary Weapon*, by the erection of a *Scolding Amphitheatre*" (Knapp 1949: 167).

Sometimes such projects had a more direct relation to charlatanism. At least one author entered the patent-medicine trade on his own account – John Hill, who began his career as an apothecary. And John Shebbeare notoriously touted the theory that, to quote a sarcastic contemporary, "the primary cause of all diseases proceeds from excess or defect of the electric fire; the novelty and *Verity* of which could not fail to recommend it to his fashionable readers" (Adair n.d.: 189). Less obviously, Christopher Smart cashed in on the success of the magazine *Mother Midnight* by adapting it as a burlesque musical which he compered, cross-dressed, as an elderly midwife. At the show's center was its satire of John Henley and his Oratory. Although as Paula McDowell is making clear, Henley had a serious pedagogical project, he was also a charlatan by almost any definition, if a self-ironizing one. He ran a bizarre advertising campaign to attract a paying audience to his "chapel," which was part place of instruction and part place of amusement, and had long been cited as the crucial instance of the threat of a charlatanized culture (in *The Dunciad*, for instance). Smart's show consisted largely of farcical music performed on vernacular instruments in a complex play with the taste canons from which Henley kept his distance. Did Smart's customers get their money's worth? Horace Walpole at least did not think so (Sherbo 1967: 80). Here Smart's critical, comic parody, in offering so much triviality and cacophony, veered perilously close to charlatanism on its own account.

Given literary entrepreneurship's intimate relations to fraud and hype, it is unsurprising that this was a period when literature in general was engaged with charlatanism as a topic. As we know, satire and commentary routinely denounced their objects precisely as involved in, or instances of, quackery or charlatanism, or, more abstractly, represented the general social and cultural scene as organized around charlatanism or (what was closely related) conjuring or trickery. Of the thousands upon thousands of instances of this, let me just gesture at one.

In his 1763 satire *The Ghost*, Charles Churchill, the stunningly successful verse satirist, represented contemporary British society, and especially the Scots, as inheritors of a long lineage of quackery reaching back to the ancient Chaldeans, moving past early eighteenth-century charlatans like Duncan Campbell (the astrologer, patent medicine and magic charm seller) into present media culture, at whose center, Churchill believes, or pretends to believe, lurks Smollett. In verses about those who belong to this genealogy of charlatanism, Churchill writes:

> Some, with high Titles and Degrees,
> Which wise Men borrow when they please,
> Without or trouble or expence,
> PHYSICIANS instantly commence,
> And proudly boast an equal skill
> With those who claim the *right* to *kill*. ...
> Some, the more subtle of their race, ...
> Came to the *Brother* SMOLLET'S aid,
> And carried on the CRITIC trade.
> Attach'd to Letters and the Muse,
> *Some* Verses wrote, and some wrote News.
> *Those*, eve'ry morning, great appear
> In LEDGER, or in GAZETTEER;
> Spreading the falshood of the day,
> By turns for FADEN and for SAY.
> (Churchill 1956: 75)

Here the world of news and most especially of criticism is pictured as continuous with that of quackery because of the falsity and indifference to cultural and social distinctions that they share. Churchill's is a politically motivated attack – he was about to be aligned with John Wilkes and the radical reform movement – while Smollett was a propagandist for George III's Ministry. But it is a sign of the power of charlatan discourse that Churchill chooses it to obscure his own political bias: anti-quackery provides him with easy access to the moral high ground. To accept that provision, however, is to join charlatanism, since to denounce one's opposition as a charlatan from a partisan position is to flirt with deceit. And here the full reach of charlatanism's cruel logic becomes apparent: as the preferred name for false promises or overweeningness, it is all but inescapable within a structure that places its participants in particular and limited positions within a commercialized and politicized field at the same time as demanding of them truth and objectivity.

Sentimentalism and objectivity

The drive to help the cause of objectivity was part of what propelled the first media organs of modern criticism, Ralph Griffiths's *Monthly Review* (1749) and Smollett's *Critical Review* (1756), both of which aimed to provide authoritative assessment of books. But, as we might expect, these journals, far from transcending the deceptions and falsities of the literary world, intensified abuse, insecurity, divisions and charlatan discourse. At just this moment literary mood and subjectivity underwent a significant transformation. Most openly this shift in mood manifested itself in the sentimentalism that swept the culture after the success of Richardson's novels and then Sterne's *Tristram Shandy*. Here we have a real break with the old tradition of denunciatory satire (whose last important figure was Churchill) as well as with popular literature-as-instruction (in which Newbery's career was largely made), both of which were entangled in charlatanism and its critico-figurative uses. In my next chapter I will argue that the literary fashion for sentimentalism was, in part, a means by which literature and drama helped compensate for the slow dissolution of rurally based communitarian connections, as if affective benevolence and philanthropic intent, nourished in fictions, might replace the responsibilities implicit in the hierarchies of the landed estates and indeed the financial burdens of the parochial poor-law system.[11] This interpretation at least has the virtue of helping to explain why sentimentalism, as a product of a loosening of social structures and connections, was accompanied by an increase of alienation and – let me emphasize – resentment among writers, as we are about to see in more detail. It also helps explain why sentimentalism – despite its break with older charlatanized literary forms – is still imbricated with charlatanism, since (as will become clearer in the next chapter) the transports of tears, benevolence and sympathy it promoted in lieu of practical responsibility were so easy to manipulate and so difficult to authenticate.

It is no accident that key instances of early sentimental writing – the well known failure in *A Sentimental Journey* of Yorick's intense sensibility and benevolence to end in practical alms-giving (except when disavowed quasi-prostitution is involved) and Mr Harley's tarnished sentimental charity towards an itinerant con man in Henry Mackenzie's *Man of Feeling* – expose the vulnerability of the new mood to costiveness and fraud, and, by the same token, reveal how close to falsity the mood itself could be. Let the dog's neat trick in this passage from *Man of Feeling* where Harley is about to give money to the fraudulent supplicant stand as an allegorization of sentiment-alism's undermining of virtue and its incorporation of charlatanism:

> Harley had drawn a shilling from his pocket; but Virtue bade him consider on whom he was going to bestow it. Virtue held back his arm; but a milder form, a younger sister of Virtue's, not so severe as Virtue, nor so serious as Pity, smiled upon him; his fingers lost their compression, nor did Virtue offer to catch the money as it fell. It had no sooner reached the ground than the watchful cur (a trick he had been taught) snapped it up, and, contrary to the most approved method of stewardship, delivered it immediately into the hands of his master.
>
> (Mackenzie 1967: 18)

As sympathetic Compassion, their "younger sister," replaces Virtue and Pity, it is exposed to a wholly manipulative environment – even the con man's dog has learnt a trick by which he can protect his master's reputation at the same time as guarding the money. Indeed, the cur expresses the sheer empiricism and materiality to which both sentimentalism and charlatanism tend.

Resentment: Smart

In abstract the social structure of the resentment that appeared alongside charlatan-tainted sentimentalism can be analyzed quite simply: an urbanized, commercialized, mediatized cultural field encouraged individual competition and, as just noted, undermined oligarchic social dependences and cultural hierarchies. But the market had not yet found mechanisms by which writers could be adequately rewarded for their work. This meant that they were habitually beset by disjunctions between their own notions of their worth (notions which they inherited from the classically orientated culture of the past) and the financial value of that work. This further meant that, as older canons dissolved under a stream of money flowing mainly to booksellers, authors' energies were often released around what was also a value crisis. For a period, this structure abetted the circulation of the discourse of charlatanism. All the more so since three means by which market instabilities and the value crisis could be managed were not in place. These were, first, institutions and collectivities supportive of social hope and reformism, which by the century's end would nurture both the romantic avant-gardes and political progressivism. Second, the extension of reading's powers of cultivation into new class layers, which would take off only from the late 1770s, accelerating through the last decades of the century (St Clair 204: 103–22). And third: the aestheticization and autonomization of non-classical literature was not yet fully under way. In a sense, the mid-eighteenth century marked a hiatus within the processes of modernization. And many individuals paid a price for working at this moment of relative disorganization. Among writers in particular, madness, aggression, poverty and imprisonment were commonplace. As I say, so too was resentment.

Let us take as instances the two writers most closely associated with John Newbery: Christopher Smart and Oliver Goldsmith.[12] Both, as we have seen, incorporated advertisements for Dr James's Powder in their work and both were supported and, indeed, housed by Newbery for a period. Although two more different kinds of writer can scarcely be imagined, socially Smart and Goldsmith shared a great deal – at least if we ignore Goldsmith's Irishness. Both were born into that sector of the middling classes bordering on the lower gentry. Both were university-trained but chose the urban writer's life over established professions and were drawn into the heart of the book-trade/patent-medicine nexus by virtue of their exceptional talent. Both spent time in debtors' prison and experienced difficulty living within their means, spending, in particular, more than they could afford on fine clothes to elicit social recognition. Both won their reputation for their poetry but turned to more entrepreneurial literary projects to make a living. Both were propelled by emotions they could not control, although only Smart was confined in a madhouse. The emotion that Smart experienced was an intense religiosity which expressed itself in a compulsion to adore God in public; the emotion that beset Goldsmith was envy, joined to an irrepressible impulse to put himself forward in social gatherings.

Although nothing seems more oppositional than envy and religious adoration, in fact once we read Smart's and Goldsmith's *oeuvres* and bio-graphies in relation to one another it is possible to regard them as two expressions of a shared experience and social structure – the structure being, of course, the literary economy, described above, within which charlatanism flourished and in which Newbery was a key player.

Smart's adoration was expressed most unguardedly and fully in the text that we know as *Jubilate Agno*, which is often called a poem although it seems more to be a spiritual and prophesizing diary.[13] It was written while Smart was confined in a madhouse, in imitation of biblical rhetorics, although Smart, appropriating the newspaper/literature synergy, called himself the "Lord's News-Writer."[14] Like much grace- and prayer-based evangelicalism, *Jubilate Agno* has a deep relation to the ontology of quackery: many of its last verses praise quasi-magical remedies: "Let Usher, house of Usher rejoice with Condurdon an herb with a red flower worn about the neck for scurvy." Some even combine bookselling and medicine: "Let Crockett, house of Crockett rejoice with Emboline an Asiatic Shrub with small leaves, an antidote. I pray for the soul of Crockett the bookseller the first to put me upon a version of the Psalms."[15]

But the primary force that the text conveys is that of an imprisoned man, less than certain of his soteriological status, encyclopedically journalizing his learning and everyday life by reference to a benevolent, if occluded, divine force, out of an overwhelming sense of bitterness and envy. "For the Tall and the Stately are against me, but humiliation on humiliation is on my side" (Fragment B, No. 112, p. 62), he writes. Or "God consider thou me for the baseness of those I have served very highly" (Fragment D, No. 223, p. 139) – a verse which may single out Newbery, who had stopped supporting Smart and may have been partly responsible for his incarceration. Only to buoy himself up by noting, "For the Sin against the Holy Ghost is Ingratitude" (Fragment B, No. 306, p. 83), and to declare, "I preach the very GOSPEL of CHRIST without comment and with this weapon I shall slay envy" (Fragment B, No. 9, p. 51) – mainly, one assumes, his own envy. Even Smart's benedictions of his associates, for all their investment in God's love, hint at resentment. Why, for instance, does he write, "God bless Charles Mason and all Trinity College" (Fragment B, No. 283, p. 81) when, in turning to the surgeon Middleton, he can declare only, "God be gracious to the immortal soul of Dr Middleton" (Fragment B, No. 282, p. 81), and pronounce less positively still on Christopher Anstey, "Lord have mercy on Christopher Anstey and his kinsmen" (Fragment D, No. 104, p. 130). Blessing, graciousness, mercy: it's hard to see these diminishing gradations of God's love as free from judgment.

Smart, then, attaches himself to a vitalist ontology in which rationalism and empiricism are marginalized, partly in flight from his everyday troubles, and partly in an attempt to deploy religio-magical forces against his enemies. In this move, he connects to a discourse of the patent medicine retailers. But finally *Jubilate Agno* does not belong to charlatanism. Its intensity and verbal brilliance, its profound sense of language as a material *thing*, along with its eccentricity and obscurity and privateness, locate it where calculation, pretension and deceit cease to operate, that is, where madness and writing meet. Nonetheless it also belongs to a moment where envy – for Smart, a sin – is being repudiated only to be almost mutely replaced, if not quite by resentment as a socio-political emotion, at least by a pervasive sense of personal injustice. It will be Edmund Burke in his *Reflections on the Revolution in France* who, in yet another return to charlatanism, will theorize and transparently politicize that mutation in relation to evangelicalism: insisting that religious enthusiasm often masks "envy and malignity" as "distinction, and honours, and revenues" and that therefore it often speaks the "patois of fraud" (Burke 2003: 104). Smart's religion cannot be thought of simply as charlatanized and displaced social resentment, but it's not quite outside of it either.

Resentment: Goldsmith

Goldsmith is a more thoroughly secular writer, whose attempt to escape the culture of charlatanism takes him in the opposite direction to Smart. As is often noted, he is the only author in the Anglophone canon to achieve lasting success in the novel, the drama and poetry, which he managed by contriving a twist to cultural conservatism. Most notably, he refused the temptations of sentimentalism as well as the kind of celebrity that Sterne pioneered, in which an author's public persona merges into that of his characters. But he did not turn to the satire tradition still maintained by his contemporary Churchill, for instance, and whose anti-charlatanism, as we have seen, was itself infected.

In the epilogue to *The Good Natur'd Man* Goldsmith invokes quackery conventionally enough:

> As puffing quacks some caitiff wretch procure
> To swear the pill, or drop, has wrought a cure:
> Thus, on the stage, our playwrights still depend
> For Epilogues and Prologues on some friend,
> Who knows each art of coaxing up the town,
> And make full many a bitter pill go down ...
> (Goldsmith 1904: 241)

This draws Goldsmith into the net of charlatanism in familiar terms. He rejects the "pill" that he is in the process of administering by demanding that the audience ignore his canvassing and "blame where you must, be candid where you can" – that is, deploy the kind of hard but fair judgment that he enjoins in the play itself. His epilogue is, in fact, marketing the play by denying its own role as advertisement.

But this is not Goldsmith's habitual move. In his poem *The Deserted Village*, for instance, he polemically resisted the social extension of market forces by drawing attention to the suffering caused by enclosures and emigration, that is, by capitalism's extension into agriculture. His politics are not, however, those of contemporary "patriotism" – of the populist resistance to infringements of English liberties. Rather, like his friend Johnson, if less assertively, he defends "traditional," quasi-absolutist, rurally based subordination against sentimentalism. But Goldsmith can also call upon a cross-cultural perspectivalism as a means of attaining distance from the modern charlatanized, capitalized scene. After all, his first major foray into journalism was his essay series *Chinese Letters* for Newbery's *Public Ledger*. Here a Chinese visitor to England casts a puzzled eye over the English social scene, revealing it as arbitrary and irrational in many aspects. It's a technique that, for all its problems and limits, allows Goldsmith to write as if he stands outside but not above his society, and to remove himself from the nationalism that was important to Smart, for instance. It is as if the cosmopolitanism of a writer who began his career largely by exploiting the experiences of a youthful trip to Europe enables the degree of detachment and skepticism required not just to avoid charlatanism but to embrace the old rurally based social institutions and hierarchies.

In *The Vicar of Wakefield* Goldsmith turns to a sunny objectivity able to contain both farce and melancholy so as to mount a critique of benevolent sentimentalism. *The Vicar of Wakefield* is a retelling of the Job story: in it a naive, openhearted rural parson with vague aspirations to primitive Christianity from the vantage point of a vulnerable, uxorious gentility, fails to act sufficiently skeptically for his own secular interests. He is beset by tribulation after tribulation, and ultimately finds himself in a debtors' prison, only to be miraculously rescued by the generosity of a member of the local landed gentry. One historical basis of sensibility's emergence, namely its displacement of institutionalized care of the poor, is here staged with exceptional lucidity. Somewhat similarly, in Goldsmith's first comedy, *The Good Natur'd Man*, young Mr Honeywood finds himself facing ruin because, in his benevolence, he falls prey to "every sharper and coxcomb" (Goldsmith 1904: 610). But in this case, benevolence is presented more as a result of a fear of offending others than of innocence of heart. The message in both texts is that modern society is crammed with money-seeking charlatans whom the cult of sentimental good-feeling only encourages. Once again, it's adherence to traditional life-ways and hierarchies, armed with a rational skepticism, that can resist the tide of fraud, emotion, and huckstering.

Goldsmith's reputation was at odds with his public values. It is almost as if he separates his private life and his textual values in resistance to the sentimentalism which, of course, hoped to join these two domains. He became famous for his private insecurity and enviousness. Anecdotes to this end are one of the bass notes of Boswell's *Life of Johnson* as well as of more contemporaneous accounts.[16] Goldsmith was resentful that, for all his fame and recognition, he was still required to write compilations, popular science books and so on for the booksellers in order to live something like a gentleman. He was especially bitter because, unlike Johnson, he was never granted a government pension. In sum, he took it hard that for all his success he remained, to many, an Irish scribbler of little social note and dignity. But again this did not quite add up to *ressentiment* in that his personal envy and bitterness did not take a consciously politicized turn.

Otherwise put, he was responding precisely to the lack of fit between his literary success and his social success. Indeed, we can interpret his mode of subjectivity as at least in part a consequence of the contradictions involved in his rejection of sentimentalism and his appeal for traditional subordination from within the heart of the charlatanized book trade. Yet it seems as if Goldsmith in mainly eluding the cultural economy of charlatanism opened the way for another less nameable situation in which the writer's private affective life begins to exist not so much extrinsically to, or barred from, the work but in systematic and dynamic contradiction to it. Goldsmith's personality negates his work almost algebraically: he personally possesses no defamiliarizing eye; he is incapable of subordinating himself; he knows no tranquility; charity is difficult for him. Yet he goes on preaching subordination, charity and traditional order.

In more abstract terms still: charlatanism dominated mid-eighteenth-century culture and began to lose its capacity to provide an interpretative grid in the century's last decades (despite the denunciatory rhetoric of a figure like Thomas Carlyle which is still partly organized around it) partly because the book and medicine trades move apart but also because relations between literature, politics, and the market are reorganized so that literary writers, decreasingly reliant on patronage, can become primary agents in forming new political, social, cultural, and affective structures. This capacity for agency decreases tensions between the commercial and cultural aspects of their work, and enables a new "romantic" insistence on authenticity and expressiveness based on the requirement that writers' lives and their message cohere in terms which move past those of sentimentalism. That is another story, but it is worth gesturing to here since it helps us see that Goldsmith and Smart – so connected to the patent-medicine trade and so unable to harmonize their lives and their works except, in the case of Smart, at the threshold of sanity – stand as exemplars of the disorganized and charlatanized literary scene out of which romanticism and *ressentiment* both emerged.

Chapter 3

Interesting

The politics of the sympathetic imagination

This chapter examines the relationship between what Luc Boltanski has called the "politics of pity" and the eighteenth-century modernization of the literary field which was briefly outlined in my first chapter (Boltanski 1999: 3–19). It presents a case for the political utility of sentimental literature. And its larger purpose is to show how sympathy (the core category of a sentimental politics of pity) has, in the development of modern culture, been entangled with a more powerful but much less visible and contested category: that of the "interesting."

This topic is not simply academic for me. I began thinking about it from out of a sense of outrage and helplessness in the face of a particular public event – the refusal, in August 2001, of the Australian government to allow the MV *Tampa* to enter Australian waters. For those readers unfamiliar with this events: the *Tampa* was a Norwegian tanker carrying 430 refugees who had been rescued from a sinking ferry and who wished to claim asylum in Australia under the 1951 UN Convention relating to the Status of Refugees (Marr and Wilkinson 2003). Without warning or precedent, the tanker was refused permission to dock in Australia, boarded by troops, and sailed under duress to Nauru, a remote, poor, ecologically devastated Pacific island whose leaders, after prolonged negotiation, allowed the asylum-seekers to be disembarked in return for the provision of health care and other benefits to their own citizens by the Australian government.[1]

This intervention was part of a policy change towards asylum-seekers around the world, one which has been politicized most fiercely in France, and which, as Alain Badiou and others have noted, marks a change in the governmentality of global capitalism in which walls and barriers between different populations (i.e., between the rich and the poor) have become much more prominent (Badiou 2007b: 71–95). In Australia in 2001 laws were introduced by the Howard government to allow refugees to be processed offshore, a policy dubbed the "Pacific Solution." And the *Tampa* affair was presented through a strenuous public relations campaign that pictured the government's refusal to allow the asylum-seekers permission to land as an expression of the nation's right to determine entry into the country. This rights rhetoric encoded a hard xenophobia tinged with racism. It helped the Liberal Party to be re-elected under Howard's leadership in an election that it had been expected to lose. And it helped produce widespread tolerance for a series of tricky moves, including the government's claim during the election that another group of refugees threw children off a boat to win sympathy. This was later shown to have been false, and to have been widely known to be false at the time it was made.

As I say, these events – which in some ways presaged the West's panicked and opportunistic reaction to September 11 – reduced me to powerless outrage. Why powerless? First, because no viable political resistance to the government emerged: opinion polls showed that most Australians supported its policies in the face of which the opposition Labor Party, which formally (but not in fact) occupied the position of a left alternative, did not contest them either. Second, because the language of rationality had largely been pre-empted. As is so often the case, rights discourse had splintered into competing rights, in this case between Australia's sovereign rights and the Iraqi refugees' right to freedom from persecution – an impasse no exercise of practical reason could easily resolve. The law too failed the refugees: legal challenges to the Pacific Solution stalled in the nation's highest court. And the limits of the public sphere became apparent. There was no covert censorship; knowledgeable, impassioned voices put the case for an open policy towards asylum-seekers repeatedly in the media. But to no effect.

The *Tampa* affair made it clear that political horizons had shrunk. Ineffectual opposition to the Pacific Solution came not from the traditional left; not from workers (many of whom were xenophobic; many of whom felt economically threatened by immigration as such, and, indeed, by any hint of deregulated transnational labor flows); not from most Aborigines or from earlier migrants, but from the "liberal professional-managerial class" allied with political humanitarian agencies, many associated with religion and, for obvious reasons, with Islam. What the *Tampa* affair brought home was that my position on this issue, which was not "liberal" except in the mouths of those who disagree with it, could not be attached to any powerful political agency. It has no widely recognized name, no overarching organization, no coherent collectivity, even though it is quite well articulated, at least in the media, even though public political protest can be mounted on its behalf, and even though a raft of small single-issue groups, think tanks, new social movements, rights organizations, charities and NGOs work towards its ends in specific situations. This powerlessness became even clearer in the American political failure to oppose George W. Bush's invasion of Iraq in 2003 as well as the failure to prevent draconian and inhumane immigration policies taking hold in the United States too after 2006. In that powerlessness, the shape of hegemony in endgame democratic capitalism (as outlined in my final chapters) became clearer. And it helped pave the way for the much more radical politics expressed in my final chapters.

In this situation, it came as something of a surprise to realize that the *Tampa* moment was determined by an emotion across a distance – by what we can provisionally call sympathetic compassion. And the reason for this was the distance between me as (then) a member of the Australian "liberal" bourgeoisie and the *Tampa* refugees. Had we shared a collectivity, or at least shared access to formal political institutions, then this form of affective politics need not have been invoked. It is not just that, in Australia, organizations working on behalf of those whom the French call *les sans-papiers* are relatively undeveloped; rather the Howard policies were aimed at preventing refugees from arriving in mainland Australia at all. They were not permitted into our space.

I realized that, in turning toward sympathy and political "sentiment," I was swimming with at least an academic tide. It was not just that I seemed close to joining avowed liberals like Richard Rorty or Martha Nussbaum, for whom, in Rorty's version, progress in the recognition of others' rights will "owe nothing to increased moral knowledge and everything to hearing sad and sentimental stories" (cited in Robbins 1999: 133). Or for whom, in Nussbaum's more rationalist terms, it is politically crucial to develop "the capacity to see one another as fully human" so that "the sympathetic imagination" becomes an "essential ingredient" of a "rational argument" (Nussbaum 1995: xiii). It became apparent that, within cultural studies, more critical and nuanced work on the public and political use of intimate feeling was being written, much of it by Americanists, towards new understandings of the politics of affect. Many of us, it seemed, were renegotiating our relations with public sentiment and its history as we increasingly become subject to that deinstitutionalization of the formal political sphere in which we are invited simply to feel rather than to participate or think.

Yet most critical cultural studies work starts from a different place than where I found myself in relation to the *Tampa* affair. It focuses on the uses of suffering, intimacy, and innocence in modern national politics, especially where these emotions are assigned mainly to women or, conversely, are deployed by the right. It is not primarily concerned with the emotional motivations for political action across large social and cultural distances and at the very limits of state politics, as in the *Tampa* case. After all, at the time, there was almost no representation of the *Tampa* refugees in the Australian media (just as there was to be almost no representation of the suffering of the Iraqi people in the US media as the second US–Iraq war wound on). There was certainly no PR campaign based on their privations. It was, as I say, because they were so remote from the public, so easily placed outside the care of the state, that a form of sympathetic imagination seemed all that remained to reach out to them, at least by those of us not professionally involved in human rights, international aid, NGOs, and so on.

Let me clarify this difference by taking an early example from the new work on the politics of affect which deals with somewhat similar issues to my Australian case – Lauren Berlant's chapter on representations of immigration and minorities in *The Queen of America goes to Washington City* (1997). There she argues that, in the United States, citizenship has become more and more connected to images of intimate life, as against, for instance, being conceived of as a legal right or a basis for political agency. This "intimate citizenship" is seductive in part because it is through the play of feeling in the private domain that a promise of the good life flickers into being, especially for the poorest and weakest members of the community. At the same time, the public appropriation of affect implicitly regulates private life because (to speak abstractly) political representations of innocence and hurt contain controlling judgments upon such states, and so can be easily harnessed to a "compassion" or to "family values" that replace policies which do materially aid the disadvantaged. Berlant's essay, which focuses on various *Time* cover stories on immigration, argues that the United States is increasingly defining itself as the nation where normative private, familial life and intimate relations (most of all: love) can be almost perfect, the rest of the world being relegated to the abstractly institutional and public, where it is figured neither as exotic nor weird (Berlant 1997: 205). Obviously this requires denial on a massive scale, and Berlant ends her chapter with an appeal for her readers to agitate against the privatization and emotionalization of the political imaginary and to invent "new scenes of sociality that take the pressure off the family form to organize history for everything from individuals to national cultures" (1997: 220).

However persuasive this analysis may be, it doesn't speak to situations like the *Tampa* immigrants or the suffering of the Iraqi people. What is at stake there is not how to resist a clammy and overwhelming public imagery of private suffering, intimacy, love, etc., turned to hetero-normative ends but how to produce a sense of connection with, and responsibility to, strangers within a political situation marked by a hardness of heart that belongs not simply to the government, the media, the right, big business, and so on, but pretty much to the community as a whole, *sans* a few co-religionists, activists, and liberal intellectuals.

It's at this point that my professional interest in eighteenth-century literature – as the corpus in which compassionate and imaginative sympathy becomes a principal component of fiction – is brought into play, just because no clearly recognized collectivity has taken charge of the kind of compassion that might resist the geopolitics of which the Pacific Solution and the Western attitude to the Iraqi people in the second US–Iraqi war have been instances. The professional stake that one has in literature which aimed to popularize compassion stands where this absent political grouping might be. So my interest is less in critiquing the contemporary dissemination of sentiment in the political sphere than in understanding the underpinnings, the effectiveness, and the historicity of those forms of public compassion and imaginative sympathy across a distance that canonical literature has long been thought to nurture. Yet to understand these we need to remind our-selves of the limits under which sympathy-based politics operates – to which I now turn.

Most obviously, sympathy for the suffering – let's use that phrase as shorthand – may supplant rather than supplement rational thought about unjust systems that cause suffering, as well as sidelining actions to reform those systems. Indeed, sympathy breaks through all conceptual schema that propel praxis: in Herbert Marcuse's words, it tends to undermine the "dis-tinction between the true and false, the good and bad, the rational and irrational … " (Marcuse 1988: 113). As such sympathy tends to block more radical politics which might transform the system more totally. This argu-ment can be regarded as a variation of a classical objection to pity (one that Friedrich Nietzsche reinvigorated) – namely, that it "enfeebles the soul" and corrodes the steeliness required both to live life to the fullest and to act resolutely (Nietzsche 1986: 38). Behind such suspicions lies the knowledge that feeling sympathy may bring its own pleasures, interest, and compla-cencies that can become their own reward, so as to deflect from action and solidarity.

In somewhat similar terms, sympathy does not recognize hierarchies of responsibility and connection: do we owe the same moral attention to a stranger as to our parents, say? Most would contend not. David Hume, one of sympathy's most influential defenders, went further: he thought (rightly) that the capacity to feel it was in part a function of geography. Spatial dis-tance weakened it. But sympathy is no respecter of social connections or identities, which was also one of the eighteenth century's most often expressed complaints against it.[2] So in cases like the *Tampa*, in which the distant suddenly becomes close, the architectonics of politicized pity quickly begin to totter.

Sympathy is also structurally connected to liberalism. It presupposes a fundamental distance between people (and in particular between the sym-pathizer and the sympathized with) which binds it to the individualism whose most powerful political expression liberalism has been. It was against this aspect of sympathy that Jean-Jacques Rousseau mounted his (deeply ambivalent) critique of what he called "pity," attempting to replace a con-cept of society in which justice depended on compassion by a very different model in which all individuals were equal participants in the articulation and realization of a unified social will.

Yet sympathy is also both structurally projective and self-alienating. Its capacity to humanize others comes at a cost, since it humanizes them into partial versions of themselves. So it is that, when acted upon bureau-cratically, sympathy may produce administrative apparatuses that – in the language of post-structuralism – turn others into the same. At the same time, and from the other direction, acts of sympathy empty the sympathiz-ing self, since to sympathize with others is not simply to make of them versions of oneself but also to make of oneself a version of them. It is this that allows David Hartley, one of the great theorists of sympathy, to think of sympathy mystically, as a stage in the annihilation of self which will ultimately lead to the reign of *agape* conceived of in orthodox Christian terms as a form of selfless love that causes us to "embrace even the most wicked with the most cordial, tender, humble Affection" (Hartley 1759 II: 437). At any rate, there exists a residual tension between sympathy and identity.

Along other lines, this loss of selfhood also lies behind the Stoic critique of compassion. For the ancient Stoics, compassion jeopardized that detachment from the world and that control over the passions that are required for personal well-being.

Then too, sympathy tends to lose its objects. At one level (as Catherine Gallagher has contended and as Rousseau also insisted), sympathy is easier to solicit for fictional characters than for real people to whom one might have practical responsibilities.[3] Indeed, as already noted, those with whom one sympathizes are always to some degree creatures of our imagination. At another level, in the public sphere, suffering is presented in an avalanche of stories about, images of, and testimonies to particularized hurt and deprivation, since, to cite Hannah Arendt's eloquent arguments to this end, sympathy cannot be effectively directed toward "a whole class or a people" but only toward individuals (Arendt 1965: 85). It is not just that such messages cannot consistently confirm their own truth or even sincerity, they overwhelm the compassionate, burying judgment beneath "universal sympathy," as Oliver Goldsmith put it in *The Vicar of Wakefield*, which itself may transform its subjects into what Goldsmith elsewhere called "machines of pity" (Goldsmith 1974: 21). Consequently "compassion fatigue" is accompanied by a certain skeptical wariness (Hartman 1997: 143–44). From the media there flows too much suffering – suffering which may not always be quite what it seems. Indeed, it is not just that fictional victims are easier to sympathize with than real ones, it is that public sympathy actually tends to fictionalize and sensationalize its objects (Boltanski 1999: 183).

At the very least, there exists a structural disjunction between sympathy in private and in public, since the former is out of general view (its academic analysis requires ethnography at best) and its precise force, causes and motives may elude both those who feel it and those who receive it. On the other hand, public sympathy focuses upon the readable and fully meaningful object, and it stereotypes the sympathizer too. Any theory that attempts to derive the sources of a politics of sentiment from flows of feeling in everyday life risks running aground on this disjunction.

And sympathy bears no values by itself. Although compassionate sympathy, in the West at least, has long been associated with benevolence and a certain progressive politics as a flow of emotion from the privileged to the suffering, from the secure to the vulnerable, in principle sympathy can extend to any being who is defined as simultaneously like and other to ourselves –

to victims of oppression, say, or to victims of the system which structures oppression, who might well include the oppressors themselves. To sympathize with the emperor Nero might be an act of greater emotional virtuosity than to sympathize with his persecuted slaves. (Thus, for instance, the emotional force of Herman Melville's *Billy Budd* depends on its presentation of a (Christ-like) victim who sympathizes with his persecutor.) So sympathy as an affect is fickle and capricious, since we have no duty to be sympathetic except under principles that are independent from sympathy itself. Otherwise put: sympathy is not an essence of human nature, as many eighteenth-century moral philosophers (notably Francis Hutcheson and Hume) believed. Indeed, sympathy occurs not on the basis of deep-seated dispositions, or as guided by moral principle, but at the social level, as the result of more or less consensual norms into which individuals have been trained (usually invisibly to themselves), and, at the personal level, contingently, in a mood or captured by an image, a person, or a story. Indeed, although I have been speaking of sympathy as if it were an emotion, it is not quite as simple as that. It is also a thought, an imaginative act, and an intention: indeed, it is in the dislocations between sympathy as feeling, as intention, and as action that it begins to fall apart as a practical basis for ethical and political life.

Finally, it is never clear that sympathy is disinterested. It was one of Jeremy Bentham's most incisive departures from the Whiggish, naturalist moral philosophy of his time that he joined the argument that, as a motive, sympathy was as self-interested as any other (Bentham 1817: 14 ff.).[4] For Bentham this did not matter, since he contended (against David Hartley) that all motives are interested, but from both the Hutchesonian and the idealist positions, it deprives sympathy of much of its legitimation.

The literature of sympathy is shaped by these limits and constraints when it emerges as a specific, highly commercialized, genre in the eighteenth century – as the novel of sensibility – which represents and encourages sympathetic feelings within the routines of everyday life. As is well known, that literature marks no radical break in cultural history. It draws upon various traditions, including the Latitudinarian emphasis on benevolent charity; the celebration of the public virtues of emotional openness by civic republicans; the ontology of esoteric Neoplatonism, which consists precisely of sympathies that bind the world together; the evocation of tears and pity in public-theater tragedies; the hyperresponsiveness ascribed to melancholia by old-fashioned medical theorists, and the grounding of emotional responses in neurology by more modern ones, as well as the repositioning of sympathy as a moral emotion after Joseph Butler, Hutcheson, and Hume in particular.[5]

However, it has not been sufficiently recognized that what was at stake was less a new role for emotion in public life than a transforming intensification of an old one. Let's use this formula: across the eighteenth century compassion was transformed into "sensibility" – where, on the one side, compassion is to be thought of as a moral emotion in which recognition of another's suffering typically led to charitable action on the basis of an acknowledged responsibility (and which was rooted in the traditional Christian virtue of charity as practical *agape*), and where, on the other, sensibility is to be thought of as involving an empathetic identification across a distance with another to whom one's acknowledged responsibility might be minimal – its object might be a fictional character or an animal – and in which the feeling itself had a value independent of its outcome. In terms of the later eighteenth century, Samuel Johnson stands as an exemplar of compassion (especially as described by James Boswell) while Laurence Sterne stands as a (problematic) apostle of sensibility.[6]

At least some of the forces that allowed this transformation are clear from recent scholarship.[7] This takes both a social and a more narrowly literary form. As to the first, the man of feeling is an ideological figure who is to be understood sociologically as a product and a vehicle of the extension of market forces, who carries with him: the hopes for a privatization of charity; resistance to the anti-economic production and anti-market effects of what is today called "welfare"; and, in more concrete terms, for a repeal of the old parochial poor laws through which property owners took care of the poor at the parish level under legal compulsion. (See Watts 2007: 98 for a somewhat similar historicization of sentimentalism.) The man of feeling, however, decides for himself when to feel pity and when to give, and regularly detaches the affect of sensibility from the act of charity.[8] He needs no poor law; he stands in the place of institutionalized charity.

In terms of literature, the sentimental novel, which became a key tool for dispersing sensibility as against compassion, was structured by sympathy's limits and constraints as presented in specific characters on specific fictional occasions (Ellison 1999: 6). Of course, these occasions themselves belonged to the transformations of the literary field caused (to put it bluntly) by commodification – in which, as we have seen above, the book became a purchasable or borrowable commodity for a larger proportion of the population, and in which so-called "extensive" reading practices became more usual. One fictional narrative after another was read for transitory and private pleasures and utilities, rather than a small number of books being read repeatedly, often aloud. As a result, the production of private intensities became increasingly important to the book trade (Engelsing 1974). These commodified intensities helped the domain of fiction imagine a society democratized not through actual political participation but through collectivized good will, benevolent action, acute sensitivity to suffering, and tears. In particular, in this situation a characterology of "the man of feeling" quickly appeared (gender is of course crucial here) around a number of particular literary names and most of all around Laurence Sterne in his persona as Yorick – a character who first appears in *Tristram Shandy* (1760–67) and then again as the author's *alter ego* in *A Sentimental Journey* (1768). Sterne exploited the constraints of sympathy like those I have just listed to create texts capable of producing more powerfully engaging – but also more specifically literary – responses (which include irony) in his readers. Paradoxically, sympathy in the guise of sensibility helped autonomize literature. To put this more generally, as men of feeling and women of sensibility circulate through the ordinary world in novel after novel in resistance to the old charitable institutions and processes, sentimental reading's capacity to insert itself into everyday life intensified awareness and fear of fiction's autonomy. As fiction further entangled itself with the ordinary it produced a new order of its own.

The novelization of imaginative sympathy in terms that depart from charitable deed occurs early in the culture of sensibility. In the first scene of *A Sentimental Journey*, for instance, Yorick finds himself in a mood in which "every power which sustained life" is working "without friction" so much so that "was I a King of France ... what a moment for an orphan to have begged his father's portmanteau of me" (Sterne 1987: 28). In this mood he meets a poor Franciscan monk upon whom he deploys the full force of his sympathetic imagination but to whom, on a whim, he declines to give a farthing, although with whom he later exchanges snuff boxes. It's a complex moment: it is, for instance, a corrective reminiscence of *Gil Blas*'s second chapter, which also describes, but non-sentimentally, an encounter with a beggar. It also implies a critique of Catholicism's mendicant orders. But its main thrust is to divert attention from compassionate sympathy as an ethical emotion towards sentiment and sympathetic imagination as a feature of the social type to which Yorick belongs – a type we can call the modern literary subject. In the end, readers find themselves identifying, more or less ironically or at least in some puzzlement, with Yorick and his fancies rather than simulating flows of social compassion and charity. They find themselves engaging in the imaginary, unlocalized democracy of feeling which is available through commercialized fiction rather than bound to a hierarchized society largely organized around parochial government and charity.

The story of literary sensibility's deflection from the politics of compassion into its own autonomous domain needs to be told very carefully especially because, as sympathy becomes detached from compassion in the old sense, it itself undergoes a rapid transformation. In Britain, William Wordsworth, in particular, extends the concept beyond charity and benevolence by imagining what Raymond Williams called a "general common humanity" unified by a shared emotional power – the power, simultaneously, of creativity and of sympathy. This (to reference Williams again) is "one of the principal sources of the idea of Culture as such" (Williams 1958: 59). At this moment a diffused sympathy connects individuals into a collective culture but can also extend beyond shared traditions and customs to form the basis of the moral and affective idea of humanity as such. But it need not lead to particular action.

This is not to suggest that relations between popular literary sensibility and compassion were much influenced by the abstraction of sympathy into the culture-idea, at least until the mid-nineteenth century. I would suggest that one specific category is more important in ordering the split between sensibility and compassion. That is the neglected para-aesthetic category of the "interesting" in something like our current sense, a usage which the *OED* claims first appears nowhere else than in Sterne's *A Sentimental Journey* but which can in fact be found earlier. At any rate, "interesting" becomes a familiar category through which both the world and cultural objects are apprehended at the same time that sensibility was being disarticulated from compassion, so to become a key term through which modern literary (and indeed cultural) production would be received.[9] This makes its neglect by historians and critics puzzling. While there exists a whole library on the history of sensibility and sentimentality, there is almost nothing on the history of the "interesting."[10] It's as if "interesting" belongs to the conceptual air we breathe rather than to the vicissitudes of history and culture.

I hope that we can, with Raymond Williams, simply agree that today and long since "interesting" has become (probably) the concept most often used to endorse cultural objects (Williams 1976: 144). It routinely performs more conceptual labor than it seems fit for. To take two canonical nineteenth-century examples: William Wordsworth describes the purpose of his and Coleridge's *Lyrical Ballads* (1798) in the famous preface to the second edition (1800) like this:

> The principle object ... proposed in these Poems was to choose incidents and situations from common life, and to relate or describe them, throughout, as far as was possible in a selection of language really used by men, and, at the same time, to throw over them a certain colouring of imagination, whereby ordinary things should be presented to the mind in an unusual aspect; and further, and above all, to make these incidents and situations *interesting* by tracing in them, truly though not ostentatiously, the primary laws of our nature: chiefly, as far as regards the manner in which we associate ideas in a state of excitement.
>
> (Wordsworth 2000: 596, italics mine)

Here "interesting" carries an extraordinary conceptual weight, and indeed, as we are about to see, the word means something slightly different than it does today – it implies an ethical engagement now lacking. Nearly seventy years later, when, in *Culture and Anarchy*, Matthew Arnold wants to distinguish cultures based on mere science from those aimed at fulfilling human "perfection", he too turns to an ethically charged concept of the "interesting" to designate what the first lack in comparison to the second, as if the other capacities or qualities he is urging – seeing things as they are, the deployment of critical intelligence, sweetness and light, etc. – have less than the force than he needs at this juncture (Arnold 1993: 60).

These days, however, we say "That's interesting" phatically, mundanely, almost without noticing it and without meaning anything at all. At most, the phrase signals a qualified, limited investment of feeling in an object – a detached engagement, so to say. As such, it might be understood as an indication of how little ethical, aesthetic, or political commitment is demanded of contemporary cultural participants. But this kind of understanding, while not altogether mistaken, risks underestimating the term's complex past and the discursive structures in which it first appeared.

In the eighteenth century, "interesting" meant something more than it does today. Indeed, it could possess a specifically political force within the debates over sentimentalism and compassion. At one level there is a transition from the old meaning of "interest" as a stake, and more particularly a competitive and/or precarious stake in some finite good or advantage, as in the current phrase "interest group" to a more personal "interest" – a soldier's in R&R, for instance, to something vaguer still, the interest or interestingness of a fiction, say. It seems to be Samuel Richardson in particular who (possibly under the influence of French usage) popularizes the term in a new, adjectival sense of "attention-gripping".[11] He does so, for instance, in this passage from *Sir Charles Grandison* (1753–54) about a masquerade in which the bounds of propriety were being exceeded: "She put me upon recollecting the giddy scene, which those dreadfully interesting ones that followed it, had made me wish to blot out of my memory" (Richardson 1753 II: letter XXXI). Here "interesting" has lost connection with "interest" as a stake in a good such as property or even a pleasure like sex but it remains a stronger, more threatening, and restricted concept than it will become.

Similarly when Boswell used the word in his *Life of Johnson*, it is generally applied to literary biography or tourism, which is "interesting" because it engages readers in what they share with authors, life itself.[12] Johnson's own criticism entangles itself around the concept, for that matter. He too repeatedly argued (as in the sixtieth number of *The Rambler*) that literary biography is especially valuable because we have so much "interest" in it – this interest operating at the borders of an old and a new sense of the term, as it also does when the young Frances Burney, on starting her diary in 1768, self-mockingly declares her adventures to be "wonderful, surprising & interesting" in a sequence of adjectives which did not seem as anticlimactic then as it does now (Burney 1988: 1). In his *Life of Milton*, Johnson, citing Addison, declares Milton's *Paradise Lost* to be interesting in the old sense, because its topic – the Fall – concerns us all, while at the same time insisting that it lacks "Human Interest" because, being too remote from everyday life, it tends to dullness.[13] In this appeal to what is not boring (a word that would come into being only in the middle of the nineteenth century) we glimpse one reason why the sense of "interesting" shifts at the very moment that the novel genre becomes commercialized and the novel of sensibility becomes popular – the interesting and the sentimental both *engage*.

But the interesting has a wider reach than the sentimental in part just because it is vaguer and because it loses its ethical charge: it can cover, in particular, narrative pleasures such as those stimulated by suspense, which become a driving force in fictional narratives (both in prose and in drama) from the 1780s onwards. The theater critic James Boaden talks of the "search after great strength of interest" around this period, and marks Elizabeth Inchbald's dramas as being at the forefront of this pursuit (Boaden 1825 II: 79). Indeed, being interesting becomes an important criterion for reviewers of fiction in the new serious review periodicals – the *Monthly* and the *Critical* – that were established in the middle of the eighteenth century, as a term able to mediate between readers and novels delivered to the market. That particular setting for the term "interesting" would appear to have accelerated its dissemination. And indeed the new novel of the 1770s – increasingly concerned with "typicality" and fashion, multi-volume, often published or at least reprinted serially – needed precisely to be interesting above all things.

However, the modern sense of "interesting" also untangles itself from interest-as-a-stake during a period when "interest" was a loaded term for social theory. Famously, interest had been first singled out as a reliable, calculable key to human action against the unruly passions in Machiavelli's theorization of statecraft, and then, as "self-interest," had been set against moral sentiment, sociability, and sympathy in debates between the Hobbesians and the school of Shaftesbury at the beginning of the eighteenth century.[14] As a young man the Anglican churchman and theologian Joseph Butler made an influential contribution to this debate by arguing that benevolence and the "pursuits of public good" were as involved in self-love and "our own interest" as the "pursuits of private good" and that only a false analogy between private property and private interest allowed this to be overlooked (Butler 1860: 134 ff.).

By the century's end interest itself was figured as a concept that binds individuals together into society rather than as the predictable spring of individual action, that is to say, there existed (what William Godwin among others called) a "public interest" of a different order than the sum of individual interests, and which could not be confined to more traditionally transindividual entities like the nation (Godwin 1985: 466). Thus Thomas Paine argued in *The Rights of Man* (1791) that almost all the work of government ought to be carried out not by an unrepresentative administration but by society instead, and ground his case on the pervasiveness of interest:

> It is to the great and fundamental principles of society and civilization – to the common use universally consented to, and mutually and reciprocally maintained – to the unceasing circulation of interest, which, passing through its million channels, invigorates the whole mass of civilized man – it is to these things, infinitely more than to anything which even the best instituted government can perform, that the safety and prosperity of the individual and of the whole depends.
>
> (Paine 1969:186–87)

Here widely dispersed interests, both shared and individual, but especially shared, "invigorate" the "mass" of man into a civilized social whole. Interest has been generalized: it connotes not self-servingness but a commitment to the social good – while still denoting a personal engagement.

This move owes much to Claude Adrian Helvétius, whose *De l'Esprit* (1758) and posthumous *De l'Homme* (1776) both circulated widely in Britain, including in plebeian circles, after their translation into English in 1759 and 1777 respectively. For Helvétius, interest determines action because, in an expansion of the concept, it mediates between internal states and the outside world: "interest and want are the principles of all sociability," he writes, being driven by "corporeal sensibility," which he construes straightforwardly as the desire for pleasure and the avoidance of pain (Helvétius 1777: 137). An orderly and just society will exist only when all its members have an interest in it – and not just a material interest. Indeed, the public has its own specific interest in itself, namely that the greatest happiness of the greatest number be the measure of social value. Interest is not simply driven by "self-love", it is rather (as it was in Hume) "the powerful and general spring, that source of action in all men, which carries them sometimes to vice and sometimes to virtue" (1777: 181). But if interests are determined by pleasure, they are also determining, since, to some degree, man perceives, believes, and feels that which is in his interest: this is the idea that Helvétius's follower Jeremy Bentham will formularize as "interest-begotten prejudice" (Bentham 1989: 180).

Along with his development of the "greatest happiness of the greatest number" principle (which had already been formulated, of course, by Joseph Butler and John Brown in theological terms) and his insistence that all human beings have the same quantum of natural intelligence, it is this insight that marks Helvétius out. He insists that imagination is itself driven by interests, and that imagination, especially in religious narratives, has driven history and inhabits morals. Differences between peoples and customs are differences in the ways that interests have congealed into beliefs. But he also insists that, because of this, the mind can be educated so that the empire of observation and fact may colonize that of morals and imagination. Through education, interests are, so to speak, brought back to earth in the form of "principles of morality and politics," and most of all in the form of the utilitarian calculations of happiness that, in different forms, Godwin, Bentham, and the later English philosophic radicals all took from him.

In effect, then, after Helvétius, "interest" is associated less with Thomas Hobbes, Bernard Mandeville, and Hume and more with the promoters of enlightened governance. So William Hazlitt, in his early contribution to philosophy, *An Essay on the Principles of Human Action, to which are added some Remarks on the Systems of Hartley and Helvétius* (1805), mounts an argument for the primacy of disinterestedness as against self-interest as a motive for action not by denying interest's importance but by increasing it. Interest in and for others and also for one's future self is as powerful a psychological force as interest for the present self. In particular, for Hazlitt, sympathetic imagination is not in conceptual or psychological opposition to interest, in the first place because one can have no interest in one's future self without the capacity sympathetically to imagine that projected self, and, second, because the power to identify with a future self is not in principle different from the power to sympathize with others. By this point, then, interest can be regarded as a form of social participation, and its circulation in interesting narratives and images as a means to tighten and extend social bonds. In this sense, unlikely as it may seem, interest is doing something like the work of compassion without (so far as the radical thinkers were concerned) relying on sensibility or the false hypotheses of innate sympathy or of Rousseauvian "good nature" or of Christian benevolence. Being "interesting" then becomes a popular and autonomous property of narratives, images, scenes, persons, pulling them out of the realms either of the merely diverting or of the properly moral or aesthetic, and drawing them into what Godwin in *An Enquiry concerning Political Justice* (1798) called "social communication" (the condition, Godwin noted, for pursuing the "best interests" of mankind). At this point the concept acquires a particular socially progressive force as it does, to take just one instance, in the loaded title of Olaudah Equiana's *The Interesting Narrative of the Life of Olaudah Equiana or Gustavus Vassa the African, written by Himself* (1789).

Yet it bears that force only marginally and for a short period. Very quickly "interesting" becomes almost wholly banalized. If it does not mean merely amusing it means more than that only by suggesting that there exists a motive or reward for attending to what is "interesting" without that motive or reward requiring – or necessarily being capable of – specification. At the same stroke, in the first decades of the nineteenth century, interesting becomes primarily a qualifier of cultural rather than of political or ethical things (although, censoriously and somewhat archaically, pregnant women in particular remain "interesting" across the nineteenth century). Indeed it becomes the cultural equivalent of that "calm passion" which, as Albert Hirschman pointed out, was deemed the (desirable) emotional basis of an economy based on capital and exchange rather than on landed property (Hirschman 1977: 66). And, in a different sphere, it becomes a category that undermines those theories that emphasized "disinterestedness" as the primary quality of the aesthetic response. However, the difference between the disinterested attention of the aesthete on the one side and the vernacular pursuit of the interesting on the other is less than the terms themselves, embedded in the old senses of "interest", would lead us to suppose. In fact, Immanuel Kant, who argued most influentially that an aesthetic relation requires the spectator's disinterest, floundered when trying to account what it was that drew the spectator's attention to the object in the first place. As Hans-Georg Gadamer has contended, Kant needed to have it both ways: while the aesthetic object does not engage interest, at the same time "only the beautiful thing speaks meaningfully to us and evokes our total interest" (Gadamer 2006: 43 ff.). "Interesting" as a para-aesthetic concept at least has the virtue of avoiding that paradox.

In returning to the scene of sensibility's literary emergence, then, it may seem that we do not find support for the politics of compassion that the powerlessness of the modern liberal demands but rather a fugitive moment that quickly deliquesces into the autonomization of literature, the intensities of reading as consumption, the phantasmal promise of public engagement and, most of all, the interesting, interested reader. That reader, prefigured in Sterne's Yorick and his eccentricities, continues to organize our own public image and position as literary professionals, situated at a slight remove from our fellow citizens, including those citizens for whom, today, the Pacific Solution, or the panicked, opportunistic politics of anti-terrorism, seem all but unassailable.

But this may be a little precipitate. For in the end – speaking generally – it may be that political compassion across a distance can be rescued from the public uses of intimacy and feeling and the para-aesthetics of the interesting. Why, after all, are professors of literature almost all cosmopolitan liberals (although before about 1960 we tended at least as often to be conservative)?[15] Is it because we imagine ourselves ultimately to belong not primarily to the nation but to a collectivity of the literary and the cultivated across national borders? Is it because we stand to gain relatively little from the social and economic structures that (seem to be) protected by hard patriotism, conservatism, and strategic indifference to the suffering of those culturally different from oneself? Or is it that, in a Bourdieuean sense, it is in our interest to mark ourselves out from the dominating fraction of the dominant classes, as well as from most mass media, by embracing a broader, less materialist politics which is, unlike theirs, partly based on imagination and sympathy? Or could it indeed be that (as we mostly like to think) our training provides us with a capacity for critical analysis and for openness to difference along with a relatively strong sense of history?

Does the canon itself shape our sympathetic liberalism? Does its content, and specifically its excitement of sympathy, count? My sense (or hope?) is that it does, if in highly qualified ways. I want to insist that it's not just that certain fictional techniques – the identification of readers with realist characters, say – may tie sympathy and interest together, it's that literary subjectivity remains (however tenuously) open to those flows of compassion from the privileged to the suffering which have (despite everything) helped legitimate and motivate reform and philanthropy. It does so because, in many of its moments – and most of all in the novel of sensibility – literature continues its interesting tease of charity and compassion, repeatedly invoking, rejecting, and deforming it.

As the slightest of gestures towards this topic, let me offer three very cursory anecdotal examples, historical rather than textual, all focused on

Sterne as a founder of one school of sympathy-based fiction, to remind us of the complex relations between the literature of sensibility and social action. Take the Tory and evangelical abolitionist William Wilberforce's harsh judgment of Sterne: "Instead of employing his talents for the benefits of his fellow creatures, they were applied to the pernicious purposes of corrupting the national taste, and of lowering the standard of manners and morals" (cited in Woodard 1999: 81–82). Compare that to the ex-slave Ignatius Sancho's appeal to Sterne to join his work against slavery since, according to Sancho, a fan, Sterne was one of only two famous authors humane enough to do so. And finally consider Leonard O'Malley, the Irish lawyer and member of the revolutionary political association the United Irishmen, who in the 1790s defended many of his comrades in their trials for treason but who was simultaneously the spy who betrayed them. It absolutely fits the logic of sympathy that O'Malley was a popular sentimental lyricist and a Sterne imitator who wrote an adaptation of *Tristram Shandy* for the stage. Let O'Malley stand for the separation of the literary tease of sympathy from actual moral behavior; let Wilberforce stand for the reformer's scorn of literary pleasures and interests; let Sancho stand for the recognition that literary sensibility retains a compassionate charge containing at least the promise of political solidarity across differences.

Since Sterne's time, literature may have increasingly subsumed compassion into the interesting and the sentimental but it is in literature's self-interest that it does not wholly forgo the intricate, unstable promises of the sympathetic imagination, or to disjoin itself from the ideal of a politics of compassion. Sympathy itself may be a poor political resource, useful mainly when communication falters and organized joint action is all but impossible (as in the case between the privileged academic and the *Tampa* refugees); but it remains a rich quarry for literature whose social utility is so difficult to specify and affirm and whose public appeal depends more on its promise of interest, including the interest of compassion, than on its social power.

In my first chapter I argued that one reason for us to pay attention to eighteenth-century Tory literary practice was its chill message of mortification. It presents us with a rebuke to the pride excited simply by being of our moment; it invokes the death that haunts all literary fields, especially now. But I am beginning here to argue something like the opposite: that the pursuit of the interesting is valuable at least in so far as it contains traces of nearly occluded history of charity and sensibility. This, however, does not seem to me a logical contradiction – after all there is no logical difficulty in sometimes engaging with the dead and sometimes engaging with the living. But it may seem ethically unsatisfactory, since it does not imply an especially coherent framework for literary criticism/history. And indeed professional literary criticism is today not so much a coherent as a dispersed and appetitive formation, one in which it is almost possible (but probably not quite) to defend even the deadly boring archives of a figure like John Nichols as ... interesting.

Part II

Towards endgame capitalism

Literature, theory, culture

Chapter 4

World literature, Stalinism, and the nation

Christina Stead as lost object

Christina Stead was a novelist who began publishing in the Popular Front era and finished her career during the Cold War. Born in Australia, she lived most of her life, and set and published most of her novels, abroad. She wrote about three continents (Australia, Europe, and North America), developing a powerful and distinctive style and narrative technique along the way. Although few writers have more to tell us about mid-twentieth-century Western society and culture, she is not widely known, except, perhaps, as author of *The Man Who Loved Children* (1940) and, in Australia, as author of *For Love Alone* (1944) as well.

For all her adult life, she was a committed, if heretical, Stalinist, and her writing was thoroughly informed by her Stalinism. This makes her a particularly fascinating and instructive case in considering relations between the modern – globalized – literary field and resistance to capitalism. In this chapter I argue that her hatred of capitalism was a basic source of her literary power. In that light, turning to a concept of the global literary field (a.k.a. "world literature") I uncover the institutional forces which enabled her work to circulate into the Cold War as well as those that blocked her reputation from fully flourishing. This requires me not just to present quite a detailed account of her career and *oeuvre* but to examine a development of the modern literary field, posthumous to Stead, within which a wider economic and cultural globalization intersected with what Goethe long ago named "world literature."[1]

Today, world literature (and cognate concepts) are receiving increased academic attention after decades of neglect. Indeed, the interest in world literature obviously follows the recent rapid extension of cross-border flows of tourists and cultural goods around the world, including literary fictions. And those fictions are today attached to a complex leisure industry involving writers' festivals, literary-prize junkets and publicity, literary tourism, adaptation and spinoff opportunities – an industry only rather indirectly dependent upon the actual reading of books.[2] Indeed, there is a complex dynamic between literature's increased participation in the genteel leisure industry and the relative decline of literary writing's importance both in the education system and in the market: the renewed attention to world literature being as much an expression of anxiety concerning literature's decline as a response to its commercial cross-media globalization. In this situation Australia, like many other more or less peripheral nations, is strenuously concerned to place its literature (henceforth Auslit) inside the global canon. After all, there's an increased sense that a lively and rich culture, including a literary culture, whether or not attached to actual reading, possesses economic value (direct or indirect) to those nations and cities which nurture it. Once we come to think of it, it is clear that Shakespeare's contribution to the British economy, for instance, must have been immense. And governments and certain interest groups are still, if only fitfully, concerned to maintain the habit of literary reading, partly (in the Arnoldian tradition) in obeisance to cultural standards set against (allegedly) inarticulate, superficial and labile populisms.

Bearing this in mind, I want to begin by examining what is arguably the most subtle recent account of world literature – that put forward by Pascale Casanova in her *The World Republic of Letters* (1999). I will go on to consider the adequacy of Casanova's model to Christina Stead, and in particular to her 1965 novel, *Cotters' England*. As I have already suggested, I have chosen Stead because I believe that she is a writer with an exceptionally, perhaps uniquely, strong claim to joining the global canon (which is not necessarily to say, strong enough). And I have chosen *Cotters' England* not simply because, although often recognized as one of Stead's most successful novels by specialist critics, it is still largely unknown and can thus test the likelihood of her being more fully canonized and also help us focus on the kind of work required to succeed in the task of transnational canonization.

It is necessary to concede at the outset that the quantifiable evidence for Stead's claim to canonicity is weak. This is not the place fully to enumerate her institutional standing but some indications are worth noting, particularly in comparison to her (in this context) closest peer, the Australian novelist Patrick White. During her lifetime Stead won no major international award, whereas Patrick White was a Nobel Prize winner. Stead has two novels currently in print in the United States, one in the United Kingdom, one in Germany, and none in France, while White has one novel in print in the United States, two in the United Kingdom, none in Germany, and six in France. Stead is widely translated, but not nearly so widely as White. Both Stead and White are the subject of expert biographies and collections of letters, but only White has a professionally assembled bibliography. The MLA bibliography, which lists academic critical works, contains about thirty items on Stead published over the decade 1997–2007, against forty articles and books devoted to White. Since 1980 there have been approximately twelve academic monographs written on Stead (all in English) while there have been twenty-five on White, two of which are in German and one in French. (But tellingly, of those, three on Stead were published since 2000, against two on White.)

Given Stead's weakness in these terms, it is clear that she can be more fully canonized only by insisting on her "quality." (The scare quotes signify a dislike for the reductive force of the word's bureaucratic usages in this context.)[3] That's one reason why evaluative close reading is required to make the case.

Casanova's *The World Republic of Letters*

Casanova does not often use the term "world literature" at all, preferring the hallowed metaphor "republic of letters" even though she is concerned with a select literary canon and her work ultimately derives from Marx's comment that capitalism's drive towards the unification of the world market will take intellectual form when "from numerous national literatures and local literatures there arises a world literature."[4] For all that, Casanova's republic of letters does not belong to a vaguely defined transnational public sphere. It is a highly structured, partially autonomous field, with clear hierarchies and functions that allow it to reproduce and extend itself in an ordered fashion. It is, however, not controlled: no central body representing world literature (like the French Academy, for instance) creates and monitors canons or organizes resistance to any waning of literary interest.

Casanova's world republic of letters covers and transcends particular linguistic and national territories across whose borders texts and reputations circulate, mainly in translation, in a unified worldwide import and export book trade. So it's a concept that borrows from the "world system" as posited by Immanuel Wallerstein. Yet, for Wallerstein, capitalism has created an interdependent system of core, semi-peripheral, and peripheral regions across the globe in which core regions maintain an interest in maintaining the "underdevelopment" of the peripheries, and there's no sense in Casanova that the metropole seeks to "underrecognize" writing from the peripheries for its own cultural gain. Indeed, the workings of the literary field remain invisible to participants, who are likely to resist cold sociological analysis of their seemingly unmediated relation to the works they admire. In this sense, then, Casanova's concept of field also owes much to that established by Pierre Bourdieu in his work on relation between cultural tastes and class, although, unlike Bourdieu, she does not confine herself to a national formation. We can put it like this: Casanova's important theoretical move is to break with the old concept of world literature, and the comparativist model which was derived from it, by conceiving of it as a system in terms drawn from Wallerstein, and a field in terms drawn from Bourdieu.

In Casanova's model the national vernacular literatures comprising the global literary system view one another as rivals, given that immense symbolic and material rewards are available to those nations and languages which produce internationally recognized geniuses of the order of Shakespeare, Cervantes, Proust, or Goethe. Historically, it is through competition for such rewards that two new formations developed – a national literary canon written in various vernaculars (rather than in the classical languages) and an international canon in which literary works achieve their widest possible cross-border recognition. Canons of this type first appeared in Europe in the early modern period as French replaced Latin as the language of Continental learned communication. The international canon gradually expanded and enriched itself when writers and texts from peripheral territories and languages joined it, and as competition compelled writers within national literatures to continual innovations of form and content. In this process a certain sector of writing detached itself from political, moral, and religious functions and uses. That is to say, by the time Flaubert was writing in the middle of the nineteenth century, a certain sector of the literary field had become partially autonomous.

At this point, according to Casanova, literature also becomes divided between anachronistic and modern writing, in a structure where peripheral areas in the world system tend to produce anachronistic works, while the centers, where literary autonomy has been more nearly achieved, split between modern and anachronistic works. This division helps the literary field create that "literary capital" which can be attached to individual writers, nations and languages, and which is measurable through indicators such as bookstore numbers in a particular nation or language community, proportion of average leisure time spent on discretionary literary reading, honors given to writers, number of books and translations published, and so on. My crude numerical accounting for Stead and White's relative canonicity is an attempt to measure such literary capital for these particular authors.

For Casanova, too, those territories with the oldest literary heritage are able to acquire most literary capital. As a result, peripheral territories become increasingly dependent on the metropole, since only nations and languages with a great deal of literary capital and a strong autonomous sector have the power to consecrate writers from abroad. This power lies in the hand of metropolitan intermediaries – publishers, translators, critics – who consecrate texts, current or past, by making judgments as to what works are fully literary and which are not. Although these gatekeepers do not necessarily see themselves as engaged in canon-building, their acts of consecration habitually compare current works with those "universal classics" in which literary value has become incarnate, and which have been removed from the temporal orders of fashion, novelty and contemporaneity into a transcendental domain of the "timeless and immortal" (1999: 92). Thus the fully developed world republic of letters contains a tripartite scheme of literary temporality: works are either anachronistic, modern or timeless, with modern works produced in literary fields of maximum autonomy having the greatest capacity to pass the threshold out of mere modernity into eternal posterity.

Casanova goes on to argue that, in the development of the international literary field, Paris has possessed a unique advantage which ultimately derives from its revolutionary history, or, to put this somewhat differently, from that long-standing commitment to enlightenment which has enabled the city to define a political modernity focused on republicanism and universal emancipation. Paris has been able to convert this political capital into literary capital. But it has also been a world-city of culture whose highly developed, relatively uncensored literary institutions have long provided the environment in which great texts can be written, and which has therefore attracted writers on the periphery trapped within their minor languages and inside their limited, often censorious societies.[5] Yet Casanova recognizes that internationalized writers who expatriate themselves because of censorship or lack of recognition, or simply because of provincial torpor, may be instrumental in their choice of a place of expatriation. For example, the kind of Irish writer who moved to France in the first decades of the twentieth century might today move to the east coast of the United States (1999: 124). Nonetheless, Casanova believes that Paris remains the world's literary capital because its political and ideological history can still be cashed out as literary capital and implicitly because it does not share Anglophone loss of interest in literature. (One sign of this might be that Patrick White has more books in print in France than in the United Kingdom or the United States even today.)

Casanova also fully acknowledges that literature capable of joining the global canon is not always produced in the metropolitan centers. Indeed, peripheral nations can cause literary revolutions especially at the moment when they join the global literary field – Casanova points to Ireland and Czechoslovakia in the first half of the twentieth century as instances. That was when Joyce and Kafka appropriated "the literary and linguistic assets of the European countries whose heritages they claimed" in order to overturn them (1999: 241). For Casanova, the timing of a particular national literature's entry into world literature may, once again, be politically rather than culturally determined. But the metropolitan act of consecration which is required for the revolution to succeed is not itself political, it is literary. Indeed, as she insists, a particular *oeuvre* can join world literature only at the point when it has achieved a measure of independence from political and cultural-nationalist interests and purposes (1999: 86). Here too France has a continuing advantage just because it was the first nation to produce an autonomous literary field. But this also means that specific national literatures contain an opposition between those writers who write for international readerships and those that don't, which roughly maps on to the anachronistic/ modern distinction which is, as far as she is concerned, centered on France.

As noted above, Casanova's model is partly derived from Bourdieu. But it differs from its precursor in one particularly pertinent regard. In Bourdieu's description of "distinction" those without cultural capital don't understand the notion of cultural autonomy at all. In accounting for their tastes, working-class men and women do not appeal to purely aesthetic criteria, or to art as an end in itself. Indeed, they make a virtue of their ignorance (Bourdieu

1986: 372 ff.). But, in Casanova, nations whose literatures do not count in the world literary system are not wholly outside the protocols which constitute the literary field as autonomous: serious writers the world over recognize the greatness of Joyce, Kafka, Dostoevsky and so on, even if as models to reject. When popular fiction writers claim major literary value for their work, they too compare themselves to established canonical authors. Certainly it is impossible to be an art-writer without this recognition, so there's a sense in which everyone is playing the same game. This, indeed, is what enables those on the margins periodically to revolutionize literary style and form.

That Bourdieu's scheme is rigid while Casanova's is fluid in this regard makes it even more important to note that she remains limited by Bourdieu's structuralism and hard binaries. For Casanova, literature is either linked to autonomy or not; it is either modern or anachronistic, either consecrated or unconsecrated, either national or international, even if over time the status of particular works may change. For this reason, her model stands at some distance from the messy world in which literary works may be ambiguously autonomous; may belong to no specific national culture; may be placed in some more or less undefined location between or outside the anachronistic and the modern; where claims to international status may be debatable or unclear, or exist in a hazily defined zone of quasi-canonicity, as well as where various highly developed literary communities may make different judgments from one another and create different canons from one another, and where, in particular, pedagogical/scholarly canons may take very different forms than market/journalistic ones. In a revealing omission, Casanova (unlike Bourdieu) discounts the education system's powers of canonization, presumably because to do so would diminish Paris's claim to influence over the world republic of letters.

Casanova's is finally a less materialist account than Bourdieu's. For him, the distribution of cultural capital is underpinned by factors like the distribution of economic capital and restricted access to higher education, so that its accumulation is finite. That's less the case in Casanova. Although she does have a strong sense of the economics of the publishing industry, for instance, and locates the gatekeepers of global canonicity institutionally, in the end she is not especially interested in the actual social settings and rhetoric in which texts are disseminated, translated, reviewed and acclaimed. Thus, on the one side, the acts of judgment by which works are deemed canonical are strangely absent in her work, a point to which I will return. On the other, restraints upon canonicity – for instance, limits to the number of reading hours a community can muster; to the size of the book market; to the number of literature courses an education system can offer; to literary interest in general – do not concern her. Does the global canon consist of 1,000 works? Or would 100 be a more realistic number? Whatever the answer, it is clear that there exist real restraints upon how many books can be read, taught, reviewed, bought, translated, and hence that the global canon is relatively small for reasons unrelated to purely literary quality, and which cannot be wholly accounted for in structural terms either. This poses specific problems for conscious, organized efforts of canonization like the "internationalizing Auslit" movement. In the end it may be that there is only room for no, or only one or two, classic Australian texts in the world's bookshelves and classrooms.

Stead's career

Rather than elaborating a critique of Casanova's model, I want now to inquire into how it might apply to Christina Stead, so as to assess Stead's potential for global canonicity. And for that, as I say, we need a reasonably detailed and analytic narrative of her work and career. But this analysis is not extrinsic to the processes of canonization, which, indeed, partly depend on the compellingness of narratives that bind together texts, authorial lives, and social settings. This means that the story I am about to tell is itself a potential canonizing agent.

Stead was born in Sydney in 1902. She belongs to the same generation as William Faulkner (b. 1897), Elizabeth Bowen (b. 1899), Vladimir Nabokov (b. 1899), Ernest Hemingway (b. 1899), John Steinbeck (b. 1902), Evelyn Waugh (b. 1903), Graham Greene (b. 1904), Christopher Isherwood (b. 1904), Henry Green (b. 1905), Anthony Powell (b. 1905), Samuel Beckett (b. 1906), and Henry Roth (b. 1906), to name some fiction writers writing in or around the Anglophone world with at least a threshold claim to global canonicity. Although Casanova makes little room for the concept of the generation in her analysis, her emphasis on dynamic rivalry as a driving force behind global canon formation implies it, since, at least initially, competition happens primarily between writers of the same generation, and since, in practice, the "timelessness" that she invokes is first granted across discrete periods and generations. (It is worth noting that the concept of the "generation" was to be brought to bear on literary history in Paris – by Albert Thibaudet – just as Stead's career was gaining traction.)[6]

One specific feature of Stead's generation is worth noting: it came to literary maturity after the first wave of modernism during the Depression and Popular Front era (which resulted from Stalin's allowing European communist parties to ally themselves to social democratic parties in the struggle against fascism). It went on to experience World War II and then the Cold War, and entered old age in the 1960s, when Western culture did indeed undergo a further major transmutation. This was an especially difficult generation for women: I have been able to place only one other woman in the canon listed above – Elizabeth Bowen. Other highly talented and productive female writers of that generation – Anna Kavan (b. 1901), Kay Boyle (b. 1902), and Rosamund Lehmann (b. 1903), for instance – have a weaker claim on canonicity than the male writers just listed. There is a greater degree of gender equality in the canons of somewhat earlier generations (Woolf, Mansfield, Compton Burnett, Rhys, Wharton) if not those immediately following.

Stead, born into a progressivist middle-class family, was trained as a teacher and studied psychology at tertiary level but left for Europe in 1928, not just in pursuit of the energy, choices, styles and prestige of metropolitan life but also to escape from familial and peer-group surveillance and judgment (see Stead 1995). These were of course not then unusual motivations behind the metropolitan diaspora of the cultivated colonial bourgeoisie. Stead was also, typically enough for a heterosexual young woman of her time, in pursuit of a young man, Keith Duncan, who held a postgraduate scholarship at the LSE. Once in London, Duncan turned out not to be especially interested in her, and while working as a secretary in an international grain-dealing firm she began an affair with her boss, William Blech (later known as William Blake), a highly cultivated Jewish American (he claimed to have studied in Germany with Max Weber) and a married man. Stead and Blake went on to form a stable partnership (they themselves married in 1952) which lasted till Blake's death in 1968.

In 1929 the couple moved to Paris, where they worked in a shady private investment firm, the Travelers' Bank, while Stead wrote during her leisure hours. Her writing was, in Casanova's terms, committed to being *modern* in the sense that Paris then embodied. But by this time Paris was not quite the world center of cultural experimentalism and liberation it had been in the 1920s – Stead's friend Samuel Putnam thought of 1929 as ending that era (Putnam 1947: 168). And indeed Stead and Blake left Paris in 1935. Over the next forty years or so they lived a nomadic, cosmopolitan life in Britain, Europe (Spain, Belgium, France, Switzerland) and the United States (New York and Hollywood), moving in the search for sustainable employment or in flight from political or legal risk.

Blake was a committed communist, although he seems to have been a signed-up member of the party only for a year (1938) in the United States. (I will use the word "communist" rather than "Marxist" where some kind of commitment to the Stalinist program is in question. For me, "Stalinism" means both a commitment to the Soviet Union-directed policies of the Comintern and a commitment to the anti-social democratic Leninism which officially legitimated that policy.) Stead became a communist too, though apparently she never formally joined the party at all. Through the 1930s and 1940s the couple's social and intellectual world was primarily that of the Stalinist or fellow-traveling left; in the late 1930s Stead fell in love with the charismatic communist intellectual Ralph Fox, and during their years in the United States (1935–47) one of their very closest friends was the political economist Henrych Grossman, a founding member of the Frankfurt school who had moved to New York with Max Horkheimer and Theodor Adorno.

Unlike his colleagues, Grossman remained a committed Stalinist who not just continued to believe that capitalism was unsustainable in the long term but who was also loyal to the political argument that Stalin, for all his counterrevolutionary statism and murderous proclivities, was working in the interests of the only state (the Soviet Union) that might resist fascism and ultimately ignite world revolution and the liberation of the international working class.[7] These were opinions that Blake and Stead shared. During the late 1930s, in the United States, Blake was one of the Communist Party's most successful orators and fund raisers. In 1939 he published a long, if not very lucid, textbook on Marxist political economy in which he defended the necessity of precisely Marxist theory for political thought against liberals and revisionists, and he later wrote an unpublished book on imperialism (in collaboration with Grossman) for Paul Sweezy and Leo Huberman's Monthly Review Press. During the 1950s he had hopes of an academic job in the German Democratic Republic. And there are indications that he may have been on the Soviet payroll in the 1940s and 1950s (Rowley 1994: 401).

Across the Popular Front and war periods Stead was herself active in left causes as a literary intellectual of some reputation. For instance, she attended the huge gathering of writers "The First International Congress of Writers for the Defense of Writers," held in Paris in 1935, and reported on it for the *Left Review*, the British radical left's most widely read periodical. In her piece she energetically attacked liberalism, and celebrated internationalism in an amalgam of Comintern rhetoric and Casanova-like French republicanism: "The great spirit of revolutionary France, of red France, return to her true tradition. ... It is not by ice, but by fire, rather by sharp blades that we can hope to blaze a trail to the new masses that are arising," she declared (Stead 1935: 456).[8] In the States she wrote reviews for the Communist Party organ *New Masses*, attended and delivered a lecture to the Third American Writers' Congress in 1939 and joined the Joint Anti-Fascist Refugee Committee, which was declared a subversive organization by the US government. In 1940 both she and Blake wrote glowing introductory essays to the modernist sculptor David Smith's "Medals for Dishonor" exhibition, which was directed both towards a communist celebration of laborism and against the anti-Nazi war as then required for good communists by the short-lived Hitler–Stalin non-aggression pact. In 1950 she signed a petition of expatriates protesting the Liberal Party's banning of the Communist Party in Australia. Blake and Stead continued to defend the Stalinist position after 1956, the year of Russia's invasion of Hungary, Khrushchev's revelation of Stalin's crimes, and of the Cominform's demission, and which marked the end of official communism as a viable political possibility for most Marxist intellectuals. As late as 1959 she was reviewing Soviet writing for the Communist Party journal *Friendship*. Unlike almost all their contemporaries who had been communists in the 1930s, neither she nor Blake ever publicly renounced Stalinism at all.

As a writer, Stead had been in training ever since her childhood, taking detailed notes on people and settings around her. Ambitious, disciplined in her preparation for a literary career, she had submitted a children's book to Australia's biggest publisher, Angus & Robertson, before she left for England. But they rejected it. In the early 1930s, encouraged by Blake, she sent the manuscript of her first novel, *Seven Poor Men of Sydney*, around London publishers. It was accepted by Peter Davies, whose small literary house published both it and *The Salzburg Tales* in 1934, with Appleton-Century distributing both books in the United States.

The Salzburg Tales was published before *Seven Poor Men of Sydney* and remains at some distance from Stead's later work. Written under the influence of German expressionism and its primitivism, it consists of a series of stories told by a group attending the annual Salzburg Festival. It is interested in the rudiments of narrative form, somewhat in the spirit of the Russian formalists and proto-structuralists like Vladimir Propp, whose *Morphology of the Folk Tale* was published in 1928. It is not primarily interested in the novel form as such: interactions between social formations and character, between speech and action, between experience and place are not at its center: it gives us just stories. Coming to the work retrospectively, and using it as a point of contrast, one can say that it shows that Stead's later interest in fiction is not plot-driven. She is interested not so much in helping her readers narrativize their experience, let alone in being, before everything, *interesting*, but rather in character-based fiction (in which the relation between speech and action is always problematic) as a mode of social description, analysis, and critique.

Seven Poor Men, a very different kind of work, describes the constricted, mainly tragic lives of a group of young Sydney men, most intellectuals, working hand-to-mouth in the printing trade. It belongs to that extended moment when literary experimentalism and communism could be joined, deploying the modes of international modernism then associated with Joyce, Lawrence, and Woolf (along with reminiscences of George Meredith's earlier, mannered proto-modernism). It is indeed sometimes cited as the first high-modernist novel by an Australian writer.[9] Formally, its characters exist in a powerful amalgam of typification, individuality, and discursivity, by which I mean that they represent knowable social types as orthodox Marxist literary aesthetics required but they do so without forgoing a thickly depicted inner life, often presented in passages whose language threatens to exceed and break down both individuality and typification through a non-mimetic prose lyricism.[10] That breakdown had, of course, been pioneered by the modernist experimentalists and in one form or other would reappear in some of Stead's later novels, although her career trajectory moves away from modernism, as we will see.

Thematically *Seven Poor Men of Sydney* engages what will become abiding concerns for Stead. First, the hollowness and self-deceptions of bourgeois political radicals who are, from the communist point of view, continually tempted by revisionism and prone to false consciousness. It has two favored characters, one a communist who becomes an expatriate (Baruch Mendelssohn), the other (Joseph Baguenault), no radical, no intellectual, goes on to live a modest life of outer suburban normalcy in Sydney in retreat from the active, questing, larger world. But as such he's placed outside the novel's own readership, and is, for that reason, finally a sentimentalized figure of a kind who will not reappear in Stead's work.

From the boss's side the novel represents business activity as a ceaseless scramble for credit and staving off of employees' rightful demands, a tight-rope act between extravagant consumption and bankruptcy, involving a histrionic life of serial deceit. Indeed, here capitalism invades and pathologizes inner life, especially at the intersection of oppressive familial and institutional power and sex.[11] But the communist movement itself, which promises gender equality and liberation, ends up by neglecting and condescending to women, thereby tightening the tensions under which communist women live. The novel ends with one of the main characters, the idealistic and intelligent Michael Baguenault, killing himself after declaring his love for his half-sister, the communist Catherine, who in turn commits herself to a mental hospital.[12] And in *Seven Poor Men of Sydney* Australia itself is conceived of as a restricted place for those seriously engaged in the world. In the novel's closing chapters the Jewish communist intellectual, Baruch Mendelssohn, flees the country and an intellectually rigid local party for a career as a revolutionary activist in the States. He leaves Catherine behind while Michael's crippled friend Kol Blount, citing Henry Handel Richardson, bitterly declares of the settler colony that as the land of Europe's "rags and tatters" it "should never have been won" (Stead 1981: 309). At one level, then, the novel is an acrid celebration of colonial intellectuals' diaspora.

By and large Stead's first two books were well received by reviewers in the United States and United Kingdom but sold only moderately. Two years later, in 1936, she published *The Beauties and the Furies*, a more fully achieved high-modernist novel, this time tinged with surrealism, which shares something formally with Djuna Barnes's *Nightwood*, published by Faber the same year, even if it deals with material more like that of Jean Rhys's novels of the period. (Rhys, another – older – colonial expatriate, was living a still more marginal (and less politicized) life than Stead's in Britain and France in the 1920s and 1930s.) *The Beauties and the Furies* describes a beautiful and respectable *rentier* Englishwoman, Elvira Western, who leaves her husband Paul in London to live in Paris with Oliver Fenton, a young radical historian who is reading in the archives for his dissertation on the French labor movement after the Commune, and who is inspired by the Popular Front's fervid political atmosphere. Popular Front mass rallies allow him the illusion of being a "foot soldier in an army of millions" (Stead 1982: 138). Elvira and Oliver's affair in Paris is observed and disturbed by the *bon*

vivant Trotskyite, Marpurgo, a lace buyer in an industry undergoing industrialization and commodification. He possesses the knowledge, intelligence,
and sophistication that Elvira and Oliver lack. But he's in drift and is finally
a voyeur – in part, one infers, because, as a Trotskyite, he is not committed
to the Stalinist party, and is antagonistic to the Popular Front.[13] He, like
many of Stead's characters, represents not just the crippling paradoxes
involved in bourgeois radicalism but the larger gap between desire and
opportunity under capitalism: what Blake in his book on Marx's economics
would call a life lived inside "a maximum of temptations with a minimum
of resources" (Blake 1939: 72). By the novel's end, Elvira, having undergone
an abortion and been exposed to Oliver's infidelity, returns to her husband in
London. Oliver too travels back to England, headed for a career as a left-
wing academic, a *Kathedersozialist*, as the radical German communists used to
say – a career which, as Stead makes clear, amounts to another form of
hypocritical rentierism.[14] Perhaps the character who comes off best is
Blanche d'Anizy, an articulate Parisian actress/prostitute whose work offers
her the least mystified understanding of how romance and money actually
operate in contemporary capitalist Europe, a character who exemplifies one of
Stead's central insights – that the materialism required of the prostitute or
the prostituted businessman shares much with theoretical Marxist materialism.

In 1938 Stead published *House of all Nations*, a long, ambitious, multi-
character novel, set in Paris and about the collapse of a fraudulent private
bank, catering to the very rich, in the depression years of 1931–32, just
before the Stavisky affair broke and invoking the period during which the
gold standard came undone (brilliantly described in the first chapters of Karl
Polyani's *The Great Transformation*, 1944), in which, for the first time in
history, transnational capital flows began to shape politics.[15] Flirting with
the slick suspense techniques of popular fiction, organized scenically and
consisting largely of long conversations (more in Evelyn Waugh's mode than
in John Dos Passos's, say), *House of all Nations* makes less demands on its
readers than Stead's previous novels. The novel turns away from international
modernism towards a quasi-Balzacian social realism – a dark realism pertinent to a moment in which public transparency had disappeared and which
is linked to leftish *noir* thrillers of the period. Characters have relatively little
back-story and emotional depth, being identified rather by their jobs, ethical
and political principles, and their styles of consumption. They are oddly
affectless: although they do occasionally speak the language of feeling, they
don't seem to feel deeply. And because their interiorities are so occluded they
don't learn, either. Or rather: they think and react and plot and imagine
more than they feel and learn – and this will now become a fairly consistent
feature of Stead's characterization.

House of all Nations is also a more openly political work than the earlier
fictions, since the possibility of capitalism's collapse is a point of reference for
everyone, and once again many of the characters are intellectuals in the sense

that they can articulate (or are in search of) abstract principles to guide their actions. The bank's owner, the charming, imaginative, superficial, unscrupulous playboy Jules Bertillon spends most of his time inventing audacious criminal get-rich schemes. But Bertillon's bank, whose official investment policy is consistently bearish, is managed in accord with the orthodox Marxist theory of capitalist decline embraced by its economist, Michel Alphendéry, partly based on William Blake himself. The characters' sense that the revolution might be imminent deepens and clarifies Stead's perception of the ways in which the finance world's cynical materialism may join hands with her own Bolshevik anti-capitalist materialism.

The novel was published in New York by Simon & Schuster, a fairly recently established (1924) mainstream publisher which had abjured modernism from the very beginning (Turner 2003: 37). In the highly politicized atmosphere of the Depression and New Deal, they were relatively unfazed by Stead's politics, and signed her to a three-book contract. They supported *House of all Nations* with a major marketing campaign and almost simultaneously also published a novel by Blake. But although Stead's book did not sell badly, it failed to meet her and her publisher's expectations.

Simon & Schuster published her next novel, *The Man Who Loved Children* (1940) too. It was an autobiographical fiction, though for marketing reasons the publishers insisted that it be set in the United States rather than Australia (advertising it as Stead's American novel in their printings of *House of all Nations*). Here Stead in effect reimagines her childhood as if it happened in the 1930s rather than the 1910s, and around the Chesapeake Bay rather than Sydney harbor. It involved yet another change of style. Addressing itself more carefully to its characters' psychological development, abandoning both lyrical high-modernism and contemporary social realism, she grafted certain modernist techniques for narrating deep interiority on to a conventional naturalism committed to describing the physical and social settings of characters' lives – all this in the interests of a truncated *Bildungsroman* centered on family life.

The novel presents a devastating account, largely from a daughter's perspective, of a family dominated by a sentimental, idealist, tyrannical father, Sam Pollitt – another soft progressivist, who faintly allegorizes the United States of the New Deal itself. Despite not openly presenting itself as a political novel, it is related to the psychoanalytically orientated, anti-familial, anti-Stalinist (or "Western") theoretical Marxism being developed on the back of Reich's *The Mass Psychology of Fascism* (1933), most notably in the Frankfurt school's *Studien über Autorität und die Familie* (1936). This means that Stead's capacity to write brilliant, figurative lyrical prose in the modernist mode is consistently subordinated to the demands of coherent characterization, which is not the case in her earlier or indeed some of her later fictions. No doubt this shift was in part a response to Simon & Schuster's expectations for the book, which required Stead to move towards the mainstream, but it shares its retreat from experimentalism with a great deal of serious fiction-writing from the late 1930s on.

However, Stead's emphasis on family life and her turn to a kind of *Bildungsroman* do not mean that she breaks with communist *noir* realism. It's more that life's bleakness is now concentrated in the zone of the intimate and private, which is simultaneously presented as suffocatingly enclosed, and as indicative of systemic social restriction. From the beginning of her career, one of Stead's most characteristic notes was a smothering intimacy with her characters beyond the limits of literary decorum – as if this intimacy were itself a symptom of capitalist oppression. In *The Man Who Loved Children* that note becomes wholly streamlined for the first time. Perhaps, then, it is not surprising that the book, published at the beginning of World War II, also failed in the market.[16]

Stead's next novel *For Love Alone*, is autobiographical too: in effect it continues the story of Louisa, here called Teresa, into young adulthood, although the setting has been returned to Sydney. A more conventional novel than any of its predecessors (Stead hoped to sell it to Hollywood), it tells of Teresa's slow development into romantic literary subjectivity, and her realization that in Australia she would never be free. That's because there a young woman is primarily valued in terms of the marriage she makes, and in Australia there are few eligible men available to an intellectual young woman. At the same time, there's no escaping the hard judgments of acquaintances, friends, and family. So, in flight from social norms, Teresa falls in love with the manipulative cosmopolitan young intellectual Jonathan Crow, who is about to take up a postgraduate scholarship in London, and becomes obsessed with expatriation. In the end, Crow is revealed as an intellectual poseur, another academic hack. (He's even more in bad faith than *The Beauties and the Furies'* Oliver Fenton, since his progressivism is laced with proto-fascism.) Only in England does Teresa meet and have affairs with genuine radicals. And in the world of London communist intellectuals which Teresa joins, Stead can narrate a genre-twisting plot: *For Love Alone* is a romantic anti-romance in the precise sense that it subtly subverts the traditional marriage plot, since it ends both with Teresa's happy marriage and with her adultery. This ending is not, however, a form of erotic liberation, *à la* Freudo-Marxism; rather, along Stalinist lines, it is a premature practice of freedom, since it still happens under a capitalist system where personal fulfilment can neither signify nor anticipate post-revolutionary emancipation. In the end, Teresa's love of love is treated as strategical – as a woman's grasping her heterosexual desire and desirability as a costly form of power and self-expression in the limited space given to women for agency both under capitalism and on the left.

Because Stead had broken her contract with Simon & Schuster on the grounds that they had failed sufficiently to support her, *For Love Alone* was published by Harcourt Brace, a house with a long commitment to adventurous writing. But this novel too failed to find a commercially meaningful readership.

In the late 1940s and early 1950s she published three more novels in the United States, two with Harcourt Brace. The first, *Letty Fox: Her Luck* (1948) (which had originally formed part of the *For Love Alone* manuscript) is her only first-person narrative. And strangely, since it's not obviously auto-biographical at all, it is the novel that reveals most about its author, who this time reimagines herself as a young woman entering adulthood in late 1920s and 1930s Manhattan. It deals with life in an economy in which scarcity still reigns but is increasingly given over to more or less erotic marketing and in which there exists powerful encouragement for sexual and consumerist license. Young Letty, fashionably, joins the communist move-ment as a teenager (to use a suggestive anachronism): she dreams of writing a novel that will uncover "the economic basis of the whodunit" (Stead 2001: 277). As she enters into adulthood, she continues sporadically to rely upon Marxist theory to make sense of the social order, although, as Stead herself later remarked of her, "she has no roots in the class struggle" (Geering 1990: 424). And she's also the child of what Stead called the "Browder era," after the American Communist Party leader who, before his banishment from the party, attempted to promote a specifically American communism, capable of compromise with Roosevelt's social democracy. She's the child, too, of a very specific radical subculture – one which has, in practice, jettisoned premarital chastity and married monogamy for casual affairs and serial monogamy. In that regard she is also of the future. In Letty's Manhattan, the unforgiving division of women into respectable or unrespectable, mainly as defined by their relation to promiscuity but also by their relation to work, although still officially in force, is disappearing from everyday life. In the process there is no clear structure of feeling and knowledge through which Letty can orga-nize and fully enjoy her life. Her Marxism also makes it difficult for her to compete in the marriage market: she is too critical, too disabused, too out-side orthodox "ideology," which, as a Marxist theorist, is exactly the word she uses (Stead 2001: 544). But it provides her with no substantive organi-zational role, either (nor, for that matter, with any clearcut path to gender equality).[17] So she veers persistently and uncontrollably across romance, hard materialism, political radicalism, and literary aspirations. The novel ends with her marriage to a disinherited millionaire, a tacked-on ending without any of the conventional marriage plot's force, since it carries no endorsement of any particular social or moral value.

Letty Fox: Her Luck turned out to be the best selling book of Stead's career, mainly because it described the sex life of a promiscuous young woman, and did so relatively free of modernist experimentation (though without a scintilla of erotic charge). However, it caused a further decline in Stead's reputation, as if her interest in women's sexuality cheapened her work (not to mention the novel's implicit advocacy of communism, although it managed to enrage many communists too).[18] This meant that Stead was even more firmly positioned as, at best, a coterie writer on the margins of the Anglo-American literary world. Her next two books, neither of which found British publishers at all, were, however, among her very best. *A Little Tea, a Little Chat* (1948) was another withering critique of a philandering pseudo-socialist businessman and the private affairs of Manhattan businessmen, a return to the *noir* social realism of *House of all Nations* now veering towards the grotesque. *The People with the Dogs* (1952) was again set in New York in the period immediately after the war. In a tone that wavers between affection and dispassion, it describes a family of liberal petty *rentiers* who are themselves caught in a strange emotional force-field. They possess an easy, heterodox generosity of spirit and resources, not being caught up in the whole apparatus of capitalist competition and accumulation. And yet, having no particular stake either in work or in social progress, having no strong cultural attachments, their lives are in drift, precariously balanced between happiness and unhappiness, and they veer, albeit comfortably enough, into alienation in the Western Marxist sense. In this state, their lives tend to center around their dogs. What is astonishing about the novel, however, is how the severity of its critique of bourgeois life only seems to intensify its sense of how vital bourgeois life can be, exactly because that life's emotional tone, its mood, may be so ambiguously positioned between anxious selfishness and a careless generosity of spirit.

Neither novel made any impact in the States or elsewhere. Having failed to find a sufficiently large readership, Stead published no fiction at all in the fourteen years between 1952 and 1966. Then in 1965 the US publisher Holt Rinehart & Winston successfully republished *The Man Who Loved Children* with an introduction by the well known poet and man of letters, Randall Jarrell, who, using the rhetoric of global canonicity, claimed that it was "one of those books that their age neither reads nor praises, but that the next age thinks is a masterpiece" (Jarrell 1975: 37). The novel's success this time round owes something to the spirit of the 1960s, which, profiting from McCarthyism's political bankruptcy, recovered those modes of Freudo-Marxian critique with which the novel is aligned: Herbert Marcuse's *Eros and Civilization* was first published in the United States in 1962, for instance. At any rate, this intervention revitalized Stead's career: *The Man Who Loved Children* was published as a paperback by Penguin in 1975 and a further hardback edition came out in 1978; *House of all Nations* was republished by Avon in the United States in 1974 – these being the first (and almost the only) mass-market paperback editions of Stead's work during her lifetime. On the basis of this success, Holt Rinehart & Winston published a new novel, *Dark Places of the Heart*, in 1966, with Secker & Warburg, a firm well known for its anti-Stalinism during the Cold War, putting the book out under Stead's preferred title of *Cotters' England* in the United Kingdom.

Cotters' England had been mainly written in the late 1940s and early 1950s and was set in the austerity times of immediate post-war Newcastle and

London in the period after the 1945 general election when Labour swept to power.[19] Badly reviewed when it first appeared, it was another market failure. Nonetheless Stead published two further novels in her lifetime. *The Little Hotel,* also written in the early 1950s, was first published in Australia by Angus & Robertson – her first Australian imprint – with US editions following, including a mass-market paperback in 1980. Set in a small Swiss hotel among refugees from contemporary life, it can be regarded as a bleak Cold War reduction of one of Stead's favorite novels, Thomas Mann's *The Magic Mountain,* in which the novel of ideas is transmuted into a satiric novel of pathological manners. Her next novel, *Miss Herbert,* was published by the large mainstream US publisher Random House in 1976. Written and set in Britain in the mid-1950s, it is a negative portrayal of a self-deceived conventional suburban woman with literary ambitions which opens out to a larger critique of both liberalism and the increasingly commodified literary world. Both were received with merely hollow praise that did little to advance Stead's reputation.

Blake died in 1968 and in 1974 Stead returned to Australia, where she lived out her last nine years. Two posthumous works appeared: *Ocean of Story* (1985), a collection of shorter fiction, and *I'm Dying Laughing* (1986), a reconstruction by Stead's literary executor, Ron Geering, of the novel that Stead had been working on over the last thirty years of her life. It deals with communists in Hollywood and abroad in the McCarthy era, and mounted yet another critique of bourgeois radicalism. *I'm Dying Laughing* received respectful reviews and was published in Penguin's modern classics series in 1989, but it too did nothing to alter what had now become the orthodox opinion that Stead was to be taken seriously mainly as the author of a single masterpiece, *The Man who loved Children.*

What about Stead's academic reputation? It is ironic that the two most significant academic forces keeping Stead's *oeuvre* in circulation over this period both lacked Stead's endorsement. The first was feminism, which Stead is on record as disliking.[20] Her objections to second-wave feminism were, I suspect, ultimately based in orthodox Stalinism, for which an identity politics that had made its peace with capitalism could never be truly emancipatory. But, perhaps more important, she also could not accept 1970s feminism's attacks on male heterosexuality and those modes of heterosexual femininity invested in romance. After all, for Stead, romantic heterosexuality was a source of empowerment and pleasure for women as well as of exploitation. Nonetheless, for all Stead's anti-feminism, Virago, the London-based feminist reprint press, published seven of her less well known works between 1978 and 1986, three of which had never previously been published outside the United States.[21]

Cultural nationalism played a role in maintaining Stead's reputation as well. Interest in Australian writing increased over the 1960s as Auslit became an established pedagogical field.[22] An early sign of a Stead revival under the new professional Auslit paradigm was a special issue of the Sydney University literary magazine *Southerly* dedicated to her work as early as 1962, before the republication of *The Man who Loved Children* in the United States. Over the period, the local publishing industry was also expanding and becoming more adventurous. The pioneering paperback house, Sun Books, republished the long out of print *The Salzburg Tales* in 1966. But it was Australia's biggest house, Angus & Robertson, which was most responsible for repatriating Stead as an author: after 1966 *Cotters' England, Letty Fox: Her Luck, For Love Alone, The Man Who Loved Children, House of all Nations, Seven Poor Men of Sydney* and *The Salzburg Tales* all appeared under one or other of its imprints, most in paperback and aimed at the education market. In sum: Stead wrote as an anti-feminist communist internationalist but it was cultural nationalism and feminism that did most to ensure her works' circulation from the mid-1960s on.

Before turning to address Stead's career in relation to key political and cultural frames, it is important to emphasize that it was shaped at two specific moments by what Casanova calls "cosmopolitan intermediaries." And we need further to understand the context in which these interventions occurred. The first was in 1936 when Clifton Fadiman engineered her contract with Simon & Schuster. Fadiman had originally encountered Stead's work when he reviewed her early novels for the *New Yorker*. At that time Fadiman had only recently left the communist movement, and was slowly forming himself as a New York broker between serious culture and the new media publics and, thence, as one of the most powerful literary gatekeepers in the English-speaking world. As Joan Rubin has put it, in the 1940s and 1950s he "virtually personified middlebrow culture" in the United States (Rubin 1992: 320). He attained this position through a variety of offices. He was review editor for the *New Yorker* (1933–43); chief editor of Simon & Schuster through the 1930s; in the postwar era he was chair of the selection committee of the Book of the Month Club, part owner of an agency for radio talent, moderator of the popular radio quiz show *Information, Please* (1938–48) and the 1950s television show *This is Show Business* (1949–54) as well as author of books like *The Lifetime Reading Plan* and editor of many literary anthologies, from *The Short Stories of Henry James* (1945) to *The World Treasury of Children's Literature* (1984). It's a career possible only during that evanescent moment when US literature and literary intellectuals possessed real prestige in the audiovisual media industry.

Fadiman's intervention had so great an impact on Stead's work since the deal that he brokered with Simon & Schuster put pressure on her to set her work in the United States and to move away from modernism some way towards the middlebrow. *The Man Who Loved Children* was, of course, one result of this pressure and it is fairly clear that without the novel's American setting and its reduction of modernist techniques it would never have revived her career twenty-five years later, and so edged her *oeuvre* towards canonization. That is to say, Fadiman's mediation helped to dislocate Stead from the kind of pure, non-commercial "Parisian" literariness that Casanova believes to motivate canonization and yet, against Casanova, in doing so formed a foundation for her future fame.

The man primarily responsible for the revivification of Stead's international reputation in the mid-1960s, and its second key intermediary, was Stanley Burnshaw, who arranged the 1965 republication of *The Man Who Loved Children*. Burnshaw, a poet, editor, publisher, academic critic, and autobiographer, was a more considerable, if much less powerful, literary intellectual than Fadiman. He first met Stead as literary editor for the groundbreaking communist periodical *New Masses* in the mid-1930s (for which he had reviewed *The Beauties and the Furies*), at a time when he enthusiastically endorsed the Popular Front against many of his Trotskyite and Leninist colleagues.[23] In the decade that Blake and Stead lived in the States he became one of the couple's closest friends. As editor-in-chief (and owner) of Cordon Press he published Blake's Marxist theory textbook. He had worked with Stead on a theatrical adaptation of *Letty Fox* in the late 1940s. And as a senior editor at Holt Rinehart & Winston in the 1960s he committed himself to seeing *The Man Who Loved Children* republished, overcoming considerable resistance to make that happen. It was he who fixed on the mainstream charismatic ex-leftist man of letters Randall Jarrell as the best person to write the introduction, and who, of course, turned the critical tide for Stead.

Burnshaw's career exemplifies the difficult negotiations through which members of the 1930s Marxist left survived successfully in the Cold War period, negotiations in which, as we have seen, Stead herself did not succeed particularly well and would have succeeded even less well without Burnshaw's aid. Unlike Stead, Burnshaw repudiated his communism publicly in 1945, and went on to pursue a career as a poet, critic, and textbook publisher in part by attaching himself precisely to the notion of world literature, as well as by engaging with literary modernism, albeit with an ambivalence that would become orthodoxy in the 1960s.

In 1960 he published *The Poem Itself*, an anthology of modernist European poems in their original languages, aimed at placing them into university classrooms while embracing the negative bias that comparative literature (then an emerging discipline) directed against works in translation. Ten years later he published *The Seamless Web*, a pioneering materialist and ecological work of poetics in which he argued that poetry grounds all cultures, since it is the universal response of the human mind and body to the natural environment – an argument with clear cross-cultural, globalizing force. In the late 1950s and early 1960s he taught a course entitled "Studies in World Literature" at NYU out of which came the important collection of academic essays *Varieties of Literary Experience: Eighteen Essays in World*

Literature. This was where Harry Levin's essay "What was modernism?" first appeared, as did Lionel Trilling's "On the modern element in modern literature," which together did much to familiarize the concept of modernism in the US literary academy. In a historicist and quasi-Marxian move, Burnshaw's own essay in the collection, "The three revolutions of modern poetry," analyzed modernist poetry as "poetry of the joint-stock era," contending, *à la* Frankfurt school, that it was written under "the influence of a civilization which had declared war on Nature," a civilization which began with industrialism and had ended with the Second World War (Burnshaw 1962: 138). Modernist poets, he contended, had retreated first into subjectivity and then beyond subjectivity, through Freud's Unconscious, into the sheer signifying power of language itself, mounting a Joycean revolution of the word. That revolution aimed to "enrich the communicative content of language" in resistance to the intense subjectivization and denaturalization of the joint-stock era. Posing the question "What will be the course of the poetry of the postmodern period already begun?" (1962: 169), he predicts that the modernist revolution will now turn back on itself, seeking to reconcile itself both to an annihilated Nature and to social "responsibility."

It's an argument that echoes Burnshaw's own earlier communist criticism (in particular his famous review of Wallace Stevens's *The Idea of Order*), and it refigures the Marxist view of literature as materialist practice in terms that have a recognizably 1960s if not quite a hippie flavor. Here Marx's celebration of world literature in the *Communist Manifesto* has been transposed into a depoliticized ecological understanding of literature as a biological expressivity embedded in the human species. At any rate, it would suggest that Burnshaw's support for Stead was not motivated simply by loyalty to an old friend and comrade, or even by unreflective literary admiration for her work. It is as if he saw in Stead a postmodern writer who had saved the modernist revolution of the word for social responsibility. It is as if Stead's lyrical fictionalization of broken lives, as imagined from a communist position, could be reinterpreted by Burnshaw as post-Marxist naturalism. Or, to put this more simply, it is as if, for Burnshaw, one of the early American proponents of a theoretically legitimated world literature canon, Stead was a candidate for precisely such canonicity, since, in her ambiguously modernist work, communism could be transmuted into a fairly depoliticized anticapitalism.

The outside

As should be clear by now, Stead's career is formed in relation to two larger formations – her Australian expatriatism and her communism – which together shaped her *oeuvre* and its reception, and which both need further attention.

As I have noted, Stead was not so much an expatriate as a nomad, since, after leaving Australia in her late twenties, she never settled down in one place until she returned home in old age. Her nomadism as against her expatriatism was largely determined by her communism, not just because, in principle, communism remained an international movement but because, in practice, it prevented her from settling in the States, twentieth-century capitalism's home base. Despite her politics, Stead's strongest ties were with the United States, against the more common pattern by which Australian expatriates formed their primary bonds with imperial Britain. Her nomadism also distinguished her from her American and British peers, many of whom also spent time in Paris around the time that she did, but most of whom settled back home after their period abroad. All this had various effects: it meant that her novels were written either without a particular national readership in mind or for an American readership to which it had no deep personal connection. This had the effect of straining her realism, since it meant that she sometimes transposed material from one national context to another, as was the case in *The Man Who Loved Children*. It also meant that Stead's later novels had a weird temporality all of their own – appearing in the 1960s and 1970s but written in the 1940s or 1950s and set either then or in the 1930s. These disjunctions help account for the novels' lukewarm reception at the time, but in retrospect, as the mid-twentieth-century decades lose their vivid specificity, they allow Stead's work, for all its particularity of social setting, to join a more classical literary "timelessness," especially in the case of *The People with the Dogs* and *Cotters' England*. In the end the sacrifice of verisimilitude imposed on Stead by her communism and her expatriatism helped move her work, accidentally, towards literary autonomy.

Stead's nomadism also strained her realism because especially when she came to write about the States she was dealing with a social world wholly saturated in ideology and values that she contested, and which therefore took on a phantasmagoric quality for her. In fact her relation to America threatened both her modernism and her realism, since for her American life was based on the illusion of liberal individualism and premature practices of freedom; it wasn't "real" at all. At the same time, it created enormous pressures upon her to join a literary world itself tied to cultural industries with little room for either experimentation or communism. This helps account for the often noticed *sui generis* nature of her work: it has been prised loose from the patterns and logics that dominated literary fiction of her time. It's not, however, as if she can't be placed at least at the margins of certain traditions. Later in her career she increasingly turned towards novel writing as a mode of critique (of both ideology and everyday life practice) which can be regarded as finding a generic base – if only weakly – in the tradition of satire (see Pender 2002).

More important, her colonial expatriatism placed her in an extraordinary lineage of similarly positioned women writers – Olive Schreiner, Katherine Mansfield, and Jean Rhys – who had helped generate both "the modern" as a literary concept and modernism as a literary practice. For these writers, the distance between their colonial youth (with its particular gender relations) and the literary metropolis in which, still from the periphery, they wrote and found a readership, produced such powerful effects of defamiliarization and so strong a commitment to the modern that they became pioneers of key tendencies within the fictional avant-garde, and in particular the flooding of Jamesian form and Flaubertian realism by an affectively charged style, anchored in a character's subjectivity, which veers between the lyrical and the disillusioned. But in Stead's case, of course, this mode of literary modernist expatriatism and isolation is modified by her communism.

For all that, Stead's particular form of communist nomadism and colonial expatriatism has not served her well in terms of achieving canonicity, since they have fallen outside the main frameworks for thinking about national border-crossing in the academic humanities since the 1980s, dominated as they are by notions of "exile," "diaspora," "migration," and so on. This is all the more damaging because the importance of the tradition of women colonial expatriates in the production of modernism has not been sufficiently acknowledged.[24] This means that she is rarely a presence in the various scholarly accounts of modernism's internationalism. To take two key instances, Stead has little or no presence in the scholarship on modernism and exile, nor does she figure in more recent work on the relation between colonialism and modernism.[25] Stead's expatriatism also means that she falls out of the literary histories of those countries in which she spent most of her life and set many of her novels. Works on the British novel and literary world in the 1930s, 1940s, and 1950s mention Stead only in relation to her piece in the *Left Review*, often cited as an instance of Stalinist extremism.[26] It's a similar situation in the States, where, for instance, she barely exists even in the scholarship on the period's literary left.[27] And, at least as far as I can tell, no one counts her as an American writer.

In Australia, of course, the case is different, but, given the force of local cultural nationalism, there too Stead's expatriatism has posed a challenge. She left the country just as organized cultural nationalism first appeared in polemical writing like P. R. Stephensen's *The Foundations of Culture in Australia* (1935). In fact, Stephensen wrote his book in order to reply to a lecture in which G. H. Cowling, Professor of English at University of Melbourne, expressed skepticism as to whether Australia could ever produce literature capable of joining the global canon. Stephensen's book indignantly rebuts this position, developing a wider nationalist program to do so. Yet Australian literary culture at the time was in fact positioned between a local book trade almost wholly committed to imported titles, a philistine public sphere which habitually censored avant-garde writing on grounds of obscenity, an educational system largely dedicated to the values of imperial Britishness, and a counterhegemonic nationalist ideology with both left and right inflections and which, in the literary world, was often invoked precisely in order to stimulate the local publishing industry.[28] This was not a situation from which writers could easily join the international literary field: Cowling was right about that, and Stead's departure from Australia attests to it too.

Yet Stead herself refused to accept the politicization of Australian patriotism either for or against, and she rarely directly criticized Australian provincialism. This is not to say that she found a receptive readership or acceptance at home: her books received no special understanding or enthusiasm there, although, especially before the Cold War, the tone was often one of wary respect. Stead thought of returning home during the dog days of the Cold War but immigration laws prevented her American husband from residence and she realized she could not make a living in Australia's small literary/intellectual world (Rowley 1994: 384). Furthermore, UK conventions meant that she only received half copyright on Australian sales so that there was no financial reason for her to Australianize her writing. The Australian government banned *Letty Fox: Her Luck* in 1947 (the only country in the world to do so) in part because of Stead's communism. In 1967 she was refused the prestigious Britannica Award because she was an expatriate who had failed to set most of her novels in Australia. Admittedly this decision caused some outrage, and she went on to be granted the first Patrick White literary award in 1974, a marker of her reorientation towards Australia in her final years (Rowley 1994: 462–65).

Nonetheless, the most authoritative Australian literary history to appear in her lifetime, H. M. Green's *A History of Australian Literature* (1971), would admit only *Seven Poor Men of Sydney* and *For Love Alone* into the Auslit archive: for Green, the rest of her *oeuvre* belonged to other nations or perhaps to internationalism itself. She also suffered at home from lingering Cold War conservatism, despite academic Auslit's endorsement of her work from the 1960s on. So, for instance, in the collectively written *Oxford History of Australian Literature* (1981), Stead's whole *oeuvre* was claimed for Auslit, although little attention was still paid to the novels set outside Australia. However, Adrian Mitchell, who wrote the section on fiction, directed a litany of complaints at Stead's writing, and ended by declaring Martin Boyd a "much better writer."[29] This is comprehensible only as a political judgment.

The point to insist upon, however, is that Stead's expatriatism was essential to her career: those Australian writers who remained at home never produced texts with anything like the range, quality, and intensity of hers. Nor have they achieved anything like her international recognition, insufficient as it may be. Perhaps the best stay-at-home comparison with Stead is Eleanor Dark, a year older than Stead, whom Dorothy Green, forthrightly comparing the two writers, regarded as a "talent" against Stead's "genius" (Green 1971: 1007). As it happens, Stead was herself paid to write a reader's report on *The Timeless Land* for an American publisher in 1940. In a letter to Blake she called Dark's ambitious historical novel about the settling of New South Wales:

> a highminded rehash of (Australian) commonplaces – highminded com-
> monplaces, of course – all in the mood of a longwinded campfire story
> for a halfgrown boy, with something of the tearful grandeur of a mother
> about to go to a maternity ward and leaving a testament-of-the-soul for
> her child-about-to-be. ... Nevertheless, the old girl has pages in the 600
> which are ponderously woven and born to sonority, and resemble English
> genius, in the shape of E. M. Forster.
>
> (Stead 2005: 50)

These are cruel if not wholly unjustified remarks (although in my view Stead is very mistaken in condescending to Forster), and which reveal Stead's sense of the conventional Anglo-liberalism and sentimentalism she would have risked had she been able to reconcile herself to Australian society and the Australian reading public and stayed at home.

Yet, as we have begun to see, Stead's literary reputation now lies in the hands of her home country. It is as a writer within the Auslit lineage, a beneficiary of national pride, that her claim to canonicity is being most forthrightly urged, all the more so since literary feminism is now all but spent as a canonizing force. As mentioned above, there are obvious ironies in the circuit from expatriatism through cultural nationalism to cosmopolitan world literature, but at least it reminds us that contemporary cultural nationalism involves an emptying-out of Australian identity through global exchanges and flows in ways that Stead's expatriate communism enabled her partially to preempt.

Communism

The second key formation in Stead's career was indeed her communism. It is impossible to gauge its effect on her work objectively or even to gauge her exact relation to the movement and the party, and there's a division among the critics on this point. For instance, her biographer, Hazel Rowley, regards Stead's interest in communism as both dependent on her husband's and linked to deep-seated psychological needs rather than a rational political commitment. Furthermore, she treats Stead's novels as if their author's politics were not an important shaping force. But there's a mass of writing on the other side, which is brought together in Brigid Rooney's excellent doctoral dissertation "Gendering the Revolutionary Subject: The Role of Marxist Thought in Christina Stead's Authorial Production."[30] As should be clear by now, I too believe that Stead's communism was not just serious but also crucial to her writing and to her claim to global canonicity. Indeed, it is its primary condition, without which her work would be, if imaginable at all, much weaker.

This is not to say, however, that Stead's writing obeys any clear Marxian or communist protocol for fiction writing. In the 1930s, Marxian literary criticism and theory were less a unified field than a set of intensely argued debates, ranging from the official Stalinist line that communist authors should heroicize the revolutionary proletariat within the conventions of "socialist realism" to, say, the complex theory of utopianism associated with Ernst Bloch.

Ralph Fox's *The Novel and the People*, written as a contribution to these debates, is likely to have been especially important to Stead, since it was written by Fox when she was in love with him, and since it appeared (posthumously in 1937) at a time when her career at a novelist was open to aesthetic direction. *The Novel and the People* implies, if it does not quite spell out, a sophisticated literary theory. Its grounding claim is that Marxism alone can provide terms for the true knowledge of society's workings that a serious novelist needs to possess. In its most basic terms Marxism states that all social elements, including individual will, are determined by and interpretable within the social totality, i.e., within capitalist relations of production. Furthermore, under capitalism, society is constituted by struggles which no individual will can order, although revolutionary action can enable communist revolutionaries to become what Fox, citing Marx and echoing Wordsworth, calls the "sovereign of circumstances" (Fox 1944: 152). This means that, for the Marxist writer, claims to autonomy and liberty are illusory, the stuff of romance, this being the terminology of the period's important English Marxist literary theorist, Christopher Caudwell. Fox's second large theoretical claim is that each work of art (in this case the novel) forms a pattern in terms that also transcend the intention of its author, and this pattern mirrors the structures of the social totality (1944: 34). That argument implies that the traditional form-content distinction is unimportant, since structure is the necessary basis for both social existence and for literary works. That is, form does not have to be chosen, since it cannot be avoided: it's the precondition of content just as individual consciousness and will require the structuring force of social totality to exist at all. Against official communist literary aesthetics, this line of thought also implies that a Marxist writer can write about anything and still write as a Marxist, just because, for Marxists, all social phenomena are meaningful as determinations of capitalist relations of production.

Fox himself does not reach that catholic conclusion, although he does concede that "revolutionary novelists" may let their imaginative energies roam across the "active life" of the times wherever they may find it (1944: 141) in resistance to those who insisted that communist writers restrict themselves to one or other form of what we can call, riffing off William Empson and Michael Denning, the "proletariat pastoral."[31] Yet in consciously trying to formulate a program by which novelists might aid the popular front, Fox recommends that leftists (and not just communists) turn their attention to personalities vibrant and powerful enough to exceed the limiting pressures of normalcy and everyday life (1944: 56). In particular they should write about "epic heroes," actively involved in class struggle and not ensnared by bourgeois individualism: his instance is the Comintern leader and victim of Nazi persecution Georgi Dimitrov (whom Stead also mentions in *Letty Fox* and elsewhere) (1944: 152–53). Such a hero should be one in whom "no division any longer occurs between himself and his sphere of practical activity" (1944: 105) and who is thus able to contest the fragmentation of the capitalist social system.

It should be clear from this brief overview that Stead did not write as a communist in terms supported by Fox, even if her choice to critique the bourgeoisie rather than to celebrate the workers and to forgo plot as supreme structuring principle are loosely authorized by his work.[32] Which leaves us with the question: in what ways is she a communist writer? A couple of obvious ways: her communism underpinned her internationalism, as we have seen. And it enabled her to become, as she herself put it, a "philosophical" writer both in the sense that for her social reality is not given, it's determinate and open to reflection and critique, and in the sense that she is consistently (among other things) a novelist of political ideas. After all, an unusual number of her characters are intellectuals and many of them (often self-deceived) communist intellectuals, capable of talking abstractly and theoretically about themselves and a world that they regard to be saturated in politics.

Perhaps most of all, and paradoxically, she's a communist writer in that her narratives are presented at a radical remove from the society they describe. That is her solution to what Christopher Caudwell called the "epistemological problem of the observer," by which he meant the discovery of the "relativity of bourgeois norms," namely the undoing of the (false) universality of conventional Western values.[33] Indeed, Stead's characteristic narratological position is *outside the outside* of the middle-class world she describes and which, of course, she inhabited herself.

Outside the outside? Stead deploys a form of that modernist narrative developed by Flaubert and Henry James which removed the narrator/author's judgment and voice from fictions narrated in the third person. Aware that choice of a narratological position is politically normative, she writes, as Caudwell puts it, as an "alien," turning to this mode of distantiation not in the interest of literary form and autonomy but for heretical communist ends. It's the capitalist social world that demands distantiation, since it consists of struggle and cruelties at all levels leavened by illusions of freedom, independence, and agency. Nonetheless, in making this move she does not write as an engaged activist, and departs from Fox in that she does not write about epic communist heroes. (She comes closest to this in the early *Seven Poor Men of Sydney*, in which expatriatism still contains sufficient promise.) So she stands outside the bourgeois world as a communist and, then, outside communism, because she doesn't endorse the literature of engagement (and isn't herself bound to the party). She is outside the outside in another more subtle and impure form too: she is a communist in a world of radical sellouts which does not quite not include herself. Yet the bourgeois radical's self-deluded self-satisfactions are in the end not separable from the shameful compromises required for radicals to survive. In this structure (which is one of her main concerns from her very first novel), to be both bourgeois and radical is also to be neither radical nor bourgeois: another form of falling outside the outside. Let me put it like this: you're doubly outside – once because, as a radical, you know you've compromised; and once because, as a bourgeois survivor, you know you're not absolutely a radical.

Furthermore, in broad terms, for her, Marxist theory tells the truth about society under capitalism but it offers no ethical or epistemological aids for everyday and private life: as Letty Fox puts it,"I could analyze anything right under my nose, and was not in want of theory – but about my personal life, I had no theory" (Stead 2001: 467). Stead is outside the outside, too, then, in that she is a revolutionary writer, but the theory which leads her to become a revolutionary writer submits the field of private and social life which is her primary material as a novelist to a process of systematic negation which itself is not based on abstract principles or concrete possibilities for liberation and which therefore leaves private intensities – especially sexual/romantic passion – disconnected from legitimate moral or social frameworks.

This apositionality is linked to one of the more compelling and unusual features of Stead's writing: the revolutionary fire which is absent from the social world, and takes no propositional form in her texts, does seem to find expression in hidden winds of passion directed at her characters, who are imagined through a range of (mainly negative) emotions that, however, remain unlocatable. Hatred, scorn, disgust, admiration – which of these best names the energy, the smothering intimacy with which a particular moment in a particular character's life is being presented? This is all the more the case since she does not replace the omniscient narrative voice, opaque as it is, with a highly polished style and tone, as the high-modernists did, rather she positions it right in her characters' faces, as we may say.

We can restate this argument like this: the negation that Stead directs at the world means that her characters find no possibility for living fulfilled lives. They discover that bad faith is everywhere, even where they least expect it (i.e., in love) and even where pleasure is possible (i.e., in sex). To return to a phrase I have already used: practices of freedom are always premature. At the level of the plot, this communist negation means that narrative sequence and closure cannot reliably be used to impose meaning on social existence (although her stories often tend to suicide, which signifies social failure). This is another reason why Stead's novels tend towards plot-lessness and longwindedness. At the level of realism, it means, of course, that because the social field available for mimesis is a phantasmagoric mirror world – it already has a novelistic flavor, it continually invites participants to flights of literary imagination and presents itself to their aesthetic appreciation and pleasure. That's one reason why so many of her characters are so inventive and lyrical in their speech, continually falling outside of verisimilitude, or why, say, Jules Bertillon's fraudulent bank in *House of all Nations* can be called a thing of "beauty."

At the level of literariness, it means that, for Stead, literary value is provisional, and that literary autonomy, as the closing off of literature's participation in society, is another motivated delusion. But at this point, where modernist experimentation and communist critique fall away from one another, Stead's narratological position "outside the outside" is fractured. In the end, her novels recognize an unrealizable responsibility not just to tell, but to circulate, the truth, and as her career proceeded she seems to have been increasingly happy not to pursue modernist experimentation and the autonomy it implies beyond the tolerance of a (potential) wider reading public, despite the forces pushing her away from verisimilitude and commercialism. She was, as should be clear, no Samuel Beckett. It may even be that she is trading her participation in a middlebrow literary world off against her "outside the outsideness," her heretical communist negation of the social world. (The ending of *Letty Fox* is one such moment.) But that is, as I say, to write from a space where modernism and communism both risk shameful compromises.

This is a source of her strength, it seems to me. For if it is the case that Stead's compromised turn to the middlebrow and the domestic and autobiographical during her association with Simon & Schuster allowed her to achieve significant literary fame in her lifetime, and if that fame is now largely in the hands of Auslit and its nationalist cosmopolitan longings, it's her particular relation to communism that enables her work to stand apart from even the most finely achieved literary novels of the time – those of Elizabeth Bowen or Rosamund Lehmann or Jean Rhys, just to name three very gifted women near-contemporaries. Perhaps the ultimate difference between Stead and these writers (who of course differ a great deal from one another) is neither that she is restrained in her use of plot as a mechanism of signification and satisfaction, nor that her characters are usually recognizable social types, but that her texts rarely deal with that pathos which invites readers to identify with characters' suffering. In particular, the extramural (or extra-diegetic) intensities that swing through her fictions don't include pity, since pity may seed in the reader a catharsis of liberal generosity that no revolutionary materialist writer can admit: she does not belong to the Sternean tradition of sentimentality discussed in the last chapter. This refusal of compassion, which Brecht pursued along a different track but for similar reasons, is all the more powerful precisely because there is so much character in Stead's fiction, so much smothering intimacy. But, and crucially, the indeterminate pitiless negative emotion that she directs towards her characters is leavened by what I will call, in a technical sense, charity (i.e., *agape*). Charity is a traditional Christian theological virtue which, as Anders Nygren argued in his classic *Agape and Eros*, does not involve personal relations, or pity or compassion, or empathy (Nygren 1953: 77–78). It's the love of God turned earthwards and creaturely. Its logic runs like this: God loves all sinners, so in returning God's love I too must love my fellows, as it were impersonally, indifferent to their moral worth. That's charity. Stead, of course, affirms no God. But I'd wager that she treats her characters charitably, despite in many cases hating them and refusing them compassion, because for her History, not God, holds us all in its hands, and may redeem us not individually but collectively.

Cotters' England

In order to bring this conspectus of Stead's career to bear more tightly on the question of her potential for canonicity, it is important to pay detailed attention to at least one of her novels. Why? As we have seen, Casanova's account of the global literary field passes too quickly over the acts of discrimination through which texts are consecrated. It is true that consecration itself does not necessarily require detailed critical judgment, indeed a crucial intermediary in Stead's case – Stanley Burnshaw – almost never wrote criticism about Stead: his connection to her was primarily personal and political. But Stead needs concrete cases to be made on her behalf. And then, academic literary studies (whose canonizing powers Casanova of course downplays) remain committed to so-called "close reading." Although texts can be canonized without attracting academic close readings, there can be no doubt that the existence of an archive of such readings is a powerful aid to, and sign of, canonization. That's another reason why, in assessing Stead's relation to global canonicity, it's important to provide at least the basis of such a reading for one of Stead's texts.

One further preliminary point: academic close reading is itself a complex concept, which reaches across and towards an assemblage of practices, themselves often positioned against one another in debates over method. Four of these stand out: the dominant one, interpretation (i.e., an account of a text's meaning which consciously differs from other such accounts as produced by other academic critics); contextualization (i.e., a description of a text's historical setting, function or purpose); literary scholarship (i.e., a description of a text's literary allusions, its generic, structural, or rhetorical features, and so on); and evaluation (i.e., a judgment of its literary value). Of these, for better or worse, evaluation has become the least important, since academic writing increasingly piously assumes its objects' worth. But for obvious reasons, in this case, evaluation remains key even if I am evaluating the text in the context of its chances for canonization understood as an institutional process. Yet as will also become apparent in my reading of *Cotters' England* has a somewhat restrained relation to evaluation.

Cotters' England is set in the austerity Britain of the immediate postwar period – a moment of widespread poverty and shortages, but which also saw the first serious attempt to implement social democracy.[34] It's about the moods and life trajectories of a group of mainly communist activists, although Stead is not as explicit about her characters' communism here as she was in her novels of the 1930s: a concession no doubt to Cold War repression.

The novel focuses on Nellie Cotter, a woman of great, if eccentric, style and presence, who lives in London, although her family comes from Gateshead (here called Bridgehead), a working-class district of Newcastle upon Tyne. Nellie's father, who dies near the novel's beginning, was a glamorous, over-bearing figure, an inadequate parent and dominating husband: a very Steadian patriarch. The Cotters live in a terraced house along with Mary's brother, Uncle Sime, who is now over eighty and merely tolerated, even though he has supported the household for decades. Nellie has two siblings: Tom, a fey figure, trying to find a way out from his father's shadow, with whom she has had a very close, perhaps incestuous, relationship, and her sister Peggy, who still lives at home and has had a troubled past, having spent time in an asylum. The family are poor, and deeply resentful that Nellie does not help them out, having left a good paying job to live the high life in London. Nellie is con-tinually encouraging her brother Tom to return home and support the family.

In their younger Bridgehead days, Tom and Nellie both became involved in the "Jago" circle, which introduced them to bohemia and hence to intel-lectual life (both anarchism and communism) and sexual experimentation. In particular, Nellie became friends with a charismatic, wild, nomadic working-class prostitute, Johnny Strecker, committed to antinomianism. At one point two members of the circle committed suicide, one apparently under moral pressure from Strecker, the other under moral pressure from Nellie herself, who, in thrall to what Rex Warner called "the cult of power" in a 1946 essay of that title, considers this a dark sign of her personal charisma and influence (see Warner 1946). In the course of the novel, Nellie will help drive Caroline to suicide: Caroline, a middle-class woman in demoralized flight from a divorce, is unaccustomed to the ways of bohemian radicals.

At the time the narrative proper begins Nellie, almost forty, is living in a large house in Islington, London. She's sick and drinking heavily. She's working as a journalist for the communist daily, the *Daily Worker* (not named as such) but she has recently resigned from the party, on the grounds that political activity is ultimately selfish and that the Communist Party in particular lacks ordinary compassion (1966: 157). She takes in lodgers (including Caroline, and, for a short time, her brother Tom), many of whom are lost souls she nurtures and emotionally dominates in relationships that once again shore up her sense of her personal power. Her husband, George Cook, is a self-educated communist union leader, whom she met in their youth up north and for whom she has come down to London. George now has a job in Geneva with the ILO, and is becoming a member not so much of the labor aristocracy but of the bourgeoisie, in an anticipation of the Eurocommunist dream. George and Nellie's is a free relationship, which does not (at least now) involve sex. Their friends believe their days as a couple are numbered, and both have affairs with women. Nonetheless, Nellie hopes to join George in Europe. Indeed at one point she does go to Rome with him but soon returns, unable to stand her wifely role there, another victim of the left's subordination of women.

At the novel's end Tom has left Nellie's house to take a job as a foreman in middle England, where he will settle down and marry. Nellie once again follows George, this time to Switzerland (despite her often expressed solidarity with the English worker, and her complaints that George had sold out on them), and this is an important sign of her lack of integrity. But George dies in a skiing accident and she returns to London, where she shows signs of becoming interested in what today we would call "New Age" spirituality. Up at Bridgehead, after their mother's death, Peggy has cruelly stolen Uncle Sime's life savings and thrown him out on to the street in order to make a living by turning the house into a brothel. The scene in which she ejects her uncle, a fine expression of Stead's anti-familialism, is one of the most affecting in the *oeuvre* and stands against her rejection of compassionate pathos.[35] In so far as Nellie is complicit with Uncle Sime's expulsion from the family home it's another instance of her moral failure, but in so far as it solicits readers' imaginative sympathies on Uncle Sime's side it stands, contradictorily, with Nellie's anti-Marxist appeal to pity.

The novel is not quite an imaginative projection: it was carefully researched in 1949 by Stead, who spent time observing her friend Anne Dooley and her family in Tyneside, in order to provide herself with material. Dooley was a charismatic communist journalist, like Nellie employed by the *Daily Worker*. But *Cotters' England* is quite different from other British postwar novels. Certainly it radically departs from what had become the conventions for representing English working-class life by 1966, when it was first published. Fictions like Alan Sillitoe's *Saturday Night and Sunday Morning* (1958) represent ordinary working-class life from the outside and from the male point of view as bound together by complex codes and solidarities: a corporate class in Max Weber's terms. But Stead's novel knows no community, has no sense of ordinariness, and does not divide its readers off from its central characters, who aren't, clearly, workers at all, they're quasi-intellectuals with working-class backgrounds living admittedly fairly impoverished more or less bohemian metropolitan lives. The trajectory from working class to radical intellectual, or rather its emotional and political cost, is the novel's central interest. This means too that it can be read as an elegy to the Communist idea of proletarian literature, so important to left literary culture in the 1930s.

Cotters' England is also engaged in the quarrel between Marxism and what we can loosely call existentialism, at least in a sidelong fashion.[36] As we've seen, Nellie has recently left the Communist Party, which is one reason why she is drifting and talks so insistently about politics and ethics. In debate with Eliza, for instance, she remembers that in her Jago days:

> We went to the Communists and they said, Study, read the history of socialism, learn how society is composed and work for a future society. But I said to the district organizer: What is the meaning of death and hunger? Have you got some words so that I can explain that to a poor mother? Hunger, desertion and death are too stark for words! Your pals, I'm sorry to say, Eliza, didn't understand us at all … they couldn't work on us so easily, for we were damned serious. It was spiritual hunger.
>
> (Stead 1966: 212)

For all this speech's tenderness, Nellie's bad faith is clear, since desertion exactly describes her relation to her own Tyneside family. And her "spiritual hunger" ultimately cashes out as her will to gain power over others, although it takes conceptual form in her interest in the "unknowable." And, despite her denial, Nellie has an interest in history. We are told that as a girl she spent every afternoon in the library (Stead 1966: 228) as well as visiting miners' homes to learn about communism (here called socialism). But in the end this led her not to the history of the English working class in the spirit of E. P. Thompson, whose work is probably indirectly referenced, but to Mary Bateman, a criminal millennarian follower of the prophetess Joanna Southcott, who in the early nineteenth century exploited the spiritual hunger of the poor to defraud them, and whose sorry history as a post-Christian witch typologically predicts Nellie's.[37] (It was Thompson who famously wanted to rescue "even the deluded follower of Joanna Southcott from the enormous condescension of posterity" in a book published three years before *Cotters' England*, Thompson 1968: 13). It's a complex, recondite allusion requiring precisely the historical knowledge that Nellie despises, with all the irony consequent upon that.

Nonetheless, the distance between socialist history and theory and private life and private suffering is a real one for Stead, and, as we have seen, helps to organize her work's form and tone. Literary-historically speaking *Cotters' England* marks a departure from the novels that Stead published in the 1950s, although, technically and stylistically, it doesn't belong to the 1960s either. It is probably closest in style and tone to what Michael North has evocatively called the "artificial, almost papery quality" of the high-bourgeois realist accommodation with modernism worked through by writers like Henry Green (*Back*, 1946) and Elizabeth Bowen (*The Heat of the Day*, 1949) in their postwar fiction (North 2004: 452). It's a mode very dependent on the careful ordering of narrative access to characters' consciousness as well as on dialogue, but which, more important, finds its tone in idiolects at some remove from any recognizable vernacular yet without a trace of high-modernist or Jamesian aestheticism. Indeed, Stead's novel presents us not so much with a realist mimesis of its world as with a mimesis of an only-just-alternative world: it's a world that is not a copy of the one that we inhabit but of one at some slight – indefinable – displacement from it. Stead herself called it "a poetic interpretation of life" (Rowley 1994: 442).

Stead seems to have turned to this mode not just because she has so little attachment to ordinary language under capitalism but because her characters themselves are not securely socially grounded, and are adrift in flurries of social transformation (as the British war effort mutates into social democracy) and which destabilize not just their identities as social types but their discourse. A muted form of heteroglossia rules. Furthermore the characters' private thoughts are habitually concealed from us (we are never quite sure of Tom and Nellie's sexual orientation for instance) as the narrator refuses to take a position of omniscience, associated with convictions, Marxist and bourgeois, which are now under evacuation. And the characters too often talk rather than feel or learn. Nellie's voice in particular dominates the novel, and her rhetorical presence looms so large because her considerable intelligence and performative talents are blocked by her class, gender, and family history as well as her incapacity to take others seriously. Now that she's left the Communist Party her views have no institutional location, either. So she talks like no one ever has, in a highly figurative, disconnected flow of words and phrases. She indiscriminately sprinkles her speech with loving names, "pet," "love," "darling," "chick" in an extravagant extension of working-class idiolect; her habitual use of clichés is just out of kilter; she reaches for cultural references that elude her and trap her into a peculiar stiltedness. Yet her speech contains traces of her informal education in communist and bohemian circles as well as profoundly original and evocative images and inspired flashes of insight. More than anything, it's this language which covers over the real world in the novel's particular mode of irreal mimesis.

Here's one example from a prepared rave that Nellie delivers to her brother Tom and Camilla. At the time they are gingerly broaching a romantic relationship and have just returned from a day trip rather later than expected, having failed to spend the night together because Tom has sexual difficulties (although this is only implied):

> In a murmurous voice, she [Nellie] began: "It's so cosy and warm, why, it's lovely having you together. I'm glad you had a good talk. The world's shut its curtains against you. You drop into the wayside inn and there for a moment you have a few words with a fellow traveller. It's all there is, but it's warming. And then the lonely road. But it's the heart-cheering moment. It's wonderful that you two could have an hour together by a stranger's fire. You've watched the lonely black sky together, and felt adrift. And you know that destiny is individual. Destiny is

loneliness. It's mysterious and no one can share it. No one can shed his blood for you, no one can die for you, no one can live for you. It's the final truth. It's single blessedness to the end. There's no marriage in death; it's a stark commentary on our sham passions. They're sideshows on the lonely road. Eh, it's wonderful for me, chicks, it makes me humble, to meet two clear-eyed people like you, who do not believe there are any bargains in Vanity Fair. The lonely road, leading right through Vanity Fair. That's a freezing thought! What beautiful souls you are, like saints, like hermits! Eh, I'd like to have your courage. I'd get myself a canvas house, like the watchman on the roadworks, my brazier, my tent, my bunk, my black tea, sitting up all night, musing and thinking; that's my ideal existence. Nothing but the wind blowing, the blackness – that's the reality.

(Stead 1966, 154)

This passage, murmured to bring us close, displays much of Nellie's inventively teetering command of language, from the skewed metaphor "The world's shut its curtains against you" (which hints at her theatricality) to its echo in her awkward reference to "Vanity Fair," which, eccentrically, turns out to have a lonely road cut through it. This string of non-sequiturs and swerves across various topics and rhetorical registers is characteristically self-deceived in its main drift: no one derives more spiritual sustenance from their influence on their intimates than Nellie, no one is less able to face the blackness in solitude than she is – she is a ceaseless socializer and talker; no one is more manipulative in her relation to death than she is (she has in effect asked two people to die for her). It certainly does not speak at all to Tom and Camilla's actual situation. And it's banally sentimental despite its flashes into a certain existentialism, which is in the end fake: "Destiny is loneliness" (how can a socialist of any stripe say that?) and, in her case, the anti-Christian "no one can die for you" is a complex but downright lie.

But then, more imaginatively, it moves into a quasi-novelistic representation of what Nellie claims as her ideal life – being a nightwatchman for a road gang, staring at night skies in a "canvas house" (invoked in a sequence of telling possessive plosive-heavy "mys" – my brazier, my bunk, my tent, my black tea). At one level, it's a socially resonant image, given the importance of the housing issue both in the novel and to postwar Britain: Nellie and Caroline met while working in a housing agency which is implementing the Labour government's welfarist and modernizing response to the postwar housing shortage, much to Nellie's communist disgust. And Nellie's power base is the large house in Islington which allows her to shelter human strays. At another level, it is an image that plugs into other important events and scenes in the novel, including Charlotte's death, Uncle Sime's cruel expulsion from the Tyneside terrace, and Nellie's decision to follow George to a comfortable life in Geneva. Yet it's an image that tells us nothing of substance about Nellie's interiority: indeed, her outpouring of words only compounds her elusiveness.

The speech as a whole is, in effect, a little machine for producing semi-controlled connotations and links, some of which point to the actual social world, some of which allow us to understand the characters and their self-deceptions in terms other than they have for themselves, some of which engage living political ideas, some of which link back into literary history, some of which create internal thematic resonances, and which, all together, allow Nellie to invoke England's condition as an empty, cruel, glamorous society betrayed by its labor leaders. This invocation in turn stands in the place of the "real" England, namely England as represented by the conventions of orthodox realism, conventions which are now indirectly indebted to the reformism that neither Stead nor Nellie can abide. Nellie is a point of access into the condition of England although she is neither typical sociologically speaking nor even a fully given character: as we know, she's a declassed, cruel, insecure, power-hungry, renegade communist bohemian part lesbian with a thoroughly opaque interiority. We can take this further: the novel materializes that "outside the outside" narratological position preferred by Stead, and it does so by creating a net of connotative threads that reach across and beyond the text itself, although most are inserted into Nellie's characterization. As Jose Yglesias remarked in a review of the novel for *The Nation*: "didacticism and moralizing are so transmuted that they seem almost entirely absent from either the surfaces or depths of her story" (Yglesias 1966: 420). So, given that no narrator or character (including herself) authoritatively judges or interprets Nellie, it's the readerly desire to figure Nellie out, grounded in charity, that in the end sparks and vivifies the novel's network of connotative machines.

Here's a second speech of Nellie's, less strong rhetorically in many ways but closer to the novel's political concerns. Nellie is talking to Camilla and George's first wife, Eliza, about a left-wing journalist. "What gets into the men?" she asks rhetorically, and continues:

> "They lick their lips for the fleshpots. I just had to tick off that damn, pussy-footing, pale pink journalist Robin Bramble!"
>
> "Robin Bramble! Do you know him? He's a first-rate labor journalist,"...
>
> "He was edging up to me at the meeting making signs and asking me if I was going up north, so he could come along and hide in me skirts: he's afraid of the rabble. And asking me what happened at the housing meeting at Highbury the other day. He had to leave early. What's it to you? I said. Are your silk-stocking parlour pinks, behind their Hampstead cottonwool barricades, are they interested in the lives of the humble? Is it a new circulation stunt, using me for a stooge? I know you, mopping and mowing at the left-wingers, afraid the Reds might win before you've got yourself established as the people's

champion. Time server, with a foot in as many camps as a bloody centipede. I told he'd got a lot of closet theory, nicely served up in an ivied
quadrangle, when he was young. It's the life the workers lead, not
chewed-up paper, not theory. I told him. What's it to them, the history
of the British working class, and Jack Cade and the Levellers and Char-
tists? Do you think they'd join any of those lots? You've got to go down
in the street, I said, and climb the rotting staircase, cluttered with
plaster from the ceiling like here, and slipping in the unnamable from
the burst waste pipes. Give me a cup of tea, Eliza, pet! That damn
dominie Robert Peeble, me editor, says I have to go to classes for three
months, to classes on theory! Me! I don't believe in Marxian theory, I
said. Can it explain the unknowable? Can it help a working-class mother
who just lost her baby? Can it stop the concentration camps? Can it
keep a man in his country? It's too much schooling ye have and too
little experience; and that's why I'm the best journalist you've got or can
hope to have. I'm from the people."

(Stead 1966: 235–36)

Despite the speech's cliché-crammed vitality, despite its smothering intimacy, it's another exercise in self-deception: Nellie isn't "from the people"
any more. Indeed, as a signed-up member of London's bohemia she's capable
of acquiescing in the immiseration of her family up north. And the speech
involves a fairly obvious self-interest and irony as in the bathos of the quick
little leap from "Can it stop the concentration camps?" to "Can it keep a
man in his own country?" which last refers just to George's abandonment of
her, as she thinks it. All this turns the reader against Nellie's refusal of
theory on the grounds that she's the real experiential thing. But, once again,
the passage has a force that such remarks do not catch. This time, it's a force
fired by syntax: by the mix of imperatives, interrogatives, pluperfects, and
past imperfects through which the oration proceeds. It is also lexical:
"Hampstead cottonwool barricades," "silk-stocking parlour pinks," "moping
and mowing," "damn dominie," "closet theory," "chewed-up paper" have a
skewed vigor all of their own. And it's figurative once again: the timeserver
as a "centipede," for instance, but most ostentatiously in another metaphor of
a house, this time the strange imaginary house, cluttered by plaster, which is
transmogrified out of the "street" that Nellie imagines as reality's locus. This
image returns us not just to the canvas shelter of the previous passage, or
again to Nellie's work in postwar housing, and the crumbling family home
in Newcastle, but to her self-ascribed metaphysical homelessness, and so
repeats and enriches those connotative flows that produce the fiction's
"poetic" simulacrum of England. And the passage's force is further fired by
energizing slippages, of which probably the most powerful is in the oral echo
of the "unnameable" (the shit that flows in the basement of Nellie's imagined house) in the "unknowable," which will literarily be the novel's last

word, and which refers to those existential, death-centered interests which, in fact, if not in theory, seem to dominate Nellie's intellectual and ethical life and which stand in contradiction to her quasi-working-class, quasi-communist activism. In sum, in the end, her in-your-face intimacy with the reader is enabled both by her living at a remove from the society she inhabits and by her standing, *qua* character, outside the literary conventions through which that remove is frameable.

Stead's canonization

Where, after all this, do we stand then in relation to Stead's potential for global canonization? Do Stead's literary strategy and its results allow her to be placed alongside more widely acknowledged generational peers such as Faulkner, Nabokov, Bowen, and Greene? As should by now be apparent, these questions need to be addressed across two barely separable registers: the first critical, the second institutional. As far as criticism is concerned: I have made the case that Stead transposed her communist commitment into a form of reluctant literary autonomy that called upon a formally and tonally complex articulation of the gap between an (off-stage) Marxist theory and the conditions of everyday life, especially for women. This is the ultimate ground of her specificity as a writer and at one institutionally powerful level leads to the mixture of critique and irreal mimesis characteristic of *Cotters' England*. However, it's clear that this is more than a purely literary judgment, since it also requires that we assess the continuing pertinence of what now seems a lost political cause – communism.

Institutionally speaking, the question is: who will push for Stead's canonization, and how much heft do they have? It should be clear by now that Stead is unlikely to be canonized from below, i.e., via her appeal to the amateur literary reader.[38] This means that her work will need the support of the pedagogical institutions, and in particular, of Auslit and feminist literary criticism, with all the limits that implies.[39] It's worth noting, as an aside, that, as may be apparent, Stead's work engages another academic formation too – British cultural studies – because it investigates middle-class radicalism, relations between Marxian theory and everyday life, the political function of history, and the fate of revolutionary socialism in the era of social democracy's emergence. And these were among cultural studies' first shaping interests too. But, although this may increase Stead's resonance for some of us, cultural studies today is not about to help canonize Stead: its interests lie elsewhere.

Calculating the probabilities in these terms, and taking account of the misfit between Stead's literary project and both Auslit and the capitalist global literary field outlined by Casanova, it seems unlikely that Stead's reputation will change in the foreseeable future, or that she will be able to form the advance guard for Auslit's wider internationalization. She will remain something like a quasi-canonical author (a category Casanova, of course, does not admit): well known in Australia (if not widely read, especially outside *The Man Who Loved children* and *For Love Alone*), with no presence in US and UK literary histories and little presence in literature curricula, but with a significant if narrow reading-public reputation for *The Man Who Loved Children*, not least in the United States. She is unlikely to be viewed as a writer central to her generation's literary achievements, or to be recognized as belonging to world literature in anything like Stanley Burnshaw's (or even Randall Jarrell's) terms.

This is, of course, a provisional judgment. Things may change. For instance (in no particular order of probability):

1. Relations between core and periphery may alter in the latter's favor, making the argument that women colonial expatriates helped constitute global Anglophone literary modernism more widely acceptable. And Australia's position in the global literary field may also improve so as to increase Auslit's, at the moment weak, potential for global consecration.
2. Democratic nation-state capitalism may begin to lose some of its absolute hegemony so that Stead's radical distance from it may gain allure, and interest in lost-cause alternatives like communism, and communist literary culture, may increase.
3. Stead's generation when high modernism intersected with the increasingly commodified Cold War literary market may acquire greater literary-historiographical significance.

In any of these cases (and others are of course imaginable) Stead might become a more canonizable figure. But the important point is that these calculations have no relation to the reserve of intellectual and literary energy preserved in Stead's *oeuvre*. Its realizable literary capital, actual or potential, is not a simple function of its literary power as this can be felt by individual readers and publicly articulated and analyzed by critics. I'd like to think that the account of Stead I have put forward here, which draws a great deal from previous criticism, does help create extra ripples of recognition for her work, not least because her capacity to take a narratological position "outside the outside" of fictional worlds so as to fuse realism and modernism in the interests of a heretical Stalinism powerfully embodies and signifies literature's potential in a modern world in which (as I will argue in chapters to come) capitalism is neither escapable nor acceptable.

Chapter 5

Socialist ends

The emergence of academic theory in post-war Britain

This chapter presents a prehistory of British cultural studies by focusing on a widespread demand for theory within the left between about 1957 and 1965.[1] My main interest in the topic is simple enough. I seek to make the case that the academic "turn to theory" needs to be understood in social as much as in intellectual terms.[2] I do so partly in the hope of catching a glimpse of a moment when academic "theory" had clear and widely recognized social and political ambitions which might help weight it materially even today. At the same time I wish briefly to examine what intellectual possibilities were lost to the humanities across the period of theory's emergence, though let me concede in advance this is not an ambition I satisfactorily fulfill.

By its nature this project involves simplifications, of which the most obvious concerns the classification of theory itself. For me, operating under a basic nominalism, "theory" is just what calls itself such. But, patently, more than one mode of conceptualizing, with more than one disciplinary base, has been named "theory" inside the modern humanities. Nonetheless, for my purposes we can effectively divide theory into three main (and, admittedly, connected) phases. First, the theory that was imported into British socialism after the New Left's decline, whose major figures were Gramsci and Althusser. Then the literary post-structuralism that was widely disseminated mainly in the United States after the early 1970s, whose primary inspirations were Derrida and de Man, and which can be regarded (from an intellectual-historical point of view) as the attempt to import certain thematics within traditional European philosophy on to a literary field whose ethical basis had been broken both by the impact of structuralism and by the 1960s youth movement, and which thereby could, or acted as if it could, contribute to philosophy from within the discipline of literary studies.[3] It is still within that moment that theory emerges, in a third form, as a discrete formation inside the humanities after about 1970 and extends its range to include figures like Gilles Deleuze, Jacques Lacan, Jean-François Lyotard, Julia Kristeva, Michel Foucault, Luce Irigaray and Jean Baudrillard as well as philosophical Western Marxists such as Theodor Adorno and Walter Benjamin. This field produces a body of very loosely connected concepts with varying genealogies and implications (if still connected to the European philosophic tradition) that constitute a residual, unrecognized-as-such "theory corpus" not always able to be tied to particular proper names.

Of these three theory formations, only the first is fruitful for my purpose, i.e., the examination of the social preconditions for theory's emergence, the main reason being that literary post-structuralism as well as the ongoing European philosophization of the humanities were academic from the beginning, which is not true of socialist theory. Hence the latter kinds of theory can be understood (although not completely) in functionalist terms – as means through which certain humanities disciplines have reproduced themselves. Let me gesture at some of these functions. Theory may bridge divisions between disciplines, or even help federate them. Because it is recondite, it can provide intellectual capital able to hierarchize academic fields and to resource career building. More complexly, it promises a phantasmal but expressive conceptual mastery of the world to intellectuals who operate from positions of relative powerlessness, especially to young academics struggling with their field's difficulties in providing careers adequate to their aspirations. As it offers this promise, however, it enriches and divides the humanities' conceptual repertoire, injecting intellectual energy into academic work as much in being rejected and critiqued as in being absorbed.

Within British cultural studies, "theory" is doubly displaced: it was imported into Britain first from Italy, then from France, mainly by intellectuals working outside or on the margins of the university system, and then transposed into the academy in the aftermath of May 1968. If we ask, "Why did this happen?" we need to turn not just to the politics of the socialist left in the period, but to the wider situation in which the left was undergoing rapid mutation. To sum my argument in a phrase: British theory begins as a response to the crisis of socialism under welfarism.

The first significant call for theory within this milieu occurred early. In 1958 a group of writers, loosely associated with what is now known as the "first New Left" appeared in a volume entitled *Conviction*.[4] They included the young literary critics Raymond Williams and Richard Hoggart, but also politicians, economists, novelists, journalists, scientists, and historians – a breadth of contributors that would become much rarer after 1968. Williams was then writing *The Long Revolution* and contributed a characteristic piece, "Culture is Ordinary," posing suggestions for national media policy (Williams 1961: 342 ff.). Hoggart's "Speaking for Ourselves" demanded a "reassessment" of contemporary culture and society, claiming that "by a close and constant discipline of thought and feeling, working from the grounds outwards, we shall be better able to take stock of our lives for growth" – growth that he conceived of as developing towards classlessness, not along what he thought of as American lines, but towards "a merging of the considerable, lived-into virtues still to be found in all classes" (Hoggart 1958: 138).

Hoggart's wish for a close and constant discipline of thought became an explicit demand for theory in Iris Murdoch's essay for the volume, entitled "A House of Theory." At this time Murdoch was known as an ex-communist and author of two well received novels, who was working as a philosophy tutor at Oxford. She made her call for theory on the basis of a wide-ranging analysis of the current social situation, fairly typical of the first New Left, but also against the background of her first novel, *Under the Net* (1954), which can be regarded as a novel of theoretical practice in the way that other novels are novels of ideas. There, four cultural/intellectual formations are played off against one another: spectacle as conceived of in terms that shared much with the Situationists (who were just then developing out of Lettrism in Parisian circles that Murdoch knew); an existentially tinged Wittgensteinism committed to a sense that language itself may bar authenticity and hence committed to an ascetic ethic of silence and retreat; political activism of the kind that would soon be called the New Left, and, last, the difficult life of the serious imaginative writer. The novel opts for imaginative writing, supportive of but distant from New Left socialism.

But in her *Conviction* essay Murdoch argued that the socialist movement was "suffering from a loss of energy" for a variety of reasons. Welfarism and Keynianism had rescued capitalism from collapse. Working-class politics had been subordinated to the trade union movement. Old forms of proletarian collective culture were being eroded by the modern commercial leisure industries, and there was certainly no sign that working-class morality was sympathetic to socialism. (This was a line of thought that separated Murdoch from Williams's essay in the volume, as a reviewer pointed out, Alexander 1958: 112.) Drawing on the American sociologist C. Wright Mills, she further contended that the new forms of economic participation and egalitarianism, with their emphasis on education and consumption, were rehierarchizing society, partly by creating a new division between the "expert" and the "non-expert."[5] This meant that what she called "alienation" and "expropriation" were expanding, despite so-called "affluence," i.e., the lowering of barriers of entry into middle-class lifeways. "Alienation," a concept recently imported from Western Marxism, anchored Murdoch's demand for theory, since it was seen to be socially pervasive. To face pervasive alienated affluence, old policies and concepts were insufficient. The old British antagonism to theory had to be forgone.

Murdoch argued that that antagonism had taken three main intellectual-historical forms, reaching deep into the European and, more particularly, the British past, namely "Tory skepticism" (Burke and Hume); Benthamite skepticism (as currently instantiated by the Fabians who dominated the Labour Party) and a "Kantian-Protestant" fear of superstition whose latest manifestation was modern philosophy's desire for the "elimination of metaphysics" (Murdoch 1958: 226). British skepticism and empiricism especially prevented any imagination of what a good society might look like. Being means-orientated, they disabled conceptions of social *ends* in terms that didn't dissolve into liberal individualism. Furthermore, lack of theory encouraged the specialization of knowledge as well as intellectual passivity, which in turn allowed "bureaucracy, in all its senses, to keep us mystified" (Murdoch 1958: 228), a formulation which would appear to owe something, at least at a distance, not just to Wright Mills but to Trotskyite critiques of the Soviet state.

So Murdoch posited theory as an "area of translation" across knowledges which might "refresh the tired imagination of practice" (1958: 231). Or, as she put it in a more expanded statement:

> A more ambitious conceptual picture, thought out anew in the light of modern critical philosophy and our improved knowledge of the world, of the moral centre and moral direction of Socialism, would enable those of us who are not experts to pick up the facts of our situation in a reflective, organized and argumentative way: would give us what Shelley called the power to imagine what we know.
>
> (Murdoch 1958: 228)

Such statements echoed Edward Thompson's program of "socialist humanism" as promoted in his journal, *The New Reasoner*, to which Murdoch was a contributor. For Murdoch, as for Thompson, *socialist* theory was centered on the concept of labor, which needed to be reimagined and reconceptualized in moral terms, since, pinioned between capital and the unions, it was being instrumentalized and pacified. And here the difficulties that beset Murdoch's argument appear most clearly, since, in gesturing towards a body of Labourist work that might inspire future theory, she turned first to left intellectuals of the 1930s, especially Harold Laski and Richard Tawney, and, then, more insistently, to pre-World War I Guild Socialism, and its dominant figure, G. D. H. Cole, theorist of "workers' control," at this time still on the scene as an Oxford don whose political theory seminar was a breeding ground for young New Left intellectuals, including Stuart Hall.[6] Guild Socialism had, Murdoch claimed, assessed the damaging social consequences of capitalist economic relationships most accurately, even if its solutions were "impracticable" (1958: 232) – though by this time Cole himself was suggesting that world capitalism might break if workers in Britain (the global system's weak link) increased their demands on employers beyond the point where the welfare state could meet them, a prognosis that helps elucidate much radical left strategy to come (Cole 1957). At any rate, the gap between Murdoch's philosophical critique of British antagonism to theory and its social consequences and her hesitant appeal to the local socialist tradition marked out the area that future theory – Hoggart's "discipline of thought" – needed to occupy.

Over the next decade, writer after writer repeated Murdoch's call for theory, more or less directly.[7] Take Ralph Miliband as an example. Writing in the *New Reasoner* in 1958, he argued that, now that both welfarism and unionism were being deployed to maintain capitalism, what was needed was "an adequate grasp of the live forces at work in our society and, to use the jargon, of the close inter-connections between society's economic base and such superstructural manifestations of it as is possible to trace. What we need, in other words, is to relate so much that makes up the total culture of this society to the economic system which underpins that culture" – with theory being the tool to analyze those relations (Miliband 1958: 47). But its absence was first effectively filled only in a series of essays written in the early and mid-1960s by Tom Nairn and Perry Anderson when they took over the *New Left Review* from Stuart Hall and the first New Left in 1962. Anderson and Nairn were indeed the key figures behind the emergence of academic theory from out of the British New Left. The background against which they became the most innovative left intellectuals of the period, and brokers of European theory, has often been discussed, but it needs to be addressed once again, even though it requires us to grasp in some detail the history that immediately precedes their first writings.[8]

The first New Left that had appeared after 1956 was not, as Chris Rojek has argued, a Gramscian "bloc" but a more heterogeneous formation still, with some features of what is today called a "new social formation," some features of the political "campaign" (whose activists mainly concentrated on anti-nuclear politics), and some features of a middle-class urban subculture – which broached new forms of subjectivity best represented (at their most avant-garde) by the ex-communist "free women" casting about for autonomy, stability, and purpose in Doris Lessing's widely read novel *The Golden Notebook* (1962).[9]

The British New Left existed on the margins of the Labour Party, whose Fabian centrism, economism, bureaucratic structures, and US-centered foreign policy it denounced. It had no formal connection with the Communist Party, of course, which several of its leaders had left as recently as after the 1956 Soviet invasion of Hungary: if anything it emerged from the dis-articulation of the British Communist Party from the radical left.[10] The movement was partly based in the "New Left Clubs" that were established across the nation, of which the two most of important (in London and Manchester) helped popularize youth-orientated inner-city bohemia. They were places were people met to drink coffee, listen to jazz, hear talks, join in seminar discussions. And the first New Left's wide cultural support and energy came in part from its loose connections to transformations in the arts where innovative hybridizations of non-deferential realism with modernism were emerging in film (Lindsay Anderson, Karl Reisz, the *nouvelle vague*), television drama (Jim Allen, Tony Garnett), theater (John Osborne, John Arden, Joan Littlewood), the novel (Doris Lessing, Iris Murdoch, Alan Silli-toe), and journalism (Colin Wilson, Paul Johnson). The first New Left's media organs were the (relatively) glossy monthly *University and Left Review*, managed by Oxford graduates who included Stuart Hall and Raphael Samuel, and the more intellectual Yorkshire-based *New Reasoner*, edited by the ex-communists Edward Thompson and John Saville. In 1961 these journals would merge and be renamed the *New Left Review*, with Stuart Hall as editor.

It was widely recognized that the first New Left's most substantial intellectual contribution was Raymond William's ambitious *The Long Revolution* (1961), a *summa* of the British progressivist tradition. Here the work of the old anti-Fabian, anti-communist left – writer-activists like Edward Morel, John Hobson, G. D. H. Cole, Norman Angell, H. N. Brailsford, Laski, and Tawney, many half forgotten and none here acknowledged by Williams – were brought into contact with the tradition that Williams had earlier described in *Culture and Society*, namely the post-Burkean culturalist critique of modernity.[11] All this in terms that could underpin policy for 1960s Britain.[12]

Stuart Hall was later to declare that *The Long Revolution* was "the text of the break" into theory (Hall 1980: 19). And even if it makes as much sense to say, on the contrary, that, after Anderson and Nairn, the book came to exemplify what theory was not, there can be no doubt that it radically expanded and abstracted the available terms of cultural and social analysis. Its main claims remain quite well known – it proposes a "general human creativity" which is potentially shared by all but which class divisions, industrialism, and Fabian state management distort (1961: 28). Modern societies are dominated by "structures of feeling" and self-images (Williams does not have the concept of ideology to hand, although he is reaching for it) in which meaninglessness and cynicism thrive: an argument perhaps made most vividly in his description of the "vagrant" as an ideal type (1961: 91). Genuine and equal creativity requires a participatory society which the state can promote by scaling back private ownership and democratizing work-places, as well as by deploying the education and media systems against elitism and commercialism. Hence one of Williams's concrete policy proposals was that appropriate independent media outlets be subsidized by the state in order to prevent their absorption into private interests and the profit motive (1961: 342 ff.).

In summary, *The Long Revolution's* key suppositions and theses can be listed like this:

1. An affirmation of slow social reform as against sudden socialist revolution or even the kind of collapse in capitalism that G. D. H. Cole, for instance, continued to look towards.
2. A rejection of hard distinctions between state apparatuses and the institutions of civil society.
3. A willingness to posit fundamental human characteristics which are not determined socially (in particular, creativity and growth) as grounds for ethico-political judgments.

4. A sense that the deepest problem facing British intellectuals is how to bring the highly selective cultural heritage which has best articulated human "meaning" and creativity to bear upon the ordinary life of the community, and the understanding that this problem could be most cogently addressed by state regulation and ownership of the media. This marked Williams out as a literary intellectual, working within the ambits of what was to be called "left Leavisism."

5. The assumption that "participation" and "self-determination" between them could reconcile the concept of a "common culture," thought of as shared everyday life practices, with that of a "democratic society," thought of in proceduralist terms as a society in which *means* for the even distribution of the capacity for social engagement of *different* groups could be established.

For all the recognition that Williams received, his line of thought had problems in winning assent, as was revealed by the fate of its main policy outcome, a submission to the Pilkington Committee on the future of television. Williams and some colleagues drafted this document, published in Stuart Hall's *New Left Review* the same year as *The Long Revolution*. It recommended that the media should not be commercialized at all, and that commercial licenses already given be rescinded. It made the case that a television industry committed to quality and seriousness could be sustained only if the education system produced a critical public for it, and so requested more "courses in critical appreciation of the mass media" and the establishing of "an institute of communications research" along with the subsidized production of appropriate textbooks (Coppard et al. 1961: 45–46). This influenced the committee's report (partly because Richard Hoggart was a member) but the report itself was rejected by just about everyone else, including the government. The image of a media and education system governed by Williamsite values clearly lacked wider appeal.

Indeed, by 1963 the first New Left had well and truly run out of steam.[13] The anti-nuclear movement, with its policy of non-alignment, had failed to gain popular support too, largely as a result of the Test Ban signed that year by the nuclear powers. And the contradictions between the movement's various styles (between, say, academic left Leavisism, the "angry young men," and Lessing's "free women") were increasingly apparent. A politics addressed to Britain's balance of payment problems and comparative decline in productivity, along with a revitalized union movement, focused media attention back on to the economy and Labourism. We can map the exhaustion of the first New Left like this: it was being squeezed from three sides – by the gradual extension of what we might call the culture of irreverence (as expressed, for instance, in the period's satire boom (*That was the Week that was, Beyond the Fringe*)) and which had close connections to the commercialization of non-deferential, not necessarily elite youth lifestyles (most apparent two years later in the Beatles' astonishing success and the irruption of "swinging London"); by shifts in the Labour Party program from 1961 and especially once Harold Wilson, who had been a member of the party's left, betrayed his socialist pledges on coming to power in 1964 and attached the party to a policy of modernization seconded to global capital markets, as against egalitarianism and state ownership.[14] And, less obviously, by the gradual academization of intellectual life. This was not yet based on a radical extension of tertiary education (which was, however, recommended in the 1963 Robbins Report) but rather on the 1944 Education Act, which channeled a section of the working class into grammar schools. More important still, it relied on a 1962 Act which, for the first time, required local authorities to provide student grants for living costs and tuition. It was this Act, along with its successors, that enabled certain First New Left figures to establish their own academic institution, the Birmingham Centre for Cultural Studies, in 1964, precisely at the point that their movement was fading as a social force, and at which socialism was disappearing from big party politics.

Even Stuart Hall's *New Left Review* had run out of money and purpose by late 1962. It was taken over by Perry Anderson, an upper-class radical not in academic employment, who, together with colleagues, proceeded to lay the intellectual and material basis of a second New Left on the understanding that the left's impasse could be lifted only on the basis of a new theoretical grasp of the situation.[15] Anderson was joined by his Oxford friend Robin Blackburn and by Tom Nairn, from Scotland via Italy, who had read and absorbed the work of Antonio Gramsci as a student at Pisa. (This is not to imply that Nairn and Anderson introduced Gramsci to the New Left: the *New Reasoner* had already published excerpts from the Louis Marx translation of *Prison Letters* as well as a positive review of that volume by Christopher Hill, though in the *New Reasoner* Gramsci figures as a more humanist theorist than he would appear later.) At any rate, together Anderson and Nairn developed a new set of Gramscian conceptual tools which they brought to bear on two domains for two separate but related purposes. This involved an explicit turn from the kind of humanism implicit in left Leavisism and which had been proposed as the New Left's defining feature (under the name "Socialist community") by E. P. Thompson to a Marxism more in line with the current thinking of Oxford thinkers like G. D. H. Cole and the Trotskyite Isaac Deutscher (Anderson's tutor) with the aim of outlining new forms of socialist strategy.[16] In this spirit, they produced a brilliant historical account of Britain's failure to develop a strong working-class socialist lineage, in effect accepting the Gramscian notion that each individual nation-state had a particular trajectory towards radicalism and revolution determined by the economic condition of the proletariat and peasantry but only at some remove.

In sum: over the following decade, Anderson and Nairn radically recast the terms of New Left critique by openly returning to Marxism, by redefining

British geopolitics, and then by readdressing what Nairn called the left's "antipathy to theory" and its consequences.[17] Anderson and Nairn's geopolitics were (in the Trotskyite tradition) radically internationalist: in effect, Britain was seen not in organicist terms as the home of important and threatened traditions and lifeways, as it was by Thompson, Williams, and Hoggart, but as a particular state formation in a global system whose modern history turns around a highly mediated relation to imperialist capitalism.[18]

For the first time in the post-war period, then, two concepts became crucial: imperialism (introduced into left thought by Hobson around 1900 and further developed by Lenin around the period of the Third International but set aside during the anti-fascist struggle, now often to be recast as "neo-imperialism") and, more important, totality, which replaced Williams's notion of the "whole society."[19] "Totality" was thought analytically and critically whereas "whole society" had operated as a norm. And, however problematically, the notion of totality sidestepped the old Marxist base/superstructure problem, since it was conceived as a mode of production, namely capitalism, which subsumed the distinct categories "society," "culture," and "economy". Under this analysis, capitalism itself was constituted at several levels whose precise relations mutated, and which required constant intellectual legitimation and solicitation of popular support for its equally constant regrouping of interests into positions of power. At the level of theory, it was the left's failure to take account of totality, which Nairn summarized, in Gramscian rather than Hegelian terms, as "the hegemonic pattern rooted in a certain organization of the economy and certain institutions" that meant that Labour's reforms could be incorporated so consistently into a fundamentally conservative social system (Nairn 1965a: 196). And because it was theoretically impoverished, established left critique remained utopian and increasingly difficult to translate into practical radical strategy. Indeed, it was not committed to what Anderson called "the very idea of socialism – the transformation of society and politics," articulations of which, as I say, required theory, as had already been the case for Murdoch, of course (Anderson 1965: 246).

And yet the post-war period of reform, university extension, and the policies of Wilson's Labour government were bringing into being a new stratum of intellectuals who might be capable (in Nairn's words) of articulating a "theoretical response" to "liberalism and neo-capitalism", capable of nourishing working-class struggle (Nairn 1965a: 214). And it was their sense of the political potential of this group, lacking among traditional Marxists and socialists but very clearly articulated by C. Wright Mills and by the SDS's Port Huron statement (1962) in the United States, which marked Anderson and Nairn out in the British context.[20] The new *New Left Review* was addressed to precisely this group: even at the level of design it stripped away the gloss and illustrations of the Stuart Hall-edited journal, expressive of first New Left artiness, replacing it by an academic austerity.

The theory that Anderson and Nairn imported in their efforts to redress empiricism and nationalism was, as I have said, Gramscian, although its sense of social totality, which was more highly developed than Gramsci's, was flavored, paradoxically, by US sociology and in particular by Talcott Parsons' "general theory of society," with its account of society as a set of interlocking institutions each with its own structures and functions.[21] As we have seen, the New Left had already imported theoretical concepts – "alienation", and Wright Mills's vaguely Trotskyite critiques of elitism and bureaucratization. But Anderson and Nairn appealed to no British tradition at all, and, for the first time in this context, their arguments were tightly and self-reflexively controlled by theory. They pioneered a whole new style of writing under this self-regulative intellectual regime: streamlined so as not to diverge from a set of basic abstract principles, not interested in seducing a readership rhetorically, committed only to the argument. (The name for this style was later to become "rigor.") Their wholesale rejection of local conceptual traditions follows from their sense that British intellectuals, trapped in empiricism, had failed to articulate a rigorous critique of capitalism, partly because they were so remote from an isolationist "corporate" working class in flight from the hegemony of gentility. Anderson and Nairn's drive to theory also followed precisely from their understanding of capitalism as a totality capable of colonizing subjectivity, and their suspicion of *any* intellectual life developed within it. This meant that no theory could be conceived of as securely in place. Rather, in the spirit of Lenin and Trotsky, theory was conceived of as a set of strategically useful conceptual tools which would continually mutate. It was a form of praxis within the drive to socialism. For this line of thought, of course, the personal class positions or experiences of the intellectuals who developed theory was of no account, a notion which further removed the *New Left Review* group from Williams, Thompson, and Hoggart. And, importantly, it was their suspicion of capitalist culture as such that marked them out from the American New Left, which, in the Port Huron statement, called rather soggily for "a left with real intellectual skills, committed to deliberativeness, honesty, and reflection as working tools" (Sale 1973: 55).

The strongest expression of Nairn and Anderson's will to theory came not in their most famous and probably richest work – their Gramscian reformulation of British history – but in their critique of what they called Labourism, and their attempts to draft a strategy for socialism outside the Labour mainstream. As an instance of this work, let me take Perry Anderson's 1965 essay "Problems of Socialist Strategy," published in *Towards Socialism*, the last of the *New Left Review* volumes to include contributions by a wide range of left intellectuals including Raymond Williams, Labour politicians, civil servants, and policy advisors.

Anderson's argument was that a socialist party needed to unite a new "historical bloc" (1965: 242) capable of eliciting genuine popular consent by drawing together different groups and interests in pursuit of a shared goal. But a bloc is not an alliance; its structure needed to be one of "ascending integration", partly for organizational reasons but partly also just because popular consent could be won only if ideology were recast. This meant that the bloc's leadership needed to share a common theory, that is, a coherent, comprehensive, and abstracted account of the world, able to be communicated across a wide social spectrum against representations in place. And the old New Left option which proposed to use the education system and the state against the media was inadequate, since not only was it reformist rather than radical but, being in the hands of academics and teachers, it had no responsibility to any programmatically anti-capitalist organization. (This, of course, was in tension with the *New Left Review's* faith in university-educated radical young intellectual/theorists, a tension with profound consequences, as we shall see.)

Furthermore, Anderson argued, because consciousness was determined by a "total life-situation", the education and communication industries could not be separated out of everyday life as it proceeds through "family, sexuality, work" (1965: 245). In effect, he recognized that a new theory both of power and of politics is required once capitalism is understood as working across all social zones. And that theory must be based on what he, in Parsonian tones, called "theoretically adequate serious sociological research" (1965: 281). Indeed, Anderson's sense that power is coextensive with civil society owed much to increasingly sophisticated forms of social information gathering and statistics. (His essay drew heavily on Gallup polls.) And his account of power had ontological implications, too, since, as he argued, once one strips away ideology, in the final analysis, what exists in the human world structured by a mode of production is not liberal individuals but "human actions which collide, converse and coalesce to form the whole personal and social world we live in. Man and society exist only as *praxis*" (1965: 288).

It follows that a socialist's task is not to emancipate human beings so that they can fulfill their potentialities, luxuriate in their freedoms or extend their collective heritages but to articulate a "new model of civilization" (1965: 289) in which, presumably, actions will be less determined by values organized around the society–individual opposition or inherited traditions *tout court*. Iris Murdoch, like Edward Thompson, and indeed like Williams, had called for new figurations of a socialist morality and ethos, but Anderson and Nairn in effect demanded a whole new representation of Being-in-the-world based on a whole new social system. And, although I cannot spell this out here, in making this move they began to express conditions for the later academic theory corpus. Nowhere is this more apparent than in Anderson's remarks on power and his argument for a politics of everyday life, implicitly posed against the conventional notions of culture. Here his analysis opens out either towards a politics of identity or towards a Foucauldian theory of power.

At a more concrete level, Anderson understood that socialist intellectuals must examine present social formations so as to guide political strategy. Thus, for instance, he argued that a large proportion of the British working class had always voted Conservative (and that the Labour Party relies not on the votes of the industrial or manual workers but on white-collar votes).[22] More devastatingly still, women as a whole are and have long been more conservative than men. Indeed, he notes, if women had voted like men then the Labour Party would have been continuously in power since 1945. This means that the socialist left needed urgently to work to transform women's lives, not first and foremost to change their economic circumstances but to transform the ideology of deference and of gender privatization which they have internalized. As Anderson writes, in what is perhaps the first feminist statement within this theory lineage (pre-dating Juliet Mitchell's Althusserian and pathbreaking 1966 New Left Review essay "Women: the longest revolution"), "In the long run, only a creative counter-ideology, which offers a new vision of women's social role and purpose, as an integral part of a new vision of culture and society, will liberate women from their present condition"[23] (1965: 278).

Looking back, perhaps the most puzzling aspect of Anderson and Nairn's demand for theory is their apparent confidence that a strategy for socialism was indeed practicable. Where did they see a social agent able to work towards radically transforming society, given that by and large the first New Left and even the Labour Party itself recognized no such agent? Like G. D. H. Cole, they began with hopes of the trade union movement, which had been energized by Britain's increasing economic difficulties from about 1960 on, and in his essay on socialist strategy Anderson had developed a Gramscian schema by which different social groups, including the working class, would form an anti-hegemonic bloc, but, as we have seen, to bring that bloc together required a prior radical revisioning of ideology. So – to repeat – as Wright Mills had already recognized, in the present conjuncture, the answer is to be found mainly in the new educated classes, that is, in the student movement, which had begun to stir in the United States after the SDS's Port Huron statement of 1962 and the Berkeley free speech movement of 1964, events which had themselves been energized by the civil rights movement and the Vietnam anti-war protests.[24] Unlike the CND, which Anderson and Nairn dismissed along Trotskyite lines as bourgeois and idealist, this movement (it was argued) had an organic base among a group who (arguably) had not quite been drawn into the system as a whole.[25] And, following both the US dependency-theory economists associated with the socialist-internationalist Monthly Review and the anti-colonialism associated with Sartre's Les Temps modernes as well as with Claude Bourdet's nouvelle gauche, they also looked to the "peripheries" and colonial resistance movements (Cuba most of all) for anti-capitalist energy. And they had also noted the PRC's Cultural Revolution, based upon the revolutionary will to break with inherited traditions across civil society, though admittedly Maoism is only indirectly expressed in their writings (it played a much greater role in France, as we will see in my last chapter), partly because the Maoist splinter groups within British radicalism (e.g., the tiny Communist Party of Great Britain (Marxist-Leninist)) were extremely sectarian.[26]

The problem was, however, that this analysis separated the agents of revolution (colonized peoples) from the agents of theory (young First World intellectuals). This is true despite the fact that peripheral regions (and especially Latin America) played a key role in developing Gramscianism in particular, and anti-colonialist theorists like Fanon were widely read. (It is unfortunate that the work of C. L. R. James, who, then living in Brixton, might have helped bridge anti-colonialist and New Left thought, and who was published by the Anderson–Nairn–Blackburn *New Left Review*, was not more widely engaged.) In effect this meant that the Leninist problem of how to connect activist theory and leadership to the will of the people had exhausted itself. It is this collapse of Leninism which allows revolutionary theory to displace itself from politics on to language and, along one track, to become that mode of post-Marxist "discourse theory" which claimed that work on representation and discourse can have political effects formerly attributed only to activism, and, along another, to become that "revolution of the word" later disseminated by *Tel quel* (and especially by Sollers, Kristeva and Derrida) which would be transported and professionalized as theory into certain US literature departments, the ethical basis of whose discipline had, as I say, slowly waned. In this strand of radical post-Leninist theory, revolutionary will does not disappear, it just becomes academic and semiotic: political revolution being replaced by epistemological revolution.[27]

Closer to the historical moment I am concerned with here: it is Althusser who (hesitantly enough) marks a return to a certain Leninism. Althusser's insistence on science as the producer of true knowledge and, as a consequence, his resistance to historical memory, to humanism, to collective self-recognitions and consciousness, lead him to argue that only theory can produce the social models which can guide strategy. And that, at a stroke, deprives legitimacy from popular agency. In Althusser, furthermore, capitalism has become almost wholly impenetrable to revolutionary action (proletarian consciousness no longer bears any revolutionary charge) while theory bars the way to reformism. Capitalism becomes a decentred mode of production, organized around contradictions that bear concealment (in "absent causes") but not resolution; a moment in a history without *telos* – history as process. For that reason, theory no longer bears responsibility for concretely imagining a socialist society or even (to use Shelley's phrase) for imagining what we know. Nor does it seem to lead to an understanding of why revolution is necessary in the absence of any popular will for revolution. Furthermore, the production and dissemination of theory require no charisma of leadership, its proper place is the educational institution, itself partially autonomous from the state. In effect Althusser's weak Leninism becomes yet another insistence on the role of the educational institutions as guardians and disseminators of truth. In Althusser's later writing, when he came under the influence of the Maoist *gauchisme* of his "Ulmist" students, and did argue that theory needed to serve political activism, theory also passively joins the aesthetic in distancing us from hegemony, since it is at this point in his career that the both the work of art and theoretically informed readings reveal "distances" and gaps within ideological imaginaries, allowing idealist and empiricist mystifications to be revealed as such.[28]

What about theory within institutionalized cultural studies over this period? While this chapter is focused on the prehistory of academic theory, it is important to have some understanding of the relation between the second New Left's turn to theory and the institutionalization of cultural studies. As is well known, in 1964 Richard Hoggart established the graduate program in contemporary cultural studies at Birmingham, where he was soon joined by Stuart Hall. By this time Hall had, of course, been replaced by Anderson and his colleagues at the *New Left Review*, who, as we have seen, had effectively repudiated the first New Left project, to which Hoggart and Hall remained attached, by reformulating the turn to theory. Only in the aftermath of the 1968 student revolts would modern theory be taken up at Birmingham, not because that was when Hall took over as Director, but because the events of 1968 destroyed remaining sanctions for trying to academicize the first New Left's objectives and problems as articulated most clearly by Raymond Williams.

But, to complicate matters, by 1968 Althusser was replacing Gramsci as the primary theoretical force among British Marxists. This shift was profound, not because Althusser's conceptualizations are wholly discrepant with the sociological version of Gramsci that Nairn and Anderson were circulating (they are not), but because his figuration of the theorist was radically different.[29] Althusser himself was, of course, a Marxist fundamentalist in so far as he adhered to the true (non-Hegelian) Marx and, as such, had academicized Marxism in order to balance his anti-Stalinism and anti-Marxist humanism with his commitment to the French Communist Party (the PCF), of which he remained a member. Indeed, the Althusserian enemy is not so much capitalism as capitalism's supposed intellectual framework: humanism, empiricism, and historicism.

The question immediately poses itself; why did British theory between about 1968 and 1975 turn so overwhelmingly to Althusser?[30] Let me suggest that the Althusserian turn was enabled by:

1. Most obviously, its negation of the existential and experiential motifs of the first New Left, notably the concepts of alienation and reification, which depended on a more moral notion of human essence and hence of society than Althusser's. As Terry Eagleton was to write in his Althusserian

critique of Raymond Williams in the first chapter of *Criticism and Ideology*, "The essentially liberal conception of socialist organization implicit in the 'circular totality' of the New Left – 'connecting', 'cooperating', 'explaining', 'communicating' 'extending' – was politically sterile from the outset" (Eagleton 1976: 35). In this negation Althusserianism joined a tradition of literary/philosophical anti-humanism entwined within both left and right critique (e.g., at random: Louis-Ferdinand Céline, D. H. Lawrence, the Sartre of *Nausea*, John Osborne's *Look Back in Anger*). All the same, the critique of humanism enabled Althusserianism to become a weapon in a generational war used by the influx of new academics to break simultaneously with older leftist models still dependent on moral or humanist discourse and, importantly, the avant-gardes, including Situationism, that inspired the 1968 activists.

2. The continuing academization of British radical left intellectual life, which harmonized with the anti-activist and theoretical orientation of Althusserianism (which it shared, of course, with the Frankfurt school, for instance, but did not share with the first New Left). Indeed, Althusserianism was itself linked to modernizing (in France, republican) technocraticism in its fetish of scientific objectivity, and that seems to be one reason why so many Anglophone 1970s Althusserians became conformist and statist cultural policy adherents in the 1990s.

3. The rather ambivalent nature of Althusserian anti-statism. Cultural studies and academic theory in Britain depended largely on the state funding of institutions and students, as we have seen. This placed them in a difficult relation to the anti-statism pervasive in the social theory of the late 1960s left, a difficulty mainly addressed by ignoring it. But the later Althusser's critical account of Ideological State Apparatuses (ISAs) was a great deal more attentive to the state, and much more nuanced in its anti-statism, than was, say, the Nietzscheanism that Foucault or Deleuze had embraced at the time.[31] This is perhaps most clearly articulated in Stuart Hall's account of his reception of the Althusserian theorist of the state, Nicos Poulantzas, in which the state itself is described as relatively autonomous from capitalism (Hall 1979).

4. The rather mysterious but almost immediate evaporation of the radical intellectual spirit of the 1968 revolts. The academic wing of the socialist left was drawn instead towards Althusser's understanding of capitalism as obdurate, despite the fact that Althusser was himself unsympathetic to the 1968 movement to a degree that was spelled out in an important 1969 essay by Jacques Rancière, later republished in *La Leçon d'Althusser*. The Maoist offshoots of French Althusserianism had no real equivalents in Anglophone nations.

In the years that Gramsci and Althusser were being absorbed in Britain, the Birmingham Centre was primarily concerned with two more familiar projects –

first the attempt to bring a Leavisite understanding of cultural heritage into adjustment with a "whole society" thought in Williams's terms; and second, to draw on the set of philosophico-sociological concepts definitive of the first New Left to describe particular contemporary social formations. In a word, they were trying to combine sociology and left Leavisite cultural criticism. Let me point to two of the most substantial results of the Centre's work in the period as examples.

In 1965, the Centre published two talks by Alan Shuttleworth, given to the seminar on method (*not* theory) which students from all concentrations within the Centre attended. Shuttleworth had been a contemporary of Hall's at Oxford, where they had edited the *Universities and Left Review* together. He was now also working on John Rex's urban sociology project, funded by the Race Relations Council, that would result in the important book *Race, Community and Conflict: A Study of Sparkbrook*, Sparkbrook being a poor West Indian immigrant district in Birmingham, and Rex's work demonstrating relations between colonial history, racism, and migration experiences.

But Hoggart and Hall's CCCS was not yet interested in colonialism, racism, and migration. And in his paper for the Centre, Shuttleworth tried, conventionally, to connect a Weberian analysis of contemporary society to Leavisite discrimination. His basic thesis was that social relations in the end exist as concrete practices that can be assessed either sociologically as functions or types, or critically as the articulations of meanings or as experiences. These approaches can be brought together if we ask (in the idealist mode) whether a particular practice or text can be conceived of as a vehicle for experiences and expressive capabilities that might exist even in the best society that we can imagine. One path to answering this ethico-political question is to use Leavisite critical techniques to gauge the richness of experiences as they are communicated; another is to assess the degree to which social forms approach ideal typicality. As Shuttleworth asserts, referring to the Centre's current research project on youth culture:

> precisely one of the crucial points to be explored in the study of teenage culture is the relationship between the meanings and values expressed in dance, song, dress, speech and the attitudes and experiences of teenagers themselves. We need to find a way of detecting how far teenage culture (in the narrow sense) is truly expressive of teenage experience and how far it bends and twists it.
>
> (Shuttleworth 1967: 33)

I don't need to spell out the ways that this kind of idealist empiricism, with its uncritical acceptance of the category "teenage experience" as a norm, falls foul of Anderson and Nairn's Gramscianism, let alone the Althusserianism waiting in the wings.

The youth culture project that Shuttleworth was referring to was carried out by Stuart Hall, who, a couple of years later, published his results.[32] His is an eclectic and diffuse analysis, which draws largely upon Norman Mailer, of all people, as well as upon Marcuse, Williams, and, at a couple of moments, Gramsci. In brief, Hall argues that the new youth movements (he is thinking mainly of the hippies) are a consequence of left failure in so far as they confront the system through lifestyle, experiental experimentalism and psychic self-exile (drugs), not through activism. Following Anderson and Nairn, he contends that these movements will become socially effective only if they can ally with the world's dispossessed and if they gain a theoretical grasp of their own situation, a need that the essay's own lack of theoretical focus highlights.

It was only after 1968 that Hall and the Centre turned to theory in a systematic fashion. The year 1968 marked the end of the hope that humanist thought or the culturalist heritage could provide an effective counterforce to capitalism, and, in the same stroke, it ended habitual alliances between left academic theory and public policy and journalism, as if the passions and reorientations sparked by the revolution had burnt out the old "progressivist" connections. As far as the CCCS was concerned the key document in this turn was its sixth Working Paper, published in 1974, whose central essay was Hall's analysis of Marx's text known as the "1857 introduction." It's a topic that is intelligible only in relation to the Althusserian argument that Marx's *oeuvre* needs to be stripped of its Hegelianism. Here Hall revises Althusser by claiming that the later Marx is not the founder of a science but rather the originator of ideology critique, with the crucial corollary that Marxism does indeed bequeath an ongoing role for academic work – namely the "deciphering" of the "phenomenal forms" through which capitalism masks and reproduces itself. And that "deciphering" (as first spelled out in Stuart Hall's 1972 paper "The Determinations of Newsphotographs") involved a semiotics drawn from Roland Barthes and Umberto Eco which emphasized the polysemy of media representations. But their basic polysemy was hidden, since, in deploying hierarchized "codes" (denotative, connotative, expressive) they actually presented not a choice of meanings but a single "preferred" reading. These codes organize both the form and content of media representations so as to create the "effects" by which images are recognized as natural or normal rather than as socially produced. The larger (Gramscian/Althusserian) "dominant" ideology (the machinery of a society "structured in dominance") is constituted in these effects which allow it to "bind the governed to the governors" (Hall 1972: 84).

However, in the late 1970s, in a sudden new turn, ideology critique was all but left behind. A new relation between cultural studies and theory was worked out, most clearly in *Policing the Crisis* (Hall *et al.* 1978), which, deploying a rather reduced Gramscianism, all but ditched the late Althusserian concept of ideology. It argued that the recent panics concerning young blacks and violent crime should be analyzed as a divide-and-rule (or as we might say today "culture war") strategy on behalf of capitalist interests made fearful by the 1960s resistance movements. By scapegoating young second-generation Caribbean immigrants and presenting them as a threat to British community values and institutions, that is, by engineering a fundamentally racist law-and-order crisis, renewed union militantism and political radicalism were neutered. This analysis was weak because the militant unions were devastatingly unpopular in Britain on their own terms, since it was apparent that their readiness to strike was not just self-interested but also threatened national productivity. As Leninist Marxists had long argued, the problem lay rather in the structures of British laborism itself, its division into political and unionist wings, the divisions between unions themselves, and its dominance by what Lenin had called the "aristocracy of labor," whether his "minority of skilled, well paid workers" or, more recently, the managers of the Labour bureaucracies, whether in the party or the unions (Lenin 1932: 142). This structure meant that the working class had no institutions through which its power could be channeled in a unified fashion, which was especially crippling in a period when its own basis in nineteenth-century industrialism was coming undone. Indeed, the ultimate problem was the disappearance of the social and economic conditions which underpinned traditional laborist ideology. *Policing the Crisis's* analysis, which failed to recognize this, and which did indeed open the way to cultural studies' embrace of pluralism and identity politics, can also be understood as a premonition of later exchanges between neo-liberalism and cultural studies as a site and method of critical analysis.

At any rate, in this work theory reaches a new degree of sophistication and concreteness but at a cost: the turn to semiotics and in particular the acknowledgment of polysemy involve a logic by which the actual reception of the representations that constitute ideology needs to be acknowledged and explored. This required cultural studies to embrace ethnography – going into the world and finding out how media messages are received and used. In that move, empiricism returns to theory by the back door, and with it the political project which called for theory came to be stalled within pro-theory cultural studies itself.

I need to draw my story to an end. As should be clear by now, the Anglophone world nurtured no post-Leninist theorist of its own: no Althusser, no Foucault, no Deleuze, no Derrida. One of the reasons for this is that (as Ian Hunter has pointed out) the production of theory with that kind of authority requires a philosophic tradition lacking, for complex historical and institutional reasons, in Britain and the United States; another is that the legacies of McCarthyism and Vietnam had so hobbled US intellectual life in particular that it was drawn to *import* theory; a third is that the energy supplied by the failure of Leninism was lacking in Anglophone nations because the Leninist will to revolution had never existed in the first place, which was of course a version of the historical conundrum that Anderson and Nairn had set out to explore.[33] But – and this is a point that I can only leave lingering in the air – cultural studies' imported theories never provided one important intellectual capacity, namely the capacity to bring a history of the present – or, better, a history of present closures and limits – into relation with theory. After all, post-Althusserian theory was defined against historicism, which meant in effect that it could not learn from, or speak to, history, and historiography itself could not generate theory, or vice versa. Speaking for a moment as a historian of theory, this is all the more restrictive when one particular kind of historicism was rejected, namely Hegelianism, thought of as that mode of theory able to articulate its own historical conditions of emergence. This is particularly true because a theory's capacity persuasively to point to its own conditions of emergence is a measure of its capacity to have social impact, that is (to use the old lexicon), to acquire the status of praxis. And I'd suggest that the story I have told here allows us to recognize that theory's incapacity to historicize itself can be understood at least in part as an indirect cost of the extreme geographical/social distantiation of revolutionary from theoretical agency – the first belonging to the "Third World" the second to the "First World" – as experienced at a moment (1968) where revolutionary hopes flickered briefly over socialism's ashes.

Furthermore, as we have seen, Althusser claimed a critical power in certain works of art: it was this made him important to film studies, for instance, and helped him become an important stimulus to the emergence of modern academic theory. But in the period before empiricism unexpectedly returned to British cultural studies via semiotics, cultural studies had lost the capacity to align its affirmation of productive creativity as articulated by Williams with a turn to aesthetics or indeed with an understanding of the literary heritage. The kinds of interests, commitments, and values that draw on serious literature and the canon were to be routinely exposed to negation. Apart from anything else, this turned out to be a serious institutional weakness, since although cultural studies began as positioned between sociology and literary criticism, its theory moment removed it from the former without positioning it to recuperate the latter. Although after 1968 it had become clear that literary criticism and literary subjectivity could not carry out the social and cultural work that Williams, Hoggart, and the young Hall had asked of them, this did not mean that they had no autonomous value or even that they could not continue to support academic critique of contemporary capital and governmentality. Cultural studies' failure to acknowledge this marginalized it in the global academy, since it could never find a solid footing in English departments, which remain powerful, especially in the United States, but where the celebration of transgression and subversion had a decreasing relation to actual social conditions or political groupings. This meant that cultural studies became increasingly vulnerable to a reductive anti-elitism that it inherited in part from Wright Mills and the first New

Left. As many have noted, empiricism and populism led cultural studies increasingly towards limited vocational training, on the one hand, and affirmations of contemporary, non-literary fandoms, often based in identity politics, on the other. This movement was accelerated, since, as cultural studies has lost touch with the original "demand for theory" moment, it increasingly has come to occupy a utilitarian, bureaucratized, and concentratedly pedagogical institutional space in which the intellectual energy and capital that theory can provide have little purchase. And the remaining residual will to theory in cultural studies seems to be driven as much by the rhythms of continual innovation ultimately as governed by academic institutional demands as by specific social and political projects.

Chapter 6

Completing secularism
The mundane in the neo-liberal era

This chapter begins with a brief critical reading of Charles Taylor's book *A Secular Age*, which it uses to explore the "mundane" as a philosophical and historical concept before going on to present the qualities of contemporary experience in terms opposed to Taylor's own.

A Secular Age is a monument of what might be called a religio-transcendental turn in the postsocialist moment, a turn which both this and the next chapter examine. It is a remarkable achievement, an erudite, generous-minded, pathbreaking book. And it marks the culmination of a life's work. As far as I'm aware, Charles Taylor's argument first took shape in an essay he wrote forty years ago for the volume *From Culture to Revolution* (1968) as a member of the Catholic New Left. At the time he was committed to a non-Marxist "radical socialism," deeply opposed to capitalism – a system he understood (*à la* Western Marxism) to cause alienation and pervasive instrumentalism. For Taylor, Marxism was an enlightened humanism that failed to understand that each human being must "reach beyond himself and renew contact with the non-human, and ... the more than human" (Taylor 1968: 154). This means that alienation under capitalism cannot be annealed through any social movement that fails to understand that man and his works "can never have the transparency of pure project, thrown in front of him into the future" (ibid.) So the counter-capitalist restitution endorsed by Taylor was not a transcendentalizing resacralization as much as an acknowledgment that the world we inhabit is a gift from God. Such an acknowledgment can inspire forms of community based on receiving from and giving to others, that is, on Christian *agape*. From within Iris Murdoch's "new house of theory", community can be figured as a form of donation, of worship, and imitation of divine charity and love in terms that ground participatory socialism and a restored "public meaning."

A Secular Age is less politically engaged than this. Now Taylor argues that the West has indeed undergone secularization, but not because science has disproved religion or because religious interests and institutions have been separated from politics and state government. Rather it's because, over centuries, Latin Christianity, partly through its many internal reformist movements, became committed to the Aristotelian project of general human flourishing. During the Enlightenment, central elements of the Christian faith were transformed into a humanism whose ethical and conceptual framework and purposes were fundamentally immanent. In the process a cultural "nova" appeared in which new knowledges, faiths, orientations, styles of life and identities proliferated. At the same time, governmental apparatuses enabled people to form autonomous and private "buffered selves," capable of making choices between competing faiths and identities.

For Taylor, there is no renouncing either the humanist focus on happiness and health or Western modernity's cultural nova. But what has been weakened through and in both is a "higher," "fuller" orientation towards the sacred and transcendent based on tradition, although, admittedly, "tradition" is not a concept that Taylor emphasizes (but see Taylor 2007: 719). Actually, Taylor appears to offer two versions of the sacredness that modernity weakens: according to the first and stronger version what is in jeopardy is a "higher" perspective in which this world is ordinarily positioned in a (subordinate) relation to a divine order; the second, weaker version supposes just that fullness or depth is in jeopardy. We are threatened with the loss of what we might call hierarchized existentialist value through which some experiences and moments are fundamentally more meaningful and, so to say, more spiritually enriching than others. His argument's sweeping ambit partly relies on its ambiguation of these two spiritual drives, an ambiguity which Taylor accepts, I suspect, because he assumes (in my view mistakenly) that the first entails the second as a matter of anthropological fact.

At any rate, Taylor claims that what he calls "spiritual hunger" is integral to human beings: it constitutes (to rephrase Simone Weil) a theoretical limit to acceptable social transformations (Taylor 2007: 679; Weil 2006: 53). In effect (and to repeat a point Jonathan Sheehan made in his post to the Immanent Frame blog), his argument is based on an existentialized/theophanized moral anthropology. It is as if it accepts David Hartley's eighteenth-century argument that, even beginning from a Lockean, enlightened genetic psychology that refuses concepts like grace and innate ideas, it is possible to show that theophany is natural and essential to man.

So, for Taylor, orientation to the transcendent may take secular as well as religious forms, but either way it is occluded by modernity. (Of course, societies can also develop supernaturalisms that don't bear any relation either to the transcendent as "higher" in Taylor's sense, or to hierarchized existential value, but he is not concerned with these.) To restore the sacred he now looks not to participatory socialism but to a somewhat less collective "conversion into fullness" and "openness to transcendence" which takes practical form in concrete, individualized "itineraries towards faith" (Taylor 2007: 745). This individualization is important: for Taylor, following Ivan Illich, spiritual hunger is most purely felt *personally*. Its institutionalization always threatens to petrify it into norms, rules, and habits which, in turn, he contends, leads to spiritual elitism and conformism and ultimately to the dangerous identification of faith with civilization (Taylor 2007: 737–44). This surprisingly Protestant account of faith exists in a certain tension to Taylor's impeccably Catholic/sociological insistence that individual consciousnesses are formed through larger social imaginaries. But what is in effect a Protestant methodological individualism would seem to be required if the openness to the transcendental is to be saved from its modern wreckage just because modern Western society contains no institutions capable of collectivizing "conversion into fullness" on a grand scale.

One of *A Secular Age*'s most distinctive features is its genre. Taylor is the only intellectual I know who hearkened to the New Left call for theory by revivifying a genre known in the eighteenth century as "philosophical" or "conjectural" history. ("Conjectural" because it did not depend on known facts.) Speculative books like Adam Ferguson's *Essay on the History of Civil Society* (1767) and John Millar's *The Origin of the Distinction of Ranks* (1771) and their heirs, Hegel's *Phenomenology of Spirit* (1807) and Comte's *Course of Positive Philosophy* (1830) were monuments of emergent secularism, even if recent scholarship (like Taylor's, indeed) asks us to consider their connection to what Gerald Radner has called "Christian reform," namely those modes of Christian practice that found soteriological promise in civil engagement and improvement (Radner 1959). The philosophical historians' stadial theory, along with their capacity to classify historical formations and tendencies into units and moments which instantiate discrete abstract categories were important in generating the command over the past required by progressivism and were also important in reconciling readers to the historical record by sidelining conflict and violence. Ironically, if *A Secular Age* has forebears, those are they. Taylor himself, I suspect, comes to the genre through his engagement with Hegel, and in particular in the wake of his historicization of *The Phenomenology of Spirit*'s deployment of immanent critique in his influential first book on Hegel (Taylor 2007: 218, 347; also see Milbank 2006: 157).

Taylor too uses stadial theory and a historiography reliant upon more or less discrete categorical classifications. Like his forebears, Taylor has a liking for dividing history into the triplets that Barthold Niebuhr in his 1811 *History of Rome* (a devastating critique of philosophic history and a milestone in biblical criticism) thought characteristic of mythic narration. However, where the secularizing philosophic historians looked to a progressive extension of liberty and rationality able to retain civic humanist virtues (courage, independence, manliness, and so on), Taylor, of course, tentatively hopes for the containment of Aristotelian humanist flourishing (i.e., *eudaimonia*) whose merely worldly norms have come to marginalize and disperse a sense of the sacred.

Despite its capacity to claim mastery over the past, philosophic history is rarely written these days, in part because it can't well account for historical causality. Ultimately it is interested not in historical cause but in *telos*. And it seems that Taylor neglects important underlying material causes (most obviously capitalism and urbanization), not so much because the channels through which such causes operate in all their materiality remain largely hidden from us, but because he believes that to engage such causes is to risk embracing a reductive form of immanence, namely materialism.

It has to be said, however, that if Taylor believes that the secular world has lost a fullness available only through the transcendent, the secularist may feel an equivalent emptiness in Taylor's own analysis, since its attempts to explain how history happened, and how it happened differently in different places in the way that it did, are so abstracted and distanced from the events to which they ultimately refer. Admittedly Taylor has a complex account of how "social imaginaries" change: piecemeal shifts in social practices gradually come to require holistic ideological transformations in which the intelligibility and value of social phenomena may themselves be radically altered. (This is rather reminiscent of Tawney's description of the collapse of the medieval Catholic world view in *Religion and the Rise of Capitalism* 1926.) In this way, in Taylor, history's paths and circles are simplified into an ultimately unaccounted-for displacement of a transcendental orientation by the pursuit of merely worldly well-being. Why, given Taylor's commitment to an existentialized/theophanized moral anthropology, did this displacement happen? Why did modern man betray his own integral nature? At this point, there exists an absence at the centre of Taylor's narrative: it is not as if he can simply accept as natural that, to put it very crudely, so many Europeans came to prefer security, reason, and money to God. But if we regard the various forms of spiritual hunger and their satisfaction not as givens but as contingent social functions, then, like it or not, we can concede that societies may successfully do without them, and there is no particular historiographical problem about their loss.

Taylor is, in effect, and despite himself, writing a philosophic history which has turned conservative in what remains, just, a recognizably Burkean mode.[1] In summary terms, Burke's own most lasting contribution to theory was to join Western religious orthodoxy to Adam Smith's political economy in the face of the French Revolution's threat to oligarchic mixed government and church property. But, for Burke, orthodoxy and its institutions (the Anglican and Roman Catholic churches) had produced a secular, gentlemanly culture bound to classical learning, chivalry, and honor (a version of which we encountered in the first chapter). Without the churches and the social hierarchy that they underpinned, the new theories being disseminated by the *philosophes*, harnessed to the professional bourgeoisie's resentful drive to power, would lead not just to the chaos of democracy but to a collapse of, as Burke famously put it, "conscious dignity, a noble pride, a generous sense of glory and emulation" (Burke 2003: 48).

For all its efforts to avoid conservative melancholy and to resist appeals for the reanimation of past social forms, Taylor's argument is based on nostalgia for a lost fullness and coherence. This means that it is Burkean in structure if not in content. Unlike Burke, Taylor has, as we have seen, accepted the ideals of democracy, liberty, and equality, and unlike Burke he has little faith that a worldly alliance between orthodoxy, tradition and secular dignity might resist materialism and immanence. Only personalized spiritual practices, here detached from ecclesiology, can do that. In this regard, Taylor stands closer to another romantic conservative: the Jena school's Friedrich von Hardenberg (Novalis), who, arguably, inaugurates the application of a transcendental–immanent distinction to counter-revolution in Burkean terms. That is to say, Novalis attempts to buttress social organicism against rationalism by a religio-metaphysical concept (transcendence) inaugurated by Clement of Alexandria in the second century and whose great vehicle, in the West, became the pre-Reformation church. For Novalis the modernity that the revolution inaugurates threatens not just Christian faith and church power but more sweepingly our sense of an ontological otherness, hedged by mystery, in which the poetry of the ideal takes form.

But it is only right to receive a book as rich as *A Secular Age* on its own terms. And if, for me, it is not finally persuasive, that's not simply because of its genre or its echoes of religio-Burkean conservatism but because of a series of interlinked problems, many of which have been rehearsed by its commentators, and of which I will mention three, relevant to my purpose.

First, it is important to Taylor's argument that he discounts the fact that Christianity is a revealed religion most of whose central claims are, under modern truth regimes, false, unverifiable, or unproven. After all, although his concepts of the sacred and fullness extend beyond any particular religion, his central historical case remains limited to Latin Christendom. But believing or not believing Christian doctrine is not a choice for those living "in the true" of rational, probabilistic knowledge, nor is it necessarily an expression of a preference for organized eudaimonia. It is impelled upon them in approximately the same way that they are impelled to know that George W. Bush is (at the time of writing) President of the United States. Of course, when Christianity stops being true in fact – a "true truth" – it may still be true as feeling, as morality, as tradition, as a disposition, as myth – an "untrue truth". I will return to this.

As to my second point, it is clear that Taylor can elide the question of Christian revelation's untruth just because his final interest seems to be in an ontological distinction between the transcendent and the immanent rather than in religion as such. But as soon as you deontologize transcendence and immanence, you don't have to choose between them and can find other ways of avoiding Taylor's narrative of enchantment's loss. Taylor himself often points to forms of "immanent transcendence," thinking mainly of the existential spiritualizing of death as "a gathering point for life" which he believes continues the old spiritual hunger on new terms (Taylor 2007: 726). However, more flexible forms of (post-Spinozist) immanent transcendence that allow history and imagination to play a more complex role than they do in existentialism also become available.

Let me offer a rather obscure literary example. In his Epicurean 1861 country-house satire, *Gryll Grange*, Thomas Love Peacock describes a Mr Falconer, who, although irreligious, surrounds himself with the iconography of the famous fourth-century martyr and patron saint of philosophers and theologians, St Catherine of Alexandria. A friend warns Falconer against "becoming the dupe of your own mystification" (1947: 58), to which he replies:

> I have no fear of that. I think I can clearly distinguish devotion to ideal beauty from superstitious belief. I feel the necessity of some such devotion to fill up the void which the world, as it is, leaves in my mind. I wish to believe in the presence of some local spiritual influence; genius or nymph; linking us by a medium of something like human feeling, but more pure and more exalted, to the all-pervading, creative, and preservative spirit of the universe; but I cannot realize it from things as they are. Everything is too deeply tinged with sordid vulgarity. ... the intellectual life of the material world is dead. Imagination cannot replace it. But the intercession of saints still forms a link between the visible and invisible. In their symbols I can imagine their presence. Each in the recess of our own thought we may preserve their symbols from the intrusion of the world. And the saint whom I have chosen presents to my mind the most perfect ideality of physical, moral, and intellectual beauty.
>
> (Peacock 1947: 59)

In terms of cultural history this remarkable passage, which clearly draws on the Spinozism of its time, articulates a way between Tractarian and ritualist revivalism on the one side and William Beckford's transgressive, isolationist, aesthetic Catholic atheism on the other. What's remarkable about it is not its existential sense of the void, or its assumption that modernity and modern truth have barred human feeling from the universe's creative spirit, or even that the local itself has lost a spiritual power that it retained, for instance, as recently as Wordsworth and Coleridge's *Lyrical Ballads* (1798), but that spiritual practices are based on a conscious will to believe, and, then, that the individual imagination cannot itself replace the losses that such a will invents, and nor, by implication, can aestheticism.

For Falconer, literary subjectivity is helpless to overcome deadly modern materialism. What is required is an immersion in the products of a particular historical *institution*, namely the orthodox church, but without granting the church's doctrines any credence, since, of course, for him, as an enlightened gentleman, they are false. Here a fictionalization of orthodoxy, a true untruth around which a practice of life can form, does the work of supplementation and retrieval required by Novalis's iteration of cultural Burkeanism, although, as Peacock is aware, it does so only in impossible isolation from the demands of sexuality and sociability. At any rate, Falconer,'s is the privatization of orthodoxy not in the direction of Protestantism, not by displacing the long Pelagian tradition of Christian reform, but in the direction of aesthetic fiction as an ethos, to use a term that the Tractarians themselves donated to the English language.[2]

But – and this leads to my main point – what about those who neither feel the spiritual emptiness of modernity nor embrace secular reformism's promise? It's a question which, although it does not concern Taylor, arises with some force in this context, since the secular as a concept is positioned not just against the religious but also, if less visibly, against the mundane. That's because, ever since the Enlightenment, the secular has denoted not so much what lies beyond religion's interest and grasp as what contributes to its intermittent diminution, corruption, marginalization, and undoing. The mundane is the philosophical concept that names what stands outside that division between the secular and the religious. Taylor does not take it seriously just because he believes that to be properly human is to be possessed by spiritual hunger. The mundane, however, consists of those forms of life and experience that are not available for our moral or political or philosophical or religious or social aspirations and projects.

That is one of the ways in which it differs even from neighboring categories like "common sense" or "everyday life" or the "ordinary," which may contain promise of epistemic or social benefit and indeed even soteriological promise, as they do indeed for Taylor, who thinks of the ordinary as the domain in which "depth and fullness" are ultimately encountered (Taylor 2007: 711). This is not to say that philosophy has had no use for the mundane. It rises into view in categories such as the Greek *adiophora;* Calvin's realm of indifference; Hegel's bad infinity (the serial order of things governed by chance and which knows hierarchy or substantial difference), and in Heidegger's concept of *Alltäglichkeit*, or everydayness, in which everything is one and the same but is so within a fundamentally instrumental and immediate relation between individuals and things. Nonetheless these terms come clearly negatively coded against whatever is spiritually and culturally enriched, whereas, as I say, the mundane is external to the system (the various social imaginaries, if you like) in which such coding is intelligible. The mundane also falls out of academic knowledge: after all, the modern university system is sanctioned by the social utilities it produces. For all that, some philosophical ethics in particular can enjoin us to mundanity from afar. There may be a strain of Nietzsche's thought, for instance – the strain that resists metaphysical groundedness, ethical appeals to eternity, progress and salvation as well as any form of Kantian or utilitarian rationalism – which, in standing outside both the secular and the religious, asks us (paradoxically?) to be strong enough to live mundanely.

Once, in the grip of that fundamentally philosophical understanding of history which treats modernity as a contest between enchantment and disenchantment, between religion and the secular, between the transcendent and the material, we postulate the mundane as a category outside the fray, then another kind of philosophic history rises to view. This history does not begin in superstition and tyranny and end, like Hegel and Comte's, in freedom and the full human development of human capacities. Nor does it begin in a unified and coherent universe and end in an incoherent society. Rather, it moves from mundanity through progress and back again to mundanity. Admittedly, this narrative is not, as far as I know, anywhere articulated in quite those terms by philosophic historians but it is implicit in a strain of European philosophy, especially during the mid-twentieth century period of emergent European unification.

Take the first step in this history, the leap from mundanity to incipient progressive rationality. That's a concern of Edward Husserl in his famous 1935 Vienna lecture "Philosophy and the Crisis of European Man," where he isolates this transformative moment in the sixth century BCE Greek discovery of *theoria*. *Theoria*, for Husserl, is a disinterested and critical attitude towards the world ("critical" in that it is not determined by the empirical). Before theory, the Greeks, like everyone else hitherto, lived inside their beliefs, true or false; inside an endless cycle of transitory events and passages: a mundane world marked by its indifference to infinity and its internal indistinction. There, all achievements are "identical in sense and in value" (Husserl 1965: 161). Both Plato and Aristotle claimed that what ended the dominion of this mundane order was *thaumazein*, wonder, as triggered by the childlike but primordially metaphysical, question "Why is there something rather than nothing?" and a consequent reorientation from the finite to the infinite. As soon as that reorientation established a new vocation and new forms of solidarity, as soon as it produced the small elite group who named themselves philosophers, then the history of progress, led by critical European science and philosophy, was on its way.

Let's bypass the more familiar history-of-progress segment of the world-historical passage from mundanity to mundanity to turn to the question of what life might be once progress has been completed. And here a problem arises, because emancipatory secularism with all its conceptual baggage would necessarily wither away once rationality was known to have been fully socially implemented or, to state this in another vocabulary, once a maximum of goodness has been socially achieved. At that moment, by definition, there'd be no possibility of systemic social restructuring or political revolution. There'd be no politics in the classic sense: no hard contests over power's distribution across interests and identities, let alone over what kind of social system should be in place. Presumably, policy debate would involve endless reformist, and fundamentally minor, fine-tuning of relations between the sociopolitical system's component parts in the interests of economic productivity and agreed-upon principles of political justice. Certainly there'd be no world-historical hope: all traces of the "political Joachimist" eschatological tradition would have imploded.[3] From a philosophic-historical point of view, humanity would return to a condition of *geistlich* indistinction and indifference remarkably similar to that which Husserl imagined as existing prior to the Greek invention of philosophical life.

This apparently improbable scenario was of real philosophical concern for a few mid-century Continental philosophers who, either under the spell of a promised European unity that was one of the ideological props of the Vichy colloborationist regime in France or dreaming of a post-war, post-fascist European social democratic union, began, like Hegel himself, seriously to anticipate history's end.[4]

Thus, for instance, Theodor Adorno, pondering the strengths and weaknesses of Hegelian dialectics in 1946, began to imagine what living in a "society rid of its fetters" might look like. And he described it like this: "*Rien faire comme une bête*, lying on water and looking peacefully at the sky, 'being, nothing else, without any further definition and fulfillment,' might take the place of process, act, satisfaction, and so truly keep the promise of dialectical logic that it would culminate in its origin" (Adorno 1974: 156–57).

Another example. The Russian Heideggerian Hegelian Alexandre Kojève spent most of his working life as a senior French diplomat, playing a major role in the implementation of key elements in his epoch's legal and economic infrastructure – the Marshall Plan, the European Community and GATT. Able to imagine the completion of historical progress, he argued that it would reveal the species' existential dilemma in its purity, precisely because atheism would then triumph and progressive hope become otiose. At the end of his lectures on Hegel's *Phenomenology of Spirit*, delivered in 1937 and 1938, he notes that history cannot banish human mortality, but that this unsurpassable finitude actually provides for the continuation of freedom in terms that bear no relation to historical rationality. Only death releases man from the Calvinist sentence by which one's fate is determined in advance of one's birth (Kojève 1969: 249). Because man dies and can choose to die or "escape from Being," he can exit from whatever history delivers to him, and that possibility belongs to each of us precisely as individuals (1969: 248). Otherwise put: it is death that preserves a sense of serial time – of incomplete life after incomplete life after incomplete life – but at the same time releases man from the mundane indistinction that threatens us once progress is completed.[5]

Here is Kojève:

> If, in truly homogeneous humanity, realized as State at the end of History, *human* existences become really interchangeable, in the sense that the action ... of each man is also the action of all, death will necessarily oppose each one to all the others and will particularize him in his

empirical existence, so that universal action will also be particular action (or action liable to failure where another succeeds), and therefore *Individual*.
(Kojève 1969: 252, trans. modified)

Kojève's reading of the *Phenomenology* ends at this rather unsatisfactory point – unsatisfactory since it still isn't clear exactly how the *posthistoire* collective commitment to action in which individuation is granted only via death would in fact differ from something like Husserl's pre-philosophic mundanity. It sounds like another attempt to buttress social solidarity by a metaphysical (this time, existential) concept, even if one that is neither, in traditional terms, religious nor secular.

This issue was addressed by Joachim Ritter, a post-war German philosopher who was primarily interested in dissociating Hegel from statist Prussianism and showing, ecumenically, that Hegel's philosophy continues both the French Revolutionary project and Adam Smith's discovery of the market's autonomy and regularity.[6] Ritter effectively recognizes the abstract possibility that *posthistoire* will mark the triumph of the mundane, but he argues that this is forestalled by the Hegelian dialectic (Ritter 1982: 78). For him, conventionally enough, Hegelian modernity involves a division between those structures of the state/civil society nexus which will deliver emancipation and those that will extend "romantic" withdrawn interiority like Mr Falconer's irreligious cultivation of religious icons. Conventional enlightened rationality dismisses romantic subjectivity, with (as I'd contend) its roots in the Pauline/Lutheran doctrine of passive obedience, as irrelevant to the struggle for freedom and justice. For Ritter's Hegel, indeed, freedom cannot be realized through any form of individualism at all but only within rationally legitimated institutions. Nonetheless this dismissal of individuality risks an outcome in which substantial notions of justice and freedom are lost precisely at the point when practical emancipation is achieved. Only interiorized spiritual longing and a personal relation to the tradition can maintain the spirit of the emancipation project after the state and civil society have delivered substantial justice and freedom to all, in the sense that, without them, our will to emancipation will vanish as such just because it is universal and knows no other. Therefore Hegel dialectically preserves what we can call a privatized Burkeanism within the Absolute State that is history's terminus.

So, at history's end, old-style cultivated, emancipation-driven interiority and the religio-cultural tradition live on as energizing reminders of history's now completed drive forward. And, because of this, Ritter's version of Hegel, although resolutely anti-liberal, remains open to Carl Schmitt's critique of liberalism. Schmitt argues that once the friend–enemy distinction is lost to politics (as it must be in both liberalism and Hegelian posthistory) then social and individual risk and meaning all vanish, and domains of life that were once touched by national identity politics of aggression are effectively transformed into "a world without seriousness" – into what he calls mere "entertainment" and which, in the terms of the philosophic history I have been engaging, we recognize as the mundane.[7]

It seems to me that with Schmitt's formulation we approach the social system that we actually inhabit. I will think of that system as marked by the unprecedented degree to which the market, the media, finance capital, the state's disciplinary, educational, and welfarist apparatuses, its techniques of monitoring and surveillance, its formal political processes along with (in the United States especially) religion, the military apparatus, and the forces of material, intellectual, and cultural production have become technologically and ideologically integrated. Since about 1968 this integration has become so thorough as to delegitimize any imagination of, let alone any widely endorsed work towards, an alternative system: we live under what Sheldon Wolin has called "superpower," which aims to secure endless economic accumulation (Wolin 2004: 591 ff.).[8] This is particularly the case since, as Luc Boltanski and Eve Chiapello have argued in *The New Spirit of Capitalism*, capitalism, in each phase of its development (they list three), has consistently appropriated, and developed on the back of, the various critiques or tests that have been put to it (Boltanski and Chiapello 2005: 27 ff.).

Endgame democratic state capitalism, as we can name this system, has indeed become the final horizon of global society, and, bar paranoia, today is seriously threatened only by blind nature (that is to say, by pressures on the economic and political systems caused by endemic natural catastrophe).[9] As I said in the introduction, this is not to say that it marks the end of history as progressivism imagined it. Certainly it cannot be understood as an instantiation of perfection (it's better thought of as its overturning). But it does mark an end of historical hope.

By the same stroke there are signs that it makes a return to the philosophers' mundane. One such sign is exactly the pervasiveness of "interesting" as an evaluative category. Another of particular relevance to academics like us is that endgame capitalism's integrative machinery has appeared with an abridged theoretical legitimacy. It has been metonymically legitimated in the sense that only those aspects of the whole system that make appeal to various elements of universal rationality in old progressivist Enlightenment/revolutionary terms (e.g., democracy, liberty, human rights) can be *philosophically* sanctioned. But now those legitimations are required to carry out the work of sanctioning the whole. Claims that the new state formations are differently sanctioned than earlier states are unconvincing: Philip Bobbitt, for instance, argues that what he calls the contemporary "market state", which has replaced the old "nation-state," is grounded on its promise to offer its citizens maximum freedom of choice and opportunity (i.e., by providing the conditions for markets to flourish) rather than by securing universal welfare at the level of the individual citizen as the nation-state did (Bobbitt 2008: 88 ff.). But this is merely to incorporate neo-liberal preferences into a supposedly neutral description of state rationality.

Where should we look if we wish to consider more intimately what is at stake in endgame capitalism's putative mundanity? In the end, not to theory, I think. Nor to sociology. Nor to cultural studies. After all, the mundane does not primarily inhere, *pace* Kojève, in collective action or in individual behavior but rather in discourse and most of all in experience. This is to invoke the rather problematic concept we have already encountered in Alan Shuttleworth's work for the Birmingham Centre of Cultural Studies, and which I don't propose to elucidate in any detail here, except to say that I am thinking of it as what Henry James called "our apprehension and our measure of what happens to us as social creatures"[10] (James 1977: 11).

At this point we strike a barrier, since other people's interior experiences are hardly available to true truth. Where they are so available, they are best available through untrue truth (which in this case is also a virtual truth), and especially, for the past two centuries or so, through literary fiction, which has, coincidentally, become increasingly dependent on representations of what Henry James called "finely aware" feeling, or what the Bloomsbury circle thought of as the "inner life" (James 1977: 9).[11] Precisely because it is not a form of true truth, literary fiction is able to imagine and represent such inner life and thence the age's most revealing experiential forms.

In carrying out this task, literary fiction not just reveals deep interiority's complexity and interest for modernity but, by the same stroke, characteristically presents the subtleties, surprises and intensities of modern experience as a reward for continuous struggle and suffering. Modern serious fiction, in its virtuality, has the ability to report what it is like to live now – to feel, think, share, love, hate, dream, hope, despair, drift, remember – and it does so across a range of situations, identities, and types, while essaying unrealized experiential possibilities by binding characters and their interiorities to situations within new forms of language and narrative organization. Which is to say that if, in a philosophic-historical sense, mundanity is the chord struck by the contemporary flow of no longer quite "serious" political, religious, self-transformative, aesthetic, etc., experiences and discourses, then that note is most likely to be explored imaginatively via fictional characters.

Technically, that possibility is a consequence of authors' absolute power over their characters. Imagined characters possess no privacy in relation to their creators, and novelists don't need to respect their characters' rights and moral dignity. And, of course, not being real people, they are not restricted to actual social conditions. Yet, because literary fictions are necessarily finite and ordered, characters and their experiences are fixed in their bounded fictions for ever. Frozen and transparent, endlessly open to interpretation, fictional characters are available to reveal anything, even truth and experience's potentiality.

So it is that the quality of experience under endgame capitalism is a compelling theme for contemporary art novelists. And few have explored it more subtly than Alan Hollinghurst in *The Line of Beauty* (2004). This novel is set in Thatcherism's heyday (1983–87), a crucial moment in the (now finished?) neo-liberal epoch which helped refine the contemporary demo-cratic state capitalist machine.[12] Its central character, a young gay man, Nick Guest, has just come down to London from Cambridge. Nick is witty, intelligent, charming and a knowledgeable aesthete in the tradition that Schiller inaugurated out of Burkeanism. While living close to Thatcherism's centre he is writing a dissertation on Henry James. He boards with the family of Gerald Fledden, a Thatcherite MP and businessman, and for much of the novel he works for his rich Lebanese lover, Wani Ouradi, whose father is a major Tory Party donor. He's an apolitical Thatcherite himself.

The novel describes the tensions between Nick's increasingly promiscuous sex life and his proximity to a neo-liberalism which has ditched both pro-gressivist secularism and Christianity, and is, instead, committed to the reformist extension of property ownership, economic privatization and deregulation, risk-taking entrepreneurialism, and a virtue ethics based on self-reliance (which is itself, admittedly, grounded in old English Dissent). But at the same time Thatcherism promulgates a homophobic and xeno-phobic moral order based on family values. Nick deals with the tension between these two aspects of Thatcherism by never developing any kind of social conscience, nor an interest in self-transformation, nor any of the deep interiority and reflective sympathy to which most serious modern novels are committed, those of Henry James not least. Although a literary scholar, he does not even develop a romantic interiority *à la* Hegel. Against a backdrop of endless media events, self-serving political intrigues and market cycles, he wholeheartedly engages a mundanity of *luxe* consumption, cultivation of aesthetic tastes, "idle" daydreams, sexual and narcotic pleasure, and moral disengagement.

The novel reveals its full power in its last paragraph, which describes Nick packing his things after being evicted from Fledden's grand Notting Hill house for having brought scandal down upon the family. More ominously, he is privately awaiting the results of a test for the HIV virus which he believes, and for good reason, will be positive.

> The words that were said every day to others would be said to him, in that quiet consulting room whose desk and carpet and square modern armchair would share indissolubly in the moment. … What would he do once he left the room? He dawdled on, rather breathless, seeing visions in the middle of the day. He tried to rationalize the fear, but its pull was too strong and original. It was inside himself, but the world around him, the parked cars, the cruising taxi, the church spire among the trees, had also been changed. They had been revealed. It was like a drug sensation, but without the awareness of play. … None of his friends could save him. The time came, and they learned the news in the room they were in, at a certain moment in their planned and continuing

day. They woke the next morning, and after a while it came back to them. Nick searched their faces as they explored their feelings. He seemed to fade pretty quickly. He found himself yearning to know of their affairs, their successes, the novels and the new ideas that the few who remembered him might say he never knew, had never lived to find out. It was the morning's vision of the empty street, but projected far forward into afternoons like this one decades hence, in the absent hum of their own business. The emotion was startling. It was a sort of terror, made up of emotions from every stage of his short life, weaning, home-sickness, envy and self-pity; but he felt that the self-pity belonged to a larger pity. It was a love of the world that was shockingly unconditional. He stared back at the house, and then turned and drifted on. He looked in bewilderment at No. 24, the final house, with its regalia of stucco swags and bows. It wasn't just this street corner but the fact of a street corner that seemed, in the light of the moment, so beautiful.

(Hollinghurst 2004: 500–01)

This is an immensely rich passage in which Nick finds within himself the quasi-Nietzschean courage to face death and the incompletion of his life from within a carefully described mundanity (cf. Taylor 2007: 722–26).

First: time. After his death, Nick thinks, the world will go on serially, barely remembering him. He has not lived the kind of secular, reflective "full and productive" life that would secure him a place in others' memories: his friends will wake of mornings thinking of other things. His failure to ensure his future memory may indeed owe something to his foreseeing himself a victim of a virus which is, of itself, a contingent force of nature outside any human will, and which therefore cannot grant his death any Kojèvean individuality or bind it to any progressive, secular concept of history or to any Christian notion of transcendentally orientated sacrifice as the dark and bloody motivating force of collectivization (as theorized in the nineteenth century by Pierre-Simon Ballanche, for instance). So it is relatively easy for him lucidly and (in the end) almost impersonally to adjust himself to the termination of purposive individual self-realization and self-knowledge, without, of course, any prospect of eternal life. Facing death, he acknowledges his life's mundanity: this moment is not going to change what remains of his life. It's no conversion; it contains no regret; it is not spiritually "full."

Second: his attention to the Fleddens' house's stucco exterior of "swags and bows" in the penultimate sentence is symbolically resonant, not least because it exemplifies the line of beauty that gives the novel its title. *The Line of Beauty* has told a story of Nick's gradual recognition that he himself, as a gay aesthete, is, at best, merely decorative with regard to Thatcher's England's social infrastructure. Indeed, the beauty that Nick's taste so strongly inclines towards is neither (in a complex pun) straight nor weight-bearing – it's

found in stucco, after all – precisely because today beauty has become orna-
mental within the social machine. But this means, paradoxically, that his
outsider status can become socially representative: there's an important sense
in which *all* individual lives are extraneous or fodder to democratic state
capitalism's economic/political crises, processes, and cycles.

So his aesthetic experience here, his realization that what is beautiful is not
this street corner of rich people's stuccoed houses but the simple "fact of a
street corner," more ontologically secure than any line of beauty, marks a
letting go of the straight versus not-straight criterion of beauty. The
moment is particularized, it happens at and in *this* street corner. But this
street corner is not marked by distinction. Nothing in its specificity calls out
to him. Rather, the experience of shock and wonder comes from within Nick
himself.

In effect, then, this is a particular aesthetic experience of indistinction and
indifference that expresses the indifference into which Nick is to be thrown
upon his death: his becoming nothing much for anybody. Putting it like
this, the sheer existence of material things becomes not a puzzle or a limit or
a medium but an amazement that opens up from within Nick's experience of
mundanity in this precise moment as the collision of two registers of indistinction: first, the indifferent ordinariness of the street corner and, second,
Nick's absence in the hum of busy moments to come, which itself is the
result of his projectless embrace of mundanity.

Amazement is too loose a word, of course. Nick's is "a shockingly unconditional love of the world" – shocking because, coming from nowhere, it is
wild, a word which here peeps through "bewilderment," another term used
to describe his experience. And it is shocking and bewildering not so much
because it is surprising or transgressive but in the sense that to forgo discrimination, to abandon private qualifications and conditions in one's judgments, to find oneself deindividuated in that way, is, on the part of
individuals as they lose themselves, to experience shock. Nick's experience is
also felt as shocking and bewildering because his relation to the world has
until now been so conditional in two senses. He has been, as his name suggests, a guest in the world, holding it at bay, taking it on only conditionally,
not fully seriously and for that reason, in Adorno's phrase, he has been, as a
personality, rather undefined. He has lived a conditioned life, too, in the
sense that he has done just what society, in its messed-up way, conditions
him to do. His having lived so conditionally helps to explain why this
irruption of the unconditional is shadowed by abyssal terror. And yet, as
unqualified acceptance of the world, beyond resentment, beyond finite and
human pity, beyond even terror, this experience – a "love of the world" –
contains echoes of what is, for Christianity, *agape*, even if it lacks orthodox
agape's promise of binding communities together around mutual love and
charity (and even if it would be unorthodox to think of God's love as an
expression of God's pity for us). Nick's aestheticized, grace-like experience

falls outside theological virtue, since he directs it to indifferent things rather than to people. That's another sign of its mundanity.

Here, then, faced with the severest of spiritual/existential personal challenges, endgame capitalism does produce from within mundanity an experience that bears the weight of two great, but less than compatible, Western traditions – orthodox Christianity and aestheticism – and it does so, *pace* Schmitt, seriously enough, outside of any transcendent/immanent distinction, and any pathos for lost meaning.

No doubt this is, for all that, a conservative ending, since it changes nothing and aims to change nothing. Indeed, it leads us to understand that all *posthistoire* translations of experience into politics belong to conservatism just because historical hope has vanished. This means that the passage also hints that, at the end of historical hope, cultural conservativism need no longer be contained by its counter-revolutionary pasts nor attached, for instance, to any (finally limiting and essentializing) spiritual hunger as Taylor understands it, and instead may be able to generate complex, weight-bearing, posthistorical forms of living in the mundane.

Chapter 7

Refusing capitalism?

Theory and cultural studies after 1968

In this coda-like chapter I want to move forward from my accounts of cultural studies and endgame capitalism by turning to the current intellectual situation, in which academic "theory" has become simultaneously more political and more theological in its orientation. I will do so in order to explore in more detail what is at stake when the academic humanities embark on a radical critique of capitalism.

It is clear that the (so-called) post-structuralism developed by Derrida, Foucault, Deleuze, and others in the 1960s no longer figures as the humanities' avant garde. On one side, it has been displaced by an intellectual impulse to reconnect theory to radical politics more directly. In its most widely received form, we can call this impulse neo-*gauchisme*, since it is associated with the French May 1968 moment, especially with those whom Bruno Bosteels calls "post-Maoists," among whom Jacques Rancière and Alain Badiou stand out (Bosteels 2005). But post-structuralism has also been displaced by an interest in religion and a critique of secularism which takes a number of forms, including Charles Taylor's revival of a Catholic transcendentalism. Taylor's work has a distant but friendly relation with the more politically ambiguous "radical orthodoxy" associated with the English theologian John Milbank and his colleagues, whose cultural and political implications have not been fully spelled out, but which, according to Milbank himself, may return us to a form of Disraelian and anti-Erastian, Tory democracy[1] (Milbank 2008). There has also been a revived interest in the avowedly conservative and less than enthusiastically democratic thought of Leo Strauss and Carl Schmitt, developed in response to European capitalism's mid-twentieth-century political crisis, and which, most notably in Schmitt's work of the 1930s, laments the separation of politics from revealed religion, i.e., the decline of theo-politics in the period after about 1880.

What is particularly striking is that while theory's simultaneous turns to *gauchisme* and to religion happen along different tracks, they are by no means mutually exclusive. After all, a number of neo-*gauchiste* European political theorists have written quasi-theological texts over the past decade or so (e.g., Agamben 2005; Badiou 2003a; Žižek 2000). I'll argue that neo-*gauchisme* is now so engaging because it too embarks on a theo-politics, if one that is paradoxically, and like Leo Strauss's, for instance, irreligious.

In the first instance, I am interested in one particular consequence of these broad developments and which was addressed in Chapter 6, namely the fact that theory is now increasingly remote from, and indeed oppositional to, cultural studies. (It is worth noting that, to date, these latest forms of theory have barely been absorbed into Anglophone *literary* studies either.) As we have seen, cultural studies' relation to Continental theory was always beset by difficulties, but there can be no doubt but that Gramsci, Althusser, Foucault, Bourdieu, and de Certeau helped provide the new field with key concepts and analytical techniques. Today, however, exchanges of that kind have become rare. One key piece of evidence for this is that most essays in *New Cultural Studies: Adventures in Theory* (2006), edited by Gary Hall and Clare Birchall, do not even claim to reconnect theory to cultural studies but rather hope "to invent a cultural studies … and the possibilities for doing cultural studies after Birmingham and after theory, too" (Hall and Birchall 2007: 23). And in fact most end not by suggesting concrete proposals for the reinvigoration of cultural studies by way of recent European philosophy or theory (and thence, at least implicitly, by facing the historical moment in which that theory is articulated) but by making vague requests for what one writer calls an "analysis of a social formation" grounded on what has been "not articulated" so far (2007: 67), or by no less vague prophecies of radical "mutations of practices that seek altogether another name" (2007: 142).[2]

My simple contention is that the recent theoretical turn which allies theology to *gauchisme* responds to the end of hope that capitalism's triumph carries with it. More specifically, theory's theo-*gauchisme* is energized by its rejection of social democratic reformism, including the reformism which lies, concealed or not, within the identity politics that, as we know, dominated the humanities from the late 1970s on. After all, it has become all but impossible to see how any mode of reformism might interrupt the processes through which all social zones are being organized so as to second them to the requirements of global markets and their various private interests. To repeat a familiar point, attempts to align the old quasi-socialist left to the contemporary post-socialist market state – all forms of "third way" or "New Labour" or "Clintonian" politics – have failed sufficiently to extract themselves from a purely capitalist logic. This reduces the analytical and imaginative room available to any theory which aims practically and productively critically to engage the political sphere, as does cultural studies. At the same time, as socialism proper wanes, theories that can no longer have productive aims in view, like theo-*gauchisme*, become more vivid. In this situation, cultural studies and theory have become increasingly disjunct.

We can usefully address theory's current theo-*gauchisme* and its distancing from cultural studies by examining two moments: the French Maoist aftermath in which militant theory first took a philosophical and quasi-religious (or Pascalian) turn; and mid-1960s British New Left thought in its most policy-orientated mode, from which contemporary cultural studies emerged. I'll engage both by putting to them four tests or questions. In my view, these tests also help organize the terms in which anti-capitalist radicalism might now remain conceivable.

First, does a particular theoretic-political moment or theory make what Herbert Marcuse in 1964 famously called the "great refusal," that is to say, does it clearly positively reject democratic state capitalism and the forms of subjectivity and social possibilities (or neo-liberal "opportunities") that state capitalism, and its ceaseless reformist projects (e.g., its ceaseless socialization and desocialization of the economy) entail (Marcuse 1964: 65)? The Marcusean formulation is often regarded as old-fashioned in that it posits a hard and traditional opposition between reformism and revolution which, in particular, the new anti-capitalist social movements claim to have overcome (Gilbert 2008: 77). I am skeptical of this line of thought on the grounds that the claim to have finessed the reform–revolution opposition turns out in fact merely to defer the possibility of revolution to some distantly future situation when it might be more viable than it is now, while limiting activism to, for instance, attempts to restrict multinational corporations' profitability, power, and influence and/or to install democratic participation within a particular social field. On occasions, such activist movements have been successful, as, for instance, when Greens have prevented mining projects, or student groups have impelled multinational corporations not to use child labor, or, on a larger scale in Latin America, by encouraging political participation by depoliticized groups so as to enable sectors of the economy to be nationalized. But, even when successful, such activism is easily absorbed by democratic state capitalism thought of as an integrated and global system, and indeed tends to strengthen the system by the old logic of reformism. After all, the interests of no particular sector – not even those of large private-sector corporations – are the interests of endgame capitalism as a whole.

In cases where the answer to the question "Do you refuse capitalism?" is "Yes," radicalism opens out to theories whose responsibilities to the actual social situation in place are minimal. That flight from social responsibility is philosophically enriching to the degree that it is politically impoverishing. Indeed, since its social extent is all but universal, capitalism will often be refused ethically rather than politically, that is, in self-directed acts under control of the individual will. In this context, it is easy to remember that radical refusal is as available to the right as it is to the left: indeed, in Western Europe conservative resistance to capitalism has been at least as powerful a social and cultural force as left resistance to capitalism. For instance, both theo-politics in the Strauss/Schmitt tradition and current radical-orthodox theologies belong to that tradition – and this helps to enable their exchanges with the left.

The second question is: What does a particular theory adduce as capitalism's crippling insufficiencies?[3] We can outline three kinds of systemic failures: (1) distributional, (2) experiential or eudaimonic, and (3) administrative.

Distributional (or numerical) failures concern global capitalism's long-term and continuing failure to prevent continuing massive inequities in terms of income, access to resources and goods (e.g., health care and education), whether we think of these inequities as the result of oppression or exploitation or not. (These inequities are incontestable: for instance, after decades of First World social democracy 2 percent of the world's richest individuals own 35 percent of the world's capital and the difference between the life expectancy of the richest and that of the poorest 10 percent of the world's population is actually increasing, not decreasing.)

Eudaimonic failures concern endgame capitalism's inability to secure the social conditions in which individuals and collectives may live maximally good lives. For the sake of quick exposition, let's define the good life here as one in which people may consistently and reliably enjoy energized, subtle, and reflective experiences in everyday life, where (following on from my last chapter) the category "experience" is defined as a concrete state of consciousness in which thought, feeling, perception, memory, expectation, and creativity may be variously combined. (See Wollsterstoff 2008: 146 ff. for an anti-experiential understanding of eudaimonism.) The question concerning experience is connected to the question concerning equality to the degree that an uneven distribution of resources to individuals may be linked to an uneven distribution of complexly rewarding experiences. But experience and egalitarianism also come into tension to the degree that only egalitarianism emphasizes the autonomy (or, to use Gerry Cohen's useful phrase, "self-ownership") of the individual and thereby underpins anomie and alienation.

Administrative failures concern global endgame capitalism's increasing surveillance, quantification, and restrictive control of all its subjects, including its strategies of exclusion. Such measures include the building of walls and the use of militarized violence in order to prevent cross-border travel by workers and refugees; the increasing incarceration of individuals by nation-states; the use of computer networks to produce and store information about citizens or consumers ultimately for purposes of manipulation or control.

It should immediately be emphasized that the claim of eudaimonic/experiential failure is the oldest, the most contestable and the most compelling of these three critiques: its roots lie in the counter-revolutionary romantic anti-capitalism that emerged in nascent form among French and English pre-conservative Christian groupings like the Warburtonians and then, in a more recognizable form, with Schiller's aesthetics in Germany. After all, while the promise of a better ("fuller") life is irresistible, it is not easy to describe exactly what a maximally full experience actually *is*. Also equality and a minimum of surveillance and control are not the primary criteria by which societies are to be judged good. Given a spread of political positions which include an orthodoxy nostalgic for organic theocracy, for us to affirm the primacy of distributive justice, moral and legal rights, and individual privacy, for instance, is already partisan. Indeed, as many reactionary thinkers have supposed, it may be that an unequal society may be more capable of offering its members a good life than egalitarian ones: an argument whose power in part comes from institutionalized Christianity's compelling version of this line of thought, namely that (as we saw in previous chapters) demo-cratic capitalism jeopardizes grace's action in the world more than do more hierarchized forms of government. There would also be those, mainly from another political position, who hold that, in particular, to position the cate-gory experience as politically urgent is to embrace a conceptually bankrupt humanism. But this is doubtful, since it is possible to value experiences without making humanist assumptions, and in particular without either positing the happiness and opportunities of integral individual human sub-jects as the measure of social justice or thinking of capitalism as an enemy of natural human needs. The charge of experiential deficit may also allege (as in Raymond Williams) that particular social structures, in diminishing experi-ence, block creative energy, whether collectively or individually. But that charge too is less than humanist, since there is no need to think of creativity as expressing a given and integral humanness.

The third question to be addressed to radical anti-capitalist critique is the more institutional one of how those who are in possession of a particular radical theory (the educated and committed vanguard) may form alliances and commonalities with those not in such possession. In France in May 1968 this Leninist question was directed at the relation between radical students and workers, of course, but also, as we have seen in Chapter 6, less concretely between students and those engaged in anti-colonial liberation struggles outside the West.[4]

The last question is closely related to the third: does capitalism operate through forms of false consciousness? That is, does it rely on citizens' general stupefaction? Can the vast number of people impoverished by the global democratic state-capitalist system understand and engage the conditions that thwart and disadvantage them? If not, then they may, of course, fail to act politically in their own true interests – or, to put this in the terms it was articulated in the classical era, the *vox populi* (the people's will) may not coincide with the *salus populi* (the people's benefit). In that case, the people are not to be relied upon as allies in the struggle for justice. This problem is more alive than ever in practical politics: in the United States, for instance, a hard and reductive version of it is at the core of the most recent "cultural war" which is seen to pit a liberal educated "elite" who engage rational political justice against sections of the population said (but not by them-selves) to be at the mercy of their apathy, ignorance, prejudice, and insecurity to the extent that they do not vote in their own real interest.

May 1968

Let us come closer to contemporary *gauchisme* by further developing our account of the New Left and by reexamining what its key moment – Paris, May 1968 – meant in the history of Marxist radicalism.

The modern left's history in Europe begins in 1917 with the Russian Revolution. Within five years of that event it had become clear to the Bolsheviks, who had taken control of the Russian state, that no wider European revolution was imminent, the key event in the collapse of their internationalist hopes being the Red Army's defeat by the Poles at the battle of Warsaw in August 1920. Three years later, the International Communist Organization (the Comintern) formally gave up on its policy of fomenting national revolutions, at which point European communist parties effectively came under the Soviet Union's control on the grounds that, without its support, the international proletarian/communist cause was doomed. In the absence of actual sustained revolutionary drive among national working classes, this policy marked the parameter of all radical left thought at least until 1943 (when the Comintern was disbanded) and for some (especially in France) until 1956 (when Khrushchev denounced Stalinism and the Soviet Union invaded Hungary) or until 1968, or even, as in the case of Alain Badiou, until 1977, when French *gauchisme* became exhausted as an activist movement (Hallward 2003: 43).

At the same time, the diminution of revolutionary expectations in the 1920s was the trigger for those foundational works in Western Marxism, Lukács's essay "Class consciousness" (March 1920) and the later, better known "Reification and the consciousness of the proletariat" (1923), which were attacked by Gregory Zinoviev, the Comintern's leader. Lukács argued, in an ambiguously Leninist mode, that "vulgar Marxism" (i.e., the "mechanical" theory that capitalism's collapse was inevitable and did not depend on political intervention) was itself a barrier to successful revolutionary action and that "the fate of the revolution (and with it the fate of mankind) depends upon the ideological maturity of the proletariat, i.e., on its class consciousness" (Lukács 1971: 76). The problem with this argument for the Soviets was that it tended to depoliticize class warfare as well as to sideline the party's active role in preparing for revolution, since it connected proletarian emancipation to a longer, more contingent historical process. For Lukács the working class had not yet attained maturity not just because it was under the spell of commodity fetishism but because its immediate interest (namely, to grasp hold of whatever capitalism offered it here and now) contradicted its ultimate interest in the establishment of a communist society. Hence the proletariat remained trapped in a "reified consciousness" which wavered between "crude empiricism" and "abstract utopianism" such as that which marked movements like anarchism or Guild Socialism.

After 1920, and leaving aside the purely academic Western Marxism developed from Lukács's influential analysis, the anti-capitalist left was split into four main blocs. The first was constituted by the official national communist parties, whose political presence varied greatly in different countries but all of whom were continually faced with the dilemma of how much to cooperate with local social democratic and reformist left-wing parties (from the revolutionary point of view, the most dangerous enemy), and how much to submit to Soviet direction. For complex reasons, the British communist party failed to play an important role in Britain's formal politics, whereas, after the 1930s, the French (PCF) and, after World War II, the Italian (PCI) parties both did. (One often overlooked reason for this was theo-political. It is no accident that European communism flourished in predominantly Catholic societies where the politics of secularism were most intense, and that both Continental parties, but especially the PCI, appealed to peasants and laborers in rural communities where the church had most presence.) Of all the European communist parties, the PCF was the most closely tied to the Soviet Union, especially after World War II. This would be crucial in May 1968, since it meant that the party had by then lost credibility among students, allowing small disaffiliated *gauchiste* groups to flourish. The PCF's actual turning its back on the student revolt only confirmed that disillusionment.

The second post-revolutionary leftist bloc were the Marxist *gauchiste* breakaways from Stalinism, most notably the various Trotskyite groups who were committed to permanent revolution and regarded the Soviet state not as an instrument of the dictatorship of the proletariat but as a hierarchical and bureaucratic form of party dominance. In effect the state was seen to marshal new forms of oppression structurally removed from economic exploitation. After the Chinese Cultural Revolution in 1965, a significant number of young radicals also came under Maoism's spell – Maoism being distinguished from Trotskyism by its more stringent insistence on egalitarianism; by its concept of total revolution that would transform culture and everyday life, and by its preserving a Leninist insistence on party discipline while abandoning a no less Leninist supposition that possession of the correct theory was required both for party-disciplinary purposes and for revolutionary conjunctures to be realized. Situationism, which, in an original and influential move, inserted Lukácsian Western Marxism into art world avant-gardism so as to place their surrealist-inspired sense of impoverishment of experience and everyday life at the centre of analysis, was another such quasi-Marxist *gauchiste* group.

The third leftist bloc were the anti-statist, non-Marxist parties which Lukács had defined as abstractly utopian, and in particular the anarchists, workers' council advocates and Guild Socialists. In the 1960s, in some cases under the influence of existentialism, these would be transformed into the Anglophone "workers' control" movement, the Johnson–Forest tendency in the United States, the French *autogestation* movement (prepared for by the ultra-leftist Trotskyite group Socialisme ou Barbarie, led by Cornelius Castoriadis and Claude Lefort), and the Italian Autonomia movements.[5] The workers' council tradition was also appropriated by the most prominent French Maoist groups after 1968. Right-wing versions of this form of autonomizing, self-managing *gauchisme* appear, too, including, in Britain just before the First World War, Hilaire Belloc and the Chesterton brothers' Catholic distributism, which had connections to southern agrarianism in the United States and may be one forebear of today's radical orthodoxy's social policy. And a policy ("corporatism") of maintaining the autonomy of different social groups and institutions within the state was indeed central to Italian fascism.

The fourth leftist bloc was the non-Marxist socialists, who on occasion could shelter *gauchisme* but who nonetheless joined parliamentary politics, and who, when in power and under pressure from global markets and capital, routinely backtracked on their socialist policies. Post-war instances of such backsliding include Harold Wilson after his electoral victory in Britain in 1964 and François Mitterrand in France after 1981. That repeated backtracking by parliamentary socialism not just demoralized non-Marxist socialism, it gradually delegitimized it, and prepared the way for its final accommodation with neo-liberalism.

The events of 1968 in France inherit, but mutate, this structure. As we began to see in Chapter 6, they brought a new group and a new identity into the political arena – the student movement, which changed the meaning and contours of the category of the "political" itself. In sociological terms, the 1968 student was a product of the expanding university system. (In France student numbers tripled in the decade after 1959.) This expansion was driven less by egalitarianism as such than by the will to create a citizenry capable both of democratic responsibilities and of expanding an increasingly technology-based economy. Of course students were also being trained to maintain standards of civility, rationality, and experiential richness that were (so the familiar claim went) transmitted in the Western (and, in France, especially the republican) cultural tradition.

One interpretation of the French 1968 movement, worked through by Pierre Bourdieu, for instance, argues that it was caused by the perceived gap between the education system's promises and the actual conditions of students' lives and futures, particularly since the expansion of higher education was reducing the status and value of certificates. (See Audier 2008: 246 ff. for a fairly persuasive empirically based argument that Bourdieu got it wrong, see Gruel 2004.) Another, not inconsistent, view is that put forward by the French sociologist Jean-Pierre Le Goff. He makes the case that May 1968 was a result of France's uneven modernization. For him, the remarkable post-war development of the French economy and of everyday life (e.g., through the mass distribution of cars and domestic labor-saving devices, the expansion of telephony and the media, the provision of health care and education) came into conflict with a rigid authoritarian governmental centre: this division being in fact constitutive of Fifth Republic Gaullism, which offered the electorate both modernization *and* a conservative French republican national tradition. Le Goff further argues that this conflict could not be easily resolved, since the post-war generation's life conditions were so radically different from those who had grown up among scarcity and war before 1945. There were no shared experiences and values out of which a basis for negotiation between the generations could be established (Le Goff 1998: 23–39).

Whatever sociological account of the movement one accepts, the 1968 students embraced the secular left's rather than the (Catholic) right's critiques of capitalism, while emphasizing the poverty of experience and aiming to overturn the state's control of civil society. (As Patrick Cingolani 2003: 77 ff. argues, the Catholic right was in abeyance after Vatican II.) The *soixante-huitards* did so within an expanded political space, outside the state institutions, in which spontaneity was to be combined with collective discipline. Without wholly buying into those theories, first expressed by Michel Crozier in his *Société bloquée* (1971), which praise the 1968 uprising for "unblocking" French society, or those, like Gilles Lipvetsky in his *Ère du vide* (1983), which blame it for the 1980s' rampant consumerism and individualism, it is true that in the aftermath of 1968 civil society came to be, if not exactly politicized, then at least under politicization in an anti-statist discursive move which allowed culture, ethics, and politics to be identified with one another. "Everything is political," as the only slightly exaggerated wall slogan of the period went (Badiou 2007a: 150). Yet, of course, to the degree that everything is being politicized, nothing is.

May 1968's promise evaporated quickly. De Gaulle's election by a solid majority in June that year made that apparent. Yet ongoing *gauchiste* militancy along with significant labor strikes (especially at Lips, a long-established Besançon watchmaker, where the workers took control in 1973) as well as the emergence of identity politics (partly on the back of Maoism) meant that those looking back could think of the radical (as against the unblocking) spirit of '68 as lasting until about 1976. That was the year in which the so-called "new philosophers" emerged in France to an extraordinary media flurry orchestrated by two intellectual impresarios of the kind only France knows: the young Bernard-Henry Lévy, editor of the publishing house Grasset, which published most of the new work (just as it had published another "new conservative" moment (in books by Julien Benda and Albert Thibaudet) in the late 1920s), and the older, widely respected, resistance fighter, radical Catholic writer and television presenter Marcel Clavel. The new philosophers, many of whom had been Maoist activists, were celebrated as marking the end of both 1968 Marxist radicalism and structuralist aridity by returning to a recognizable Christian spirituality which knew no concept of secular progress. They are not to be confused with the liberals or neo-republicans like François Furet, Marcel Gauchet, and Pierre Rosanvillon, many also ex-communists or *gauchistes*, who came to prominence in France in the 1980s. To the contrary, the new philosophers of 1976 embarked upon a theological turn from within *gauchisme*, in a religious orientation which had always had a place among the left's various Christian socialisms (in France mainly via the journal *Esprit* and in Claude Bourdet's Parti Socialiste Unifié, of which the young Alain Badiou, for instance, had been a founding member). With (among others) the *Tel quel* group, Foucault, Guy Lardreau, Christian Jambet, and Alain Badiou, *gauchiste* theo-politics took new, inventive, and irreligious-Christian forms. This would attract widespread Anglophone theoretical attention only about thirty years later.

Jambet and Lardreau

For our purposes perhaps the most interesting of these early post-Maoist texts are Guy Lardreau's *Le Singe d'or: Essai sur le concept d'étape du Marxisme* (1973) and Lardreau and Christian Jambet's later *L'Ange* (1975). The little known *Le Singe d'or* was published before the burst of publicity in which the new philosophers appeared, and is one of the period's several philosophical Maoist interventions on Althusserianism. *L'Ange* was a major media event on publication: Levy hyped it in *Le Nouvel Observateur* as the new philosophy's "manifesto," a label that the authors themselves came to reject[6] (Bourg 2007: 277). Both books were embedded in *gauchisme:* Jambet and Lardreau had become involved in student radicalism as schoolboys (at Paris's prestigious Louis-le-Grand) and in 1969 helped establish the most prominent Maoist splinter group, the Gauche Prolétarienne (GP) (Hamon and Rotman 1988: 44–45). Lardreau's, in particular, was the classical institutional trajectory among Parisian *gauchiste* intellectuals. He had studied under Althusser at the École Normale Supérieur, where he became an ardent Althusserian, before joining those who deserted Althusser for Maoism as Althusser's adherence to the PCF and his attempts to reinvigorate Marxist theory against both Stalinism and humanist revisionists came to seem impossibly restrictive. In 1966 Jambet and Lardreau both joined the Union de la Jeunesse Communiste Marxiste-Leniniste (UJCML), the Maoist student organization out which the GP emerged in 1969.[7] The GP itself was a tightly organized *ouvriériste* group, whose members were committed to what Jean-Pierre Le Goff describes as the "sacrificial" politics of *l'establishment*, that is, to erasing traces of their bourgeois origins and to taking factory jobs so that they could learn from workers and help organize them (Le Goff 1998: 153 ff.). (See Linhart 1981 for the classic self-ethnographizing account of this strategy.)[8] But it was the GP's connection to the elite educational institution that enabled it to become the period's most publicly noticed *gauchiste* organization.

Le Singe d'or has been interpreted as a summary of the GP's thought (Christofferson 2004: 59). But its Maoism is strangely detached and elegiac:

it presents itself as a "spiritual autobiography" and, in its introduction, offers a frank account of why and how so many young intellectuals of Lardreau's generation took the exit from Althusserianism into political Maoism, which Lardreau now wishes to transform into an avowedly spiritual (and romantic) Maoism. At the center of this romanticism lies not theory, not Althusserian "science," not even political activism, but rather feeling, and, most of all, will. A number of explanations for this move into the politics of will and affect can be adduced, of course. De Gaulle, but especially Pompidou and Interior Minister Raymond Marcellin after De Gaulle's resignation in 1969, had persecuted the radical groups, imprisoning hundreds of militants, many of whom were attached to the GP (Ross 2002: 176). (Christian Jambet had been on the front line of one particularly ferocious police intervention in a GP-infiltrated workplace strike, Hamon and Rotman 1988: 425 ff.) The editors of GP's paper, *La Cause du peuple*, were arrested in June 1970, to another surge of protest and acts of solidarity by celebrities. More important, the policy of sacrificial *ouvriérisme* encountered worker indifference, and popular attitudes towards the radical left hardened after some turned to terrorism. At the same time, Mao's authoritarianism had become increasingly apparent, and in 1972 he had normalized relations with the enemy – with Richard Nixon's America. So Lardreau's elegiac tone is hardly surprising. Indeed, the GP disbanded itself just at the time that the book appeared.

Drawing on Foucault's notions of historical discontinuity and the epistemic break as presented in *The Order of Things* (1966), *Le Singe d'or* argues, against Althusser, that there can be no return to the true Marx. Rather, Marxism has undergone three distinct stages, each marked by a radical departure from its predecessor. First, the First International and Marx himself; second, Leninism and the 1917 Russian Revolution, and now Maoism and the Cultural Revolution. Lardreau follows Althusser in rejecting the dialectical method and the historical ontology that it assumes: it is not as if each Marxist moment maps on to a particular mutation of the mode of production. Rather, Marxism's continuity across each stage is to be found in the sheer will to revolution. And in removing the will to resistance from a continuous history of communism Lardreau also rejects a progressivist narrative of history as emancipation. For him, no society, not even a communist one, will be able to pacify the will to revolt, which now belongs to the individuated ethical subject. At this point, as we shall see, Maoism resonates with a long and various history of non-materialist French dissidence.

On the other side – the side of discontinuity – Marxism's mutations are most apparent in the different relations that hold in each of its three stages between true knowledge and the people. What interests Lardreau most is Maoism's radical break from Leninism and in particular its insistence that the people's will grounds revolutionary action. The masses need no intellectual guidance from a party vanguard in possession of the correct theory (although they may need organization). In a refusal of the concept and institutions of representation that Lardreau shares with the Situationists, with the Guild Socialist tradition, and with post-structuralism, no group can properly claim to represent the people. All representative politics involve new forms of institutional closure. Yet he acknowledges a communal role in the making of theory: correct theory, which is always provisional to a particular situation, is discovered collectively in revolutionary action. (In Sorelian terms, it will act out a collective, transindividual "myth" rather than a rational theory: there is a strong sense in which Georges Sorel's *Reflexions sur la violence* (1908) haunts French post-Maoism after 1968.) Theory lags practice. From this, it follows that no hard distinction between "science" (or truth) and ideology can be maintained: truth becomes in effect what revolution thinks. And in the end the capitalist system is to be confronted on the basis of a will to revolt that has no grounding rational legitimation but which requires a Pascalian wager. At the heart of Lardreau's politics there appears an unmediated and purely subjective throwing oneself into resistance, which is recognizably Christian as well as recognizably existentialist: "Revolution is a work of faith" (Lardreau 1973: 89).

L'Ange further spiritualizes *Le Singe d'or*'s argument. But it remains a Maoist book. Now the check on practical revolutionary agency that the GP had encountered is still more clearly acknowledged: indeed, it provides Jambet and Lardreau with their most startling new move. In *L'Ange* revolution is not possible, and it is not possible not just now for us, but eternally, because its enemy is figured as Mastery itself, i.e., the taking of a position of control, of coverage, of authority in any domain whatsoever. In part, that is because, in Trotskyite fashion, the state, and its penal and bureaucratic apparatuses, have become as important an enemy as capitalism. But, in a more fundamental line of thought which combines Lacan and Foucault, Mastery is embedded in the very processes through which language enables socialization and promises full subjectivity, that is, through which discourse becomes possible. Nonetheless, the will to resist resignation – the will to what is called "rebellion" now that revolution is impossible – remains ethically fundamental. The emblem of that will to believe in rebellion is the Angel, an operationally fictive figure who does not exist, and is known not to exist except as an enabling expression of the rebel's will and the rebel's Pascalian wager on rebellion.

Certainly Jambet and Lardreau's radical expansion of the Master–Rebel opposition via the figure of the Angel once again takes them out of the historicist insistence that rebellion must be understood as determined by particular historical conditions. For them, historical discourse has its uses (it helps connect activist intellectuals to the masses) but it cannot provide the basis for a philosophical or a political theory or indeed for militancy itself (Jambet and Lardreau 1975: 42). Rebellion is figured precisely as an angel because angels are disembodied and free from the sexual identities and drives which draw us into language and mastery, which, hence, attach us to the world and resign us. As such, angels are also not entangled in the cultural economy of pluralism and difference that is appealed to by identity politics: they are universal. Furthermore, by choosing the figure of the Angel, Jambet and Lardreau accept Christianity's conceptual legacy, which is now said to provide a powerful metaphorics for the will to rebellion. They have, in effect, embraced another fictionalized Christianity.

In *L'Ange* Jambet and Lardreau draw on a number of early twentieth-century French philosophic motifs. For instance, they politicize neo-Kantianism: it is not, as the neo-Kantian Hans Vaihinger put it in his *Philosophy of As if* (1911), that our epistemological constructs are always hypothetical or "fictional" because we cannot know ultimate reality. Instead we must knowingly invent an opponent to the master because no strong opponent can be discerned in our current situation. They also turn back to Alain (Emile Chartier – an influential Parisian professor of philosophy in the first decades of the twentieth century (and Simone Weil's mentor)) who, in his republican ethical thought, insisted on the primacy of resistance to the dominant social norms outside of formal politics. And their appeal to Pascal's wager bears, as I have already said, clear affinities to existential politics simply because what is important to them is the decision, rather than the reason, to resist, even if, crucially, the wager is not made in a bid for authenticity. Perhaps more pertinently, then, their politics is reminiscent of the rather theatricalized decisionism that also motivates revolutionary activism in André Malraux's novels of the late 1920s and 1930s, novels that most 1968 French *gauchistes* had no doubt read.

It is no less important to emphasize that Jambet and Lardreau are developing a mode of Maoist gnosticism. Their insistence on an antagonistic dualism ("one divides into two," in the Maoist catch phrase) as against conventional historicist or Hegelian dialectics is orthodox enough (and Alain Badiou calls it "a decisive inspiration for French Maoism between 1967 and 1975") (Badiou 2007a: 61). But now the "two" are not classes, nor, as they are for the younger Maoist Badiou, an expression of a principle of scission which limits dominant social structures' stability, but rather they are theogonized ethicopolitical domains embedded (albeit hypothetically) in the divine causes of things. There are two orders of creation – two worlds – for those who wager on the fictive rebel Angel. From the perspective of political anthropology, these two orders are radically divisive: there are those who side with the Master (the state, capital) and those who side with the Rebel. But, rather confusingly, it is also the case that, in a Lacanian spirit, the Master–Rebel opposition marks a split within subjectivity itself, just because Mastery is bound to the symbolic order. From this perspective, all Rebels contain Masters within themselves and the angelic ethicopolitical task is endlessly to struggle against the Master's power in oneself, to turn his weapons against him.

Philosophically, Mastery works by seducing us into believing precisely in a single self-contained world, whether immanent or God's creation. The

Master's realm is that of "semblance," thought of as the imaginary order which (especially under capitalism) promises emancipation, unity, plenitude, desire's fulfillment. Hence the struggle against the Master involves asceticism. Democracy itself belongs to the order of the semblant, because it supposes a fundamental social unity and strives for eternal peace (2007a: 37). Truth, on the other hand, belongs to the Rebel. But the catch here is that discursive truth is merely axiomatic in the way that mathematics are axiomatic – as soon as truth is defined empirically, as soon as it is based on a correspondence to reality, for instance, it belongs to the order of the imaginary (2007a: 19). To use Badiou's later apothegm: truth is not knowledge. However, truth can be enacted in particular practices of life – this being a line of thought that Foucault was then developing along other lines. For Jambet and Lardreau, but not for Foucault, true practices of life must be rebellious in the sense that they must aim not so much to reform the Master's world (which would ultimately be to work to the Master's ends) as to break relations to that world, to overturn it, or to become autonomous in regard to it. Jambet and Lardreau find inspiring examples of a true practice of life in two specific cultural revolutions: the recent Chinese one, and, more confidently and imaginatively, that among the early (third-century CE) Christian anchorites who, receiving Christ and Paul's message, fled the Roman Empire to live in the desert. There in the desert, removed from society, the devout could maintain an uncompromising asceticism, an unyielding chastity, a rejection of the body, a hatred of desire. They could dedicate themselves to a sacrificial, self-emptying beatitude (2007a: 36). Clearly the desert fathers in their strenuously unworldly asceticism are being invoked not just as exemplars of a rebellious ethical practice but against then fashionable philosophies of desire like those being put forward by Barthes, Deleuze, Guattari, and Lyotard, as well as the lifestyle libertarianism that was being embraced by a rival Maoist group, "Vive la révolution," to which, for instance, the charismatic champion of gay liberation, Guy Hocquenghem, was attached. In *gauchisme*'s breakup, the first split was between those who affirmed desire and those who did not; the second was between those who attached themselves to a marginalized identity and those who remained loyal to universalism.

How are we to assess *L'Ange* in terms of the four parameters within which, as I have suggested, radicalism might remain practically thinkable? First, the question of refusing capitalism. This refusal, of course, Jambet and Lardreau endorse. But ultimately theirs is a highly qualified endorsement, since it is not ultimately made on rational grounds, and has no hope of success. Why, then, reject capitalism at all? In the end, they do not do so on egalitarian, experiential, or libertarian grounds, but because capitalism is another – energizing, expansionary – guise of the invariant Semblant, another mode in which eternal authority masks, disseminates, and reproduces itself. That is why it is to be resisted ethically on the basis of an ungrounded spiritual wager, whose primary stake would appear to be self-determination for its own sake, the willed affirmation of will.

Where do Jambet and Lardreau stand in relation to the Leninist question of the relation between the theorist-activist and the masses? In *Le Singe d'or* Lardreau takes the basic Maoist line: the masses always know best, and the activist's role is neither to lead nor to educate them, but to act as a vanishing mediator, to come to know and to learn from them and then to help them to organize themselves into a revolutionary movement out of which new truths and theory will appear. In *L'Ange* this has changed: there are no exchanges between activists and the masses, since the rebellion against Mastery happens primarily at the level of the individual. Perhaps what is most remarkable about Jambet and Lardreau's work in relation to activism, however, is that it does not forthrightly address the question of false consciousness and the closely related question of why Maoist revolutionary efforts failed. It is certainly possible to imply from *L'Ange* (and even more from its successor *Le Monde*) that the turn to Freud and Lacan helps answer this question: it is the Mastery built into the symbolic order that ultimately defeats revolution, which, anyway, simply leads to the replacement of one Master by another. That line of thought ultimately does away with the false consciousness question, since there is no consciousness which is not, in a sense, "false." That is what the concept of "Semblance" suggests. Truth adheres to life practices, not to knowledge. And the practices through which we may attempt to live in the true are not, in any important ethical or philosophical sense, determined socially. So that the socially produced question of false consciousness falls away, and the whole problematic of the discrepancy between public will and public benefit is removed from the practice of rebellion.

Badiou

The most sustained body of work that emerges out of *gauchisme's* blockage and its turn to Lacan is Alain Badiou's. He too was a young Althusserian who turned to Maoism, although his Maoist affiliations were rather different than Jambet and Lardreau's. As already noted, he had been a founder member of the Christian Socialist Parti Socialiste Unifié, and in 1969 as a young philosophy teacher at Vincennes founded a Maoist group, the Union des Communistes de France (Marxistes-Léninistes) (UCF(ML)), not to be confused with the UJCML. The UCF(ML) rejected the *ouvriérisme* associated with the GP and dedicated itself to innovative political action such as their *grand magasins* project, which involved looting department stores in order to interrupt the circuit of consumption (Bourseiller 2008: 215). In 1974 the organization spawned a cultural activist group, Groupe Foudre, which became notorious (and widely criticized) for symbolic activism. They threw paint at the screen of showings of John Wayne's *Green Berets* and Liliana

Cavani's *The Night Porter;* most controversially they interrupted a class taught by Maria-Antoinetta Macciochi, an Althusserian associated with *Tel quel*, on the grounds that her feminist critique of fascist sexuality and affect was too soft on fascism[9] (Forest 1995: 491). In 1985 the UCF(ML) was disbanded on account of Maoism's political failure, and Badiou and his friends established the Organisation Politique (OP), a small militant group that engaged in occasional and limited protests and occupations according to what Bosteels calls the "Mallarméan principle of restricted action" (Bosteels 2005: 585).

As Badiou engages in an original theoretically informed *gauchiste* political practice he develops a stunningly ambitious and complex philosophic system in which a unified account of ethics, politics, ontology, and aesthetics is presented. It is not my purpose here to outline either his philosophy or his militancy in any detail; rather I want to point to features that will enable us to read them as expressions of a simultaneously enriching and impoverishing *gauchiste* powerlessness on terms which differ from those of Jambet and Lardreau's post-Maoism, whatever echoes between the two modes of thought that we might hear.

Perhaps Badiou's key theoretical move, and one that most tellingly distinguishes him from Jambet and Lardreau, and which enables him to move past the depoliticization of their ethics, is his connecting ethics and politics to an account of fundamental Being, that is to say, in Bruno Bosteels' terms, he links a "mathematical ontology to a theory of the intervening subject" (Bosteels 2005: 612).[10] And he does so by positing, with anti-metaphysical intent, a number of metaphysical categories, of which these are particularly important:

1. *Being itself*, which, for Badiou, is without substance or nature. It is not presentable; it is, in that sense, void. Nonetheless Badiou decides to conceptualize Being as a void through the purely formalist axioms of Cantor's set theory, a mathematical turn that takes us back to Galileo, Newton, and Descartes in the early Enlightenment. Because Being is void, it cannot do the work of grounding that is characteristic of traditional substantive ontologies. To affirm this non-metaphysical and empty concept of Being is to make a contingent decision which expresses a preference for radical immanence and multiplicity rather than transcendence and unity (e.g., for a Creator who produces just one universe). Crucially, in rejecting any account of Being as something, Badiou is making a move which is non- and anti-metaphysical (since ontologically there are only mathematical relations) but also metaphysical (since to reject the ontology of ultimate grounds and substance is, from the metaphysical point of view, to make another metaphysical move). Badiou is a non-metaphysical metaphysician, and his political theory depends on his non-metaphysical metaphysics.

2. *Situations*, that is, the structures in which the world exists and which include, as a subset, the multiple material conditions in which we actually

live that Badiou calls "historical situations." All situations are constituted by elements whose places have been more or less rigidly assigned to them. But situations are also structurally incomplete, since they cannot contain themselves as one placed element among the others. (In Badiou's later thought they also contain what John Milbank describes as "free-floating and yet necessary" elements "in excess of belonging parts" which can unleash disruptions of the situation as "evental sites," Milbank 2007: 128.) In particular, historical situations, which are distributed across different micro-logics and processes, are organized by elements that remain unplaced and unpresented.

3. *Events:* relatively rare moments in which truth processes begin, that is, where situations are subtracted from so as to reveal their own void or incompletion, and new elements and places appear. We cannot be objectively assured that events happen; rather, people (as "subjects") commit themselves to events hypothetically, through a Pascalian wager: events exist in the form of acted-out "as ifs." Examples of an event include Paul's conversion on the road to Damascus but also Georg Cantor's invention of modern "transfinite" set theory and Mallarmé's poetry (since, in a radical gesture, it subtracted content from verse and "named" bare and fundamental poetic forms). Events may have a "diagonal" or articulated relation to other events: they are less than singular. For instance, in political (as against scientific or aesthetic or personal) events, social structures suddenly become open to transformation, and a minimalist form of political organization may preserve the spirit of one event into another. In political events, too, elements of a situation that have previously been disavowed suddenly become present and countable (e.g., when workers who have no political or social status acquire acknowledged political agency in a revolutionary situation like the 1870 Paris Commune). Against orthodox Marxism or indeed sociology as such (but like the later Althusser) events occur as if contingently, but they happen from particular "evental sites" – the places in a situation where the uncounted, the indiscernible, the void can be presented – and in "evental declarations" (the language in which the previously concealed elements can be named). From Badiou's non-metaphysical/metaphysical perspective, events edge out on to Being in as much as the voids that they expose incarnate the fundamental nullity of Being. To put this rather differently, for Badiou those who are not counted and who are not present in a state of the situation live "at the edge of the void," where the thick connections and contents of culture and ideology (i.e., of representation) are less entangled. Importantly, events have a particular relation to truth: they can trigger the processes which "subtract" or strip away existing historical, social, or conceptual relations from the "state of the situation."

4. *Truth procedures,* of which there are four: science, politics, art, and love. These are the only zones in which it is possible for sudden transformative

and inventive breaks in situations (i.e., events) to occur. They can be knotted or "forced" into intersection with one another (as in "proletarian art"). In committing oneself to truth procedures, old specifications and relations lapse, so that situational identities and interests are replaced by true subjectivity, which otherwise does not exist in the world. (This is a Platonic account of subjectivity in which it is only possible to have a real self to the extent that one lives in the true.) Philosophy is thought that is shaped by and related to truth procedures: this is one of Badiou's more radical formulations, since it both enriches and destabilizes what philosophy does.

5. *Virtue*. Virtue names a subject's fidelity to events, a figuring out of what an event's consequences might be, a struggle with the materiality of the situation in an order of things where Events and the truth procedures quickly become corrupted and entangled in social relations. Fidelity takes the courage to face the impossible, i.e., not to be depressed and abjected by the distance between the world and truth/justice or by the rarity of events and the difficulties of truth procedures. Fidelity enjoins us both to militancy and to a philosophic (a Platonic/Straussian) orientation towards the truth, and, in the same gesture, towards universality and equality in the face of the universal (Badiou 2007b: 46–47). In the end, and para-doxically, virtue is the courage actively to work towards and resolutely to wait for subtraction after subtraction of what is presented in situations, in a process bounded only by the null mathematical structures which exist in the place of the metaphysicians' Being and the theologians' God.

There is a further category which organizes Badiou's thought but which is not accorded the same philosophical attention – let us call it "untruth." Untruth is approximately functionally equivalent to Jambet and Lardreau's concept of the Semblant. It has an everyday social aspect. The stuff of social existence and relations, the ordinary, the mundane, and the habitual belong to untruth in their philosophical languor and political resignation. Untruth has a political aspect: the promises of plenitude, of final emancipation, of completion of history as reason and the state systems that are legitimized by such humanist promises all belong to untruth (just as they did for Jambet and Lardreau), since they do not take account of their own relation to the Void and don't acknowledge their own finitude. Finally, untruth has an epistemological aspect; once again empirical "truth," whose criterion is a correspondence to reality, and pragmatic or consequential "truth," whose criterion is utility or effectiveness, are both merely embedded in situations and therefore removed from truth. Theorists who affirm such truth rather than recognizing it as untruth are, for Badiou as for Strauss and Plato, sophists, anti-philosophers.

What about politics? Politics are to be centered on the "communist hypothesis," namely the assertion, against worldly evidence, of universal emancipation from the regime of capitalist state democracy as impelled by a shared Idea of freedom and creativity, and which, philosophically speaking, is an expression of the will to universalize, to incarnate the void (Badiou 2007a: 156). Committed to this hypothesis, politics is legitimate only when it refuses reformism and all utilitarian, economistic, or pragmatic axioms of justice, since their basis is always situational and conditional. Nor can it be seconded to the rule of law or juridical notions like human rights, since they offer criteria for justice which cannot adapt to specific events, situations, and needs, and they do so because they maintain a false image of the subject as static, unified, and integral, fully in place. (Similar arguments are not unusual among Anglophone academic political theorists, see for instance Glendon 1991.) To repeat, this means that, in politics, powerlessness must be raised to a courageous attachment to the impossible (Badiou 2007b: 46).

Let me insist on three general aspects of Badiou's thought. First, it is resolutely secular and anti-transcendental, that is one way in which it belongs to the French republican tradition that it overtly fiercely repudiates. (It as if, despite everything, Badiou is a republican who believes neither in the state nor in the empirical individual.) In Badiou's strenuously post-secular enlightened thought, the death of God and the thematics of finitude lose their pathos. So Badiou's most theological work – his book on St Paul – emphasizes the suddenness and contingency of Paul's conversion; Paul's (supposed) relative lack of interest in miracles and eternal life; the universality of his message (anyone can become a Christian, according to Paul); that message's revolutionary nature (its making everything new); Paul's insistence on a non-Trinitarian doctrine of incarnation in which infinity is manifested situationally as Christ's body and humanness, and, last, the militancy and courage of Paul's apostolic mission. What Badiou's Paul reveals, in fact, are certain structures of the "evental." He is militantly and courageously faithful to his conversion to an event that changes everything and opens the world to the impossible and the infinite.

In this, Badiou assumes and encourages no faith in Christianity at all: indeed, for him it is the Gospels' fictional status that makes them available to philosophy. (There's a trace of Jambet and Lardreau's Angel in this.) Badiou can turn to Paul irreligiously out of his will to metaphysicalize militancy, to identify the processes of justice and truth-making and to detach justice and truth from historicism. It has nothing to do with an anthropology based on spiritual longing, or an ontology based in revealed religion. Badiou's affirmation of the Void works hard to avoid reinscribing Christian themes upon a dead God and to solicit negative-theological affect. Nonetheless Jambet and Lardreau's appropriative account of the Desert Fathers is more secular than Badiou's reworking of Paul because in them the saintly anchorites are presented as models of a politically legitimated practice of life, not as exemplifications of a chosen ontology.

Second, Badiou's thought is non-historicist: history is not conceived of as the consecutive passage of events (in the non-Badiou sense) in which life-structures are produced and through which they become ordered and intelligible. Rather, history is limited to the moments of creative and transformative breaks of which politics, love, mathematics, and art are capable. History happens to Badiouan subjects. And the past is politically helpful not because historical sociology may make social formation intelligible to us but because the past provides us with a powerful store of referents to evental sites. Importantly in relation to radical leftist thought, this refusal of historical sociology means that Badiou is not especially interested in capitalism as such, and develops no detailed account of it.

The third aspect of Badiou's thought that demands especial attention is precisely his militancy. It is positioned at the intersection between the secular, immanentist will to universality within which Badiou metaphysicalizes politics and his realization that the revolutionary epoch, opened up by 1789, has come to a close and with it the false hope of the proletariat as a universal emancipatory class. At this intersection, militancy courageously faces the impossibility of revolution (replacing it with the unexpected irruption of a short-lived political event) and confines itself to creating cracks in the system rather than to bringing it down. Activism cannot, however, be carried out on behalf of any specific interest or self-identified group, for all such communitarianism depend on exclusion and thence injustice. Rather the impulsion to militancy seems a matter of Augustinian/Pascalian election or grace: it descends upon a tiny group mysteriously and arbitrarily, and it does so in the form of virtue. It is not to be thought of in conventional terms as "political," a category which, for Badiou, names the busy-work through which the people are connected to the state (Badiou 1985). For that reason, philosophical universalism remains the militant's least corruptible weapon of thought against what Badiou calls the market's false universalism. The politics of identity must be especially resolutely refused because they are, in Badiou's theological terminology, evil: for him evil is the will maliciously to name those who do not count from within a situation. It attests to the "sacred quality of the name," i.e., it sacralizes a particular identity by naming and destroying an other (as in the Nazi genocides) (cited in Hallward 2003: 263). Militancy, then, operates on behalf of the excluded rather than the oppressed or the exploited, those whom Rancière calls "the part who have no part." In practical terms, as we know, this means the stateless, and in France *les sans papiers* or undocumented immigrants most of all.

The first difficulty here is less a conceptual one than an aesthetic or scalar one. There's a huge gap between (1) the Platonic scope of Badiou's non-metaphysical metaphysics and (2) the modesty of the militant's aims and (otherwise put) the mutation of militancy into virtue. Although it is undeniable that the stateless and undocumented immigrants, for instance, constitute an important failure of justice, that failure is dwarfed by other injustices, most obviously I think, by current endgame state capitalism's failure to ensure even remotely equal access to resources across the globe. This failure cannot be thought through in terms that replace oppression by exclusion even if it is true that global poverty is concealed by sanctioned ignorance. Indeed, it could be argued that Badiou bases his politics around the "uncounted" because the counted are not on his side, just as he abandons history and historicism for ontology because history is not on his side. His philosophical disdain for the lived-in known world; his refusal of the notion that what happens socially is ceaseless and only the result of complex historical forces; his replacement of historical temporality by *kairos*, for moments in which life will become true; his implicit endorsement of the spiritual election of those militants who bravely stay loyal to events. All these can be read as extreme symptoms of profound political failure.

What about the four questions through which I am proposing to compare radicalisms? Perhaps more forcefully than anyone, Badiou enjoins us to refuse capitalism. But his originality lies in part in his refusing to bolster that refusal by eschatological thinking or by utopianism, his refusing to refuse in a gesture which points to another more just future *polis*. And of course he does not refuse capitalism by suggesting any kind of Schmittian solution to the diminution of real politics within the democratic capitalist state, though he is acutely aware of it (Badiou 1985: 10–12). One striking difficulty of Badiou's thought is that it requires we reject capitalism for nothing, that is to say, for an alternative whose only knowable features are formal, axiomatic. There's no promise of a better society.

Why, then, is capitalism to be rejected? Because it is radically unstable; it causes too much speed and change; because it is incoherent; because it produces "an infinite regression of quibbling and calculating" (Badiou 2003b: 45); because its univeralism (its promise that all may participate on equal terms in the market) is false and forestalls singularity; because it arbitrarily churns out differences and rivalries and cannot secure a universal principle of justice; and because it relies on a vast machinery of surveillance and control which constitutes a scandal to autonomy as such. It thickens untruth. Importantly, however, capitalism is not rejected on experiental grounds: it follows from the turn of Badiou's metaphysicalized politics of the void that the content of people's interior lives is neither of philosophical nor of political account.

Badiou also undoes the Leninist question of the party's relation to the people, not just because for him party organizations are always too rigid, too exclusionary, or even, more profoundly, because he undoes the concept of the "people" and its implicit communitarianism, but because the people's benefit, their true interests, are essentially incalculable. For him, politically, there are those who are placed and who count and those who don't: that is it. So there can be no "false consciousness" in the classical sense. Admittedly, as in his recent book *De quoi Sarkozy est-il le nom?*, Badiou does talk of a particular mode of political resignation and cowardly abjection to the neo-liberal phase of endgame capitalism as a form of "mass subjectivity" and "passive contagion" in terms which seem to join the Lukácsian false consciousness hypothesis (Badiou 2007b: 125). But, more generally, for him the important socio-ethical division is not so much between those who know the truth and those who do not (between philosophers and non-philosophers) as between those who possess the virtues of courage and fidelity, those who can wager on events and stick by them, and those who can't or won't. Indeed, it is only through those virtues that one can reach for true subjectivity. After all, one of his most cogent examples of living in the true, St Paul, was not only no philosopher but was converted to an untruth. Badiou's virtue ethics and his endorsement of the sacrifice to the event, it barely needs saying, depoliticize, since it is not the case that education and the equitable distribution of power will enable false consciousness to be overcome (or ideology to be punctured), it is more that politics takes the form of an endlessly expectant contention of a wider abjection by a tiny band of the elect, brave and faithful enough to maintain their wager on the impossible. This of course cannot constitute a practical governmental politics in any society whatsoever. In the end, once again, the enemy is socialization itself.

The May Day Manifesto

To turn from Badiou's post-Maoism to the British New Left on the eve of May 1968 is to move from one world to another. Two national histories that had been locked in battle for centuries – France's and Britain's – press upon this difference, histories in which each nation established its own social and political organization; its own connection of the state to God; and, as a consequence, its own cultural and philosophical traditions. This large-scale historical distance between French post-Maoism and emergent British cultural studies is relevant in this contest since it can work to sharpen our sense of what's at stake at the juncture where theory encounters politics encounters cultural studies. What is at stake is not just two different theoretico-political orientations but two different (if entangled) histories. And nowadays the spatio-historical forces that bear on the distance between post-Maoism and early cultural studies give heft to questions that matter across global capitalism's empire, especially when those questions are given their most emphatic and bare form: namely, should we wholly refuse capitalism or not? Fortunately, we know in some detail how the New Left progenitors of cultural studies – Raymond Williams, Stuart Hall, and E. P. Thompson – responded to this question in 1968 because, with Williams leading the way, they collaborated in writing an ambitious policy-orientated proposal – the *May Day Manifesto*, which contended that the "major decision" for contemporary politics was precisely that "between acceptance and rejection of the new capitalism and imperialism." (Williams et al. 1968: 187).[11]

The *Manifesto* belongs to the history of the British post-war radical left's confrontation with mainstream left betrayal, but it does so at the moment when (as described in Chapter 6) the socialist wing of the Labour movement experienced a series of impasses, first after the party's 1961 repudiation of nuclear disarmament, and then, decisively, after Harold Wilson's electoral victory in 1964, as a result of which the party effectively abandoned its remaining official socialist policies. In 1968 the *Manifesto* authors feared that the British economy's serious weaknesses would only encourage the Labour Party's further submission to global capital, and would further reduce British national autonomy in regard to social and economic policies. In this situation, it seemed as if saving Britain from the ravages of global capital could also rescue an idea – and a history – of Britishness.

More specifically, Williams and his colleagues argue that a new stage of capitalism has been reached, which they call "managed capitalism." Managed capitalism, which is also "a managed political system," is now globally hegemonic to the degree that the socialist project needs to rethink its policies and reexamine its bases of support if it is to survive. This means that socialists must examine social operations at all levels and domains, and not least the economy. So the *Manifesto* presents a critique of a wide range of social fields and institutions, in some cases putting forward specific policy proposals too. It is not at all a culturalist or humanities-orientated document: indeed, Williams's own major intellectual project hitherto is effectively downgraded. Thus, for instance, despite its strong sense that the United States was now dominating Britain economically and culturally, the *Manifesto* makes only fleeting mention of the need to democratize the British culture concept, or to preserve collective experience by appeal to the "ordinary" and a "common culture," these being the claims most associated with his name at that time.

The *Manifesto* makes the case that managed capitalism operates under the sign of "modernization," a term which functions as a rationale for the imposition of "a false political consensus" (1968: 143) and which conceals actual governmental practices by managerial and bureaucratic experts on behalf of private and corporate interests. Modernization is an empty, depoliticizing term which excuses the persistence of poverty and inequality. At the same time modernization sanctions the disruption of cultural continuities between the past and the future, both in social practice and in public memory (1968: 45). Under its banner (as well as that of its cognate "efficiency") capitalism is being consolidated, and a "restless, visionless, faithless" society is being "diminished to a passing technique" (1968: 45). Thus, to take one concrete instance, work is now considered by government merely a matter of production. Workers suffer cycles of employment and unemployment with only minor social mediation. Creativity and craft satisfaction are disregarded and minimalized (1968: 37).

According to the *Manifesto*, as a managed political system legitimated as modernizing, the economy has become integrated with the state and formal political apparatuses to the degree that all social activity can be organized on behalf of private capital. Such policies are possible because political institutions too are managed: the major parties have become little bureaucracies with their own fiefdoms and interests in which radical voices are muted. By the same stroke, Parliament itself is increasingly extraneous to the actual centers of social management. In a word, it is increasingly apparent that "representative democracy" is "the surviving sign and medium of a class society" at whose center lies the global imperialist market as a zone in which private profits can be maximized (1968: 148).

At a fundamental social level, the integration of the state with the market is enabled both by the education system and the media. The hierarchical education system maintains class distinctions by restricting the "lower ranks" to vocational training: it is addressed neither to students' "creative self-expression" nor to their "preparation for personal life, for democratic practice and for participation in a common and equal culture" (1968: 35). More important still, the media, now mainly under the control of a few corporations, disseminate those "interpretations" of events and social structures that most efficiently maintain the system. But it is not through their reportage that the media make such a profound social impact, it is through the advertising that they carry. Advertising turns workers into consumers so that wants triumph over needs. It then invisibly spreads abroad the false view that "all are effectively free to choose, and that effective choice is about styles of consumption" (1968: 42). Participation in the social whole is replaced by an individual attachment to style under the destabilizing machinery through which both politics and the consumer market are mediatized.

The problem the *Manifesto* sets itself is to develop a means of resisting this ceaselessly modernizing, integrated, depoliticizing, managed capitalism. At one level, the answer is to rebut the "electoral machine" through a mass "political movement" or "general political campaign" (1968: 184) aimed not at revolution nor at incremental reformist measures ("evolution") but at a "socialist" restructuring of relations between the state, the political apparatuses, and the economy so as to end the "incompatibility between human and capitalist priorities" (1968: 158). The *Manifesto's* implicitly *gauchiste* aim is to replace the structures of political representation by direct participation and the distribution of decision-making powers to all across all social domains, from the workplace to the family. This preference for social autonomy is not that of the radical *autogestation* movement, however, since, for the *Manifesto*, the state remains the final ordering mechanism. Yet the state is unable to restructure itself without a social struggle, whose main instrument will be union-organized refusal of labor (1968: 178) in an analysis which fits the increasing militancy of some British unions through the 1970s and which would, in fact, lead to Margaret Thatcher's 1979 victory and the radical unions' (and the old left's) final defeat in the 1983 Miners' Strike. This is not to say that the movement towards socialism, thought in these terms, will be confined to the unions, it will also draw on the energies of those non-party, special-issue "campaigns" that have emerged in the post-war period, of which the Campaign for Nuclear Disarmament was the most prominent. But the *Manifesto* movement needs to articulate, and be articulated into, an understanding of the system as a whole: indeed, the proliferation of local activisms in the current left is regarded as a submission to managed politics' divide-and-rule tactics (1968: 167–68). The new socialist politics will be a politics of simultaneous autonomization and connection.

How to assess the *Manifesto* through our fourfold grid? First, does it in fact make the great refusal of capitalism? Only ambiguously: rather, it attempts to restate the question's terms. It *seems* to opt for profound social restructuration under the name of socialism, and so to reject reformism or any other compromise with managed capitalism, and certainly, in its affirmation of struggle, it points, albeit with important qualifications, to the Cuban and Chinese Revolutions as inspirations for the anti-capitalist movement (1968: 141). But nothing like a revolution is awaited. Instead it imagines a repoliticization of the actual social institutions in place, including the market and private ownership. Universal participation in decision-making across all social levels and domains (from the workplace and the education system to the family) is intended to limit the state's power, under whose protection, nonetheless, universal participation is secured.

Who will own what? It is clear that the media, health, and education systems are to be fully nationalized while public ownership of the banking and insurance industries is merely to be "extended" (although British ownership of foreign corporations is to be nationalized). There is to be state investment in mining and transport. For the rest, some kind of "controls" will be imposed on private enterprise (1968: 134 ff.). That is to say, the *Manifesto* accepts an ongoing market society still largely under private ownership, but one whose primary objectives have been redirected. Economic activity will be in the social interest rather than in that of private profit. And provision for social needs (e.g., alleviating poverty) will be thought of not as a by-product of, or as residual to, free-market activity but as a core purpose of society as a whole, whose main wealth-producing instrument, the market, remains nonetheless. In sum: capitalism's social and governmental institutions would be preserved, but they would be, in something like a Maoist sense, locally democratized to ensure that the market economy benefits the "whole society."

How this rather ambiguous and vague sociopolitical mutation might be politically achieved is not at all clear. It does not help that, just to take two instances, the law, in its various forms, plays no role in the *Manifesto*, and that the long and rich history of constitutional thought is ignored. (By the late 1970s, however, Williams had become a proponent of proportional representation in a sign that he had given up the possibility of a unified working-class voting bloc, Williams 1979: 387.) It is as if a cultural Marxism, which is rarely positively asserted in the book, returns in these absences; as if the restructuring being called for (if not envisioned) is so sweeping, so revolutionary in relation to collective identity, will, and consciousness – in relation, that is, to culture – as to trivialize such merely practical and institutional matters. This is a lapse of some consequence, as we shall see.

It should, however, be clear which features of the system the *Manifesto* names as reasons to resist hegemony. The fading promise of distributive justice, the continuing social dominance of a metropolitan elite, the enforced social passivity of the majority of the population, and the consequent blockage of communicative and creative dispositions and energies lie at the heart of democratic state capitalism's failure. Experiential poverty is not adduced, although, as just noted, it had been key to Williams's own early Leavisite criticism. Nor does the book share the post-1968 emphasis on penality and surveillance as modes of power. Although systemic racism and sexism are briefly acknowledged, the 1970s identity-politics-to-come are rejected in advance along classical socialist lines – such politics are driven by compromised, partial, and, by implication, formally liberal interests. There's a hidden relation between the *Manifesto's* difficulties in pointing to concrete means through which society is to be transformed and its particular ascription of capitalism's flaws. That relation is this: were capitalism's injustices, cruelties and distortions not concealed from the larger community by their imposed disengagement from decision-making in their workplace and everyday life, then it would be easier to list the mechanisms through which restructuring might occur, since they would have a collectively articulated presence and weight.

As to the Leninist question of the relation between the vanguard and the wider community, it is bypassed by the *Manifesto's* rejection of the political party and its embrace of concepts like "movement" and "campaign." More important, it is bypassed in the *Manifesto's* rhetorical mode, which also displaces the whole question of false consciousness. The *Manifesto* is positioned as an appeal for collective mobilization in a situation where signs are perceived that a post-party-political left might win wide and spontaneous community support. Nonetheless, this projected community occludes the real social motor of communal politicization assumed by the book – which is the education system. In a socialist society, education's social reach is to be extended, and the *Manifesto's* demand for a state-controlled, universal, egalitarian pedagogy of participation (1968: 34–35) closes the distance between the politically engaged on the one side and the ignorant and apathetic on the other, that is to say, between the imagined community of *Manifesto* readers/ activists and its working-class other. But of course this appeal to public pedagogy (shared by classical French republicanism and social democracy) involves difficulties: isn't it too a form of depoliticization in which political organization and consciousness-raising are being replaced by more neutral and necessarily hierarchical structures of compulsory state pedagogy? This call to a national and statist education apparatus to seal the division between the knowing activist and the wider community (and which, of course, cultural studies was being established to implement) is hard to square with the call for local democratization.

We can say, then, that the French post-Maoist project (like much later British cultural studies) occupies the empty space exposed by the New Left's failure. That failure is nowhere more apparent than in the *Manifesto*'s incapacity either to attract widespread support or practically to envision a path to, or shape of, a socialist society to come. In effect, post-Maoism replaces transformative theory and the effort to reinvigorate a radical mass politics *à la* the *Manifesto* by a dehistoricized, ontologized, anti-statist theo-politics with Christian echoes, only fully endorsed by the elect. It does so from within that French history in which the republican state combated and replaced the Catholic church in the name of secular Enlightenment universals in the interests of its own control and authority. It is as if the French post-Maoists have, on the one side, accepted republican enlightened universalism and, on the other, drawn key categories from its enemy – the church – to combat the enlightened state as an institution. In the end, at least after the Popular Front, France did not itself produce an informal left-wing constituency dominated by the unions and sectors of the middle class and hence the conditions of possibility for a document like the *Manifesto* that simultaneously makes an appeal to, and tries to build, such a constituency. There are approximate French equivalents to the policies and concepts expressed in the *Manifesto*, especially by intellectuals attached to the PSU, the New Left/Christian socialist party that the young Badiou himself helped establish. Thus André Philip in *Les Socialistes* (1967) proposed a wide and egalitarian dissemination of decision-making power as well as a planned economy against a market-orientated society of consumption, all in the interests of "responsible society" (Philip 1967: 232). But the PSU, which circulated the idea of "revolutionary reformism," had a troubled history, since it was crowded out both by the PCF (which dominated the French unions) and by the mainstream social democratic reformist parties, so that in the end it could not stave off *gauchiste* scissions. After all, France knew no equivalent of the corporatist, non-communist, internally divided British Labour movement (split between the parliamentary party and the unions) which could claim ownership of the post-war welfare state, and upon which Williams and his colleagues were indirectly still relying. And, as I say, these different histories matter to us, because it is in and through them that the crucial political question of our time is to be posed most concretely.

Living with capitalism

Should we indeed reject capitalism? It should by now be apparent that the *rational* response to this situation is negative. The failure of the New Left's efforts to restructure society, the discouragement experienced by those responsible for the last and most intellectually careful effort to campaign for a minimally compromised socialism, mean that, in our time, there is no rational alternative to reformism. Right reason would rather have us join those ceaseless efforts to manage capitalism's crises and growth spurts in the interests of social justice and the alleviation of suffering. By and large that has indeed been cultural studies' path since the mid-1970s. With some honorable exceptions (Lawrence Grossberg, Bill Schwartz) it has largely forgotten its more ambitious, non-reformist socialist direct-democratic heritage and rationale. In many cases (e.g., with creative industries pedagogues) it has become democratic state capitalism's enthusiastic servant.

But is the rational response sufficient? In my view the answer to that is also "No." Even if one cannot await revolution, one cannot simply resign oneself to the endless task of remitting state capitalism's insufficiencies. Capitalism's incapacity to realize justice, security, and order; its indifference to suffering; its debasement of experience and of intellectual and creative possibilities; its dispersion and wastage of energy are just too savage. Then, too, the processes of reform can too easily become further instruments of destruction as capitalism endlessly renews itself by appropriating its enemies. Yet, although these charges against capitalism are (to some degree) based on reason, the grounds for making an anti-reformist refusal are finally – to repeat – ethical and irrational, just because, to repeat some more, neither an exit from, nor an alternative to, capitalism is imaginable. In this triple bind – neither revolution nor reform nor the *status quo* – the terms that were once to hand to mount a resistance have vanished. That is partly because, in the West, those terms belonged to Christianity's long tradition of world rejection, so that once Christianity is consigned to untruth there exists no conceptual toolkit for resisting an immanent order – the world – which will never be redeemed from within.

In the difficult search to find concepts from which to refuse capitalism, it seems to me fitting to return to a vocabulary – to *names* in Badiou's sense – which, pre-dating modernity, has not been wholly appropriated either by modern instrumentality and relativism or by that discourse and apparatus of abstract rights, adapted to the condition of endgame capitalism. I want now to conclude by briefly gesturing at two such possibilities.

The first term I'd select, drawing on the philosophic tradition, is that ancient philosophical category "perfection": *endgame state capitalism is not perfect enough to be endorsed on any grounds at all.* In making this move I am not joining so-called "perfectionism," namely the contemporary political-theoretical argument that liberalism fails when it does not sufficiently take into account that some human activities are inferior to others (Haksar 1979: 1). Nor am I appealing to that Christian-Platonic formulation in which, as the young Lukács put it, "the *ens perfeissimum* is also the *ens realissimum*" (cited in Goldmann 1964: 49; Goldmann's account of the "tragic vision" is relevant here).

Rather I am appealing to a looser Aristotelian understanding of perfection as human action's (intermittently) realizable objective, that is to say, I am joining, from within a different social situation and to different ends, Matthew Arnold's affirmation of perfection as culture's final end.

The second, which goes closer to the heart of the matter, is "honor": *it is dishonorable enduringly to accept imperfect capitalism.* Other categories might seem more appropriate than "honor" in this context, of which perhaps the most obvious is "dignity" (*it affronts dignity to accept imperfect capitalism*), to which, as we have seen above, Edmund Burke (borrowing from the civic republican tradition?) appealed. But the notion of "dignity" was always imbricated in rationalism. For Cicero, its originator as an anthropological notion, *dignitas* named the responsibility to uphold reason against the world. For Kant, dignity was the quality granted in the autonomy required for a moral agent to obey the universal laws she legislated for herself: it is what is worthy of our moral respect. And Stoic/Kantian dignity has been modernized: it forms the basis of the contemporary legal rights terminology. Various UN declarations on human rights make their fundamental appeal to the inviolability of a self-attested human dignity, as, for instance, does the widely used bio-ethical "right to die with dignity." In providing the abstract props upon which the system as a whole can claim a certain legitimacy, such usage not only does little or nothing to add substance to particular "rights" but sucks ethical specificity and content from the concept of "dignity" itself.

"Honor's" attraction is precisely that it is archaic, almost to the point of emptiness. It does not have to be thought of socially in the way that, admittedly, some conservatives still do, as a modality of reputation or as shame's opposite. Let us concede that there's no compelling sense in which one might feel ashamed by capitalism. One can think of honor instead, as Samuel Johnson famously did in the first of the definitions he offered in his *Dictionary*, as "nobility of soul, magnanimity and a scorn of meanness." *Refusal of endgame capitalism is based on a scorn of meanness.* And honor is "noble," not in the sense that it is attached to privilege (although to a certain degree and inescapably it is) but because it is inherited. The honor that rejects modern capitalism has genealogical rather than rational grounds: it has been transmitted from some other time, that's why it's relatively pristine. That's why, too, honor's force has been massively diminished, which is important here because it reminds us (as the post-Maoists do) that the grounds for refusing capitalism are, as it were, under evacuation.

What might this honorable refusal of social imperfection practically entail? First, it means that as a matter of principle we ought not to be involved in the machinery of formal politics, since these are so integrated into the system as a whole. But it cannot involve complete indifference to human suffering or injustice, either, since, as I argued in my third chapter, that hardhearted indifference can be defended (if at all) only on the grounds that it accelerates a radical social transformation which is not now on the

agenda. This means that Badiou's militant group, the Organisation Politique, in the transitoriness, ad-hocness and spontaneity of its interventions,
in its finally thinking of militancy in terms of virtue ethics, is indeed (for all
its implicit appeal to grace) a model for activism, so long as, unlike Badiou, we
allow empathy as a motive for action and as long as there are no philosophical
or theoretical barriers to entry into militancy.

Putting politics aside, what about private life? How to live an honorable
and rigorous refusal of endgame capitalism? This is not a question which
reflection on the opposition between early cultural studies and post-Maoist
theory can help answer. Nor is it a topic that the contemporary academy is
geared to address. But let me conclude by succinctly offering some suggestions
nonetheless.

The question's difficulty derives from it being impossible either to live
outside the system – to achieve individual or collective autonomy – or to
base oneself on an ontologically grounded individuality (e.g., a "soul") which
is independent of society. Families, sex, work, culture, are all incorporated
within the system, if not equally tightly. And so it is not as if the split
between the self who is necessarily socially engaged and the self who is not
neatly maps on to a private–public distinction, as if it were possible to
inhabit one's interiority in a completely protected internal exile from the
world, in a *vita contemplativa*, for instance. It is more a question, on the one
hand, of occupying those social spaces that are least attached to endgame
capitalism mainly because of their history and, on the other, of living privately on terms that mute one's unavoidable social incorporation. Those
social spaces include, importantly, the academy, at least in the pure sciences
and the humanities, whose forms of thought lie at some remove from endgame capitalism. One thinks in particular of philosophy, theory, history,
criticism, as able to stand, if not outside, at least on the edges of democratic
capitalism, an argument for the humanities against society which, in a broad
kind of way, joins both Leo Strauss and Alain Badiou in their (different)
Platonic endorsements of the philosophic care for truth over sophism or *doxa*.
The academic humanities' most crippling limit is that they can employ and
engage so few and are therefore both so limited and so easily incorporated,
often despite themselves, into those social hierarchies in which systemic
injustice dwells.

Outside of work, post-Maoism (like Thomas Love Peacock before it)
reminds us that the histories of quietism, asceticism, and even of mysticism
(thought irreligiously) may offer some support for a private anti-capitalist
ethic, a retreat into the neutral in Barthes's sense. In the light of our last
chapter, for instance, it might be possible to develop an ethic of an asceticism not directed against the body or desire but for lightness and the mundane, as categories that lie, as it were, *beneath* capitalism's uses and spectacles.
But the key difficulty with following such a path is that capitalism is
imperfect partly because it impoverishes experience, and asceticism and, in

their own way, quietism and mysticism conspire with that impoverishment precisely because they subtract from pleasure, intensity, perceptual richness. As many have noted, modern capitalism promises experiential satisfaction through consumption at the same time as it systematically deprives consumers of the stability, knowledge, and time for full, subtle, thought-filled experiences. In the end, then, in trying to provide a template for a private ethic of capitalism's refusal we are driven to bind together principles that are in contradiction with one another. To live on the system's outer limits is to live ascetically; it is to aestheticize mundane experience; it is to deliver oneself over to temporalities other than those of capitalist production and consumption; it is to acquire the resources from which fully and freely to reflect on a wide range of engagements in the world; it is to engage in protests that have no truck with formally instituted politics. That wide raft of requirements is clearly unachievable for individuals, and its impossibility means that the task of imagining and analyzing the means of disengagement from endgame capitalism belongs less to practical ethics than to philosophy as the refuge of insoluble problems. But not to an unimaginable social transformation in which what is insoluble is solved.

Notes

Introduction

1 For a useful theory of the exit from an economic perspective see Hirschman 1970.
2 See During 2006 for my sense of cultural studies as a post-discipline.

1 Church, state, and modernization

1 My understanding of "literature"'s change of denotation has been most influentially articulated by Raymond Williams, most succinctly in his entry for "Literature" in Williams 1976: 152–53. Perhaps the most careful and extensive account of this change is to be found in Siskin 1998.
2 Siskin 1998: 11.
3 For useful summaries of recent understandings of the mutation of literature's meaning and extent in terms like these, see Justice 2002: 20–27 and Keen 1999: 1–22. This kind of analysis begins with Ian Watt's classic account of the "rise of the novel" in Watt 2001.
4 See Alok Yadav's useful remarks on how commerce, liberty, and the republic of letters were often understood in Britain as codependent, Yadav 2004: 69–72. Voltaire was especially important in disseminating this understanding of these relations in his *Philosophical Letters* (1734).
5 See Clark 1985, 1994a, 1994b. See also Pocock 1980.
6 See Black 1998 for a discussion of the issues involved in categorizing eighteenth-century England as a confessional state.
7 See Walsh et al. 1993 and Jacob 1996.
8 See, for example, Clark 1994b, Erskine-Hill 1982, and Higgins 1991. For a critical account see Folkenflik 2000.
9 The recent historiography somewhat exaggerates the openness of the British state in relation to those outside the Anglican fold. Certainly intellectual and religious counter-cultures remained outside the mainstream, in part because the universities and, with some exceptions, the legal profession remained out of reach for Dissenters and Roman Catholics and because, as I am arguing here, Anglicanism had such intellectual and cultural reach and power. For a good example of recent thinking about this issue, see Langford 1991: 72–90.
10 See Walsh et al. 1993 for an excellent overview of the Anglican Church in the period. The political attack on Anglicanism early in the century is described in Champion 1992.
11 It was difficult for ambitious intellectuals and scholars working around the universities to remain unordained: the career of John Taylor, son of a barber, noted Greek scholar, one-time Cambridge University librarian, editor of Lysius (printed by William Bowyer, who also acted as Taylor's London agent), onetime advocate of Doctors' Commons, and author of *Elements of Civil Law*, is instructive in this regard. His resistance to taking orders was

well known (he feared the politics involved) but the lure of lucrative preferment available by virtue of his scholarly fame was, in the end, too much for him. For a description of Taylor's career, see McKitterick 1992–2004 I: 128. For the careers of plebeian-born bishops, see Langford 1991: 262–63.

12 See Cookson 1982: 12–16 and Sack 1993: 46–50 for a discussion of the breakdown in relations between Dissent and the government in the 1780s. For a different account of the increasing distance between the Church and plebeian cultures see Thompson 1974.

13 This statement is not based on hard evidence, since no research exists that quantifies the various sources of money for literary/intellectual production in the period. But, leaving private patronage aside, in terms of scale the Anglican Church had no real competitor as a unified institution producing knowledge and discourse, at least until at some point in the last decades of the eighteenth century commercial booksellers began to fund knowledge production for the market on what was probably a comparative scale (a market which itself partly rechanneled Church incomes). For work on the imbrication of the Anglican Church within the larger society, see Clark 1985: 161–73, Gibson 2001: 148–81 and Jacob 1996. For the importance of the Church to intellectual life, see Young 1998: 6–7 and Gregory 1991.

14 The best brief summary of those publishers who turned to fiction in the period is to be found in Raven 1987: 35–42. For shifts in the publishing trade more generally, see Raven 2001: 1–60 and Turner 1992: 37 ff. And Fergus 2006 persuasively overturns a number of received ideas about the actual readership of novels. On the basis of evidence garnered from provincial booksellers' archives, she argues that books were bought about as regularly as they were borrowed, and women writers were read by men as much as by women. On this latter point see Fergus 2006: 41–74.

15 Almost all clergymen had degrees from Oxford and Cambridge, and all those who worked at these universities were required to sign on to the Thirty-nine Articles. Many fellows stayed at the university only until they were awarded a living, and the colleges controlled many livings themselves. See Bennett 1984.

16 Influential collections of sermons intended to be read aloud in the family circle were edited by the Dissenters John Mason (*The Lord's Day Evening Entertainment, containing Fifty-two Practical Discourses on the Most Serious and Important Subjects in Divinity, intended for the Use of Families*, 4 vols, 1752) and William Rose (*The Practical Preacher, consisting of Select Discourses from the Works of the Most Eminent Protestant Writers: with Forms of Devotion for the Use of Families*, 4 vols, 1762).

17 The relatively undeveloped nature of the Dissenting educational market in particular can be gauged from the fact that Joseph Priestley's popular lectures on history, delivered at the Warrington Academy in the 1760s, remained unpublished until 1788, even though Priestley was a well known textbook writer at the time. On publication they quickly became a standard text in the Dissenting academies and American universities.

18 A good summary of women's moral writing is to be found in Sutherland 2000. Two more detailed but very informative case studies of women's relation to Dissenting print cultures are to be found in McDowell 2002 and Taylor 2003. It is important to recognize that, despite the Anglican Church being a profoundly masculinist organization, women could and did play a significant role in its printed output: in the mid and late eighteenth century the contributions of Hannah Chapone and Hannah More stand out as examples. See Stott 2003.

19 A huge and varied literature exists on women's role in eighteenth-century commercial print culture. See in particular Eger 2001 and McDowell 1998. But see Fergus 2006: 41–74 for a persuasive argument that men were more important to the novel form's readership than women.

20 Printing history information on the Bowyer shop is available in Maslen 1993 and 1994. Bowyer did not become involved in printing Jacobite political polemics and reportage as

did Jacobite printers like Nathaniel Mist, Francis Clifton, and John Matthews, the last of whom was executed for printing seditious libel in 1719 (even though Bowyer did employ Mist's son).

21 For information on Leslie and the intellectual culture of the nonjurors, see Cornwall 1993 and 2005.

22 In particular Joseph Ames's *Typographical Antiquities* (1749).

23 It is no accident, however, that the Bowyer shop had printed John Le Neve's list of obituaries in *Monumenta Anglicana* (1717) and elsewhere, nor that it had printed Samuel Jebb's *Bibliotheca Literaria*, an annual record of the "labour of the learned" which ceased publication in 1724.

24 A good account of the differences between "old" and "new" bookselling modes is to be found in Hernland 1994. Knapton and Rivington, two of the cases she discusses, were very involved in what I am calling the "gentlemanly-ecclesiastical bloc" of the literary field.

25 A good sense of the readership can be drawn from Sherbo 1997. Seven of the eleven most regular correspondents to whom Sherbo draws attention were ordained Anglican clergymen.

26 See Levine 1991 for a view of this field.

27 See Cochrane 1964: 13–21 for an excellent summary of the London printing trade at the time. Anglo-Saxon was expensive to print and sets of Anglo-Saxon type were uncommon. The Bowyer firm, however, owned a set, and could thus play a significant triage role in book production in this area.

28 Gregory 2000: 157. The most developed project of this sort was Andrew Ducarel's incomplete *Repertory of the Endowments of Vicarages of all the Dioceses of this Kingdom*. See Nichols 1812 I: 388–89.

29 See Nichols 1812: 1–162 for the Spalding Society.

30 For the history behind the equation of the concept of "passive resistance" and rejection of the 1688 settlement see Bennett 1975: 109.

31 For an account of Warburton, see Pocock 1985b. The other secondary sources on Warburton from which I have drawn most are Evans 1932, Young 1998: 167–212 and Ingram 2005. Warburton is the villain of Stephen 1962 in an account which is, nonetheless, well worth reading.

32 Warburton's account of Church and state relations shares much with the ancient Roman one in Montesquieu's *Considérations sur les causes de la grandeur des Romains et de leur décadence* (1734).

33 Warburton's arrogance seems to have partly been in imitation of his models, themselves enemies, the Cambridge Whig scholar Richard Bentley and Alexander Pope of the *Satires*, who both maintained the hard abusive rhetoric of the early modern republic of letters.

34 See Balguy 1769: 5. In the Feathers Tavern petition, senior Anglican clergy, among whom Francis Blackburne (see Chapter 3) was a prime mover, requested a repeal of the Test Acts. For rational Dissent's response to Balguy see Priestley 1769. See also Page 2003: 114–18.

35 Hurd 1995: 359–61. The lower House of the Convocation, the Church's representative body, had been suspended in 1717 under George I, a key moment in the Church's loss of autonomy. This intensified the Jacobitism of Tories like Francis Atterbury.

36 Brown 1763: 222. For Brown's contribution to eighteenth-century intellectual life see Roberts 1996.

37 See Eaves and Kimpel 1971: 329–30.

38 See Sanna 2005: 62–63 for a good account of this controversy which I here paraphrase.

39 Under a ruling by Lord Hardwicke, Sutton was expelled from Parliament for insider stock trading and lying: Warburton wrote a pamphlet in Sutton's defence.

40 Gerrard 1994: 47; see also Walsh et al. 1993: 33.

41 See Nichol 1992 for the details of Warburton's relation to the book trade.

42 See Nichols 1812: 600–01, where Nichols describes his personal intimacy with Hurd. Some letters between Nichols and Hurd are printed here too: Hurd reads the first version of the *Literary Anecdotes* and advises Nichols against turning author.

43 It's ironical that, from an intellectual-historical point of view, this critique of luxury (itself ancient) took its characteristic eighteenth-century form in a Catholic and French text, Fénelon's *Telemaque* (1699).

44 Ingram 2005: 114–15.

45 See "A Sermon preached before the House of Lords in the Abbey Church of Westminster on Friday, December 13, 1776, being the Day appointed by Authority for a General Fast, on account of the American Rebellion," in Hurd 1811 VIII: 3–16.

46 *Letters from an Eminent Prelate*, 125.

47 I discuss Hurd's literary theory in a little more detail in During 2007.

48 For the importance of public happiness to Hoadly, see his 1708 sermon "The Happiness of the Present Establishment," in Hoadly 1773 II: 109–17.

49 Nichols 1812 I: 488.

2 Quackery, selfhood, and the emergence of the modern cultural marketplace

1 I have found Black 1987, Doherty 1992, Feather 1985, Ferdinand 1997, Isaac 1998, and Hargreaves 1997 useful in providing information here.

2 Fergus 2006 does not include cash sales in her account of John Clay's sales, and it is not inconceivable that patent medicines were more often sold in this manner than books.

3 The material in this paragraph is mainly drawn from Hambridge 1982 and Porter 2000.

4 Welsh 1885: 17 ff. See also the introduction to Roscoe 1973. More information on the Powder is to be found in Dickens 1929 and Pottle 1925.

5 See Stanhope 1777 II: 127.

6 For *The World*, see Nos. 24 and 176.

7 See www.rpsgb.org.uk/members/pdfs/pr040426.pdf.

8 See Mikhail 1993: 102–06 for a reprint of Haynes's pamphlet and notes on its context.

9 The formula was published in Monro 1788 I: 366, Monro having obtained it from the Chancery patent. For a rewarding account of certain cultural aspects of the Victorian patent medicine trade, see Richards 1990: 168–204.

10 For a portrait of Sterne as a mountebank, see *The Scheming Triumvirate* (1760), British Museum Catalogue 3730.

11 The mutuality of exchanges between sentimental benevolence and political economy's critique of the poor laws is nowhere clearer than in the closing paragraph of Joseph Townsend's influential pamphlet *A Dissertation on the Poor Laws by a Well-wisher to Mankind* (1786).

12 For an interesting approach to Newbery, Smart, and Goldsmith but with different interests than mine here see Branch 2006: 135–75.

13 See Guest 1989 for a pioneering account of this poem and its theo-political setting.

14 "Jubliate Agno: Fragment B, No. 326," in *Selected Poems*, in Smart 1990: 85.

15 "Jubliate Agno: Fragment D, No. 227, p. 140, Fragment D, No. 200" in Smart 1990: 138.

16 Mikhail 1993 contains a good selection of contemporary reports on Goldsmith's private life.

3 Interesting

1 The Nauru islanders are famous for being the most obese population on earth (mainly because of their island's ecological devastation), hence the importance of health care.

2 See, for instance, Henry Mackenzie's essay on the novel of sensibility in *The Lounger* 20 (17 June 1785).

3 This is one of the important arguments of Gallagher 1994. For Rousseau, see Rousseau 1968, 25.

4 This argument had already been put by Bernard Mandeville, among others. See Mandeville 1988: 1: 56.
5 The literature on the prehistory of sentimentalism is overwhelming. Informative studies include Brissenden 1974, Greene 1977, Jones 1993, Mullan 1988, Sheriff 1982.
6 This distinction is a version of the one that R. F. Brissenden draws between "sentiment" and "sensibility" (Brissenden 1974: 33 ff.).
7 See in particular Ellison 1999 and Watts 2007.
8 At the time of the emergence of sensibility, social compassion was being organized into private but organized projects such as, to cite two early instances, London's Foundling Hospital (1742) for the care of abandoned children, or the Magdalen Hospital (1758) for the penitential and disciplined reform of prostitutes. By the mid-nineteenth century these intertwined systems – literature and compassionate social reform – were much less closely attached to one another: indeed, the figure of the philanthropist and the imaginative artist could be seen not as allies but as opponents. That opposition is a key theme of Elizabeth Barrett Browning's verse novel *Aurora Leigh* (1857), for instance.
9 Giorgio Agamben makes a similar point. See Agamben 1999: 4.
10 Exceptions include the section on "Interest" in Williams 1976 and Adamson 2008 (which I encountered after writing this chapter).
11 See Adamson 2008: 108 for the French usage of the word.
12 See, for example, Boswell 1998: 81, where to visit a writer's house is described as "interesting".
13 For Johnson on Milton being "interesting" see Johnson 1952 I: 121, and for his lack of "Human Interest" see ibid., p. 127. Jonathan Richardson had already declared that in *Paradise Lost* "All is Interesting" because of its mix of "Pleasantness" and morality (Darbishire 1965: 328). In his *Lectures on Rhetoric and Belle Lettres* (1759–60) Hugh Blair echoed the remark, noting that *Paradise Lost* is "interesting" because, in its elevation, it seizes the imagination – another use of the word which seems to hover between its old and new sense (cited in Shawcross 1972: 246). In the next century Matthew Arnold, returning to the relation between being interesting and being close to life, could write, "The Greeks are internally interesting because they … keep nearer to the *facts* of human life" (cited in Murray 1997: 80).
14 For Machiavelli and the theorization of interest, see Wolin 2004: 207–09. The standard account of "interest" in this period remains Hirschman 1977. For a rather different articulation of the ways in which interest gained traction as an analytic category all the better to resist the passions, see Pocock 1985a: 115.
15 See the statistics on this in Anderson 1992: 141.

4 World literature, Stalinism, and the nation

1 There is a large literature on the category of world literature: the introduction to Damrosch 2003: 1–36 provides a useful entry point. Among the earlier articulations of the concept that Goethe framed we should recall the work of the gentlemanly English Anglican literary historian and editor Thomas Percy, discussed in the first chapter.
2 That a fundamentally European concept of literature was expanding was important to Erich Auerbach's argument in Auerbach 1969, where it becomes part of the process through which "our earth, the domain of *Weltliteratur*, is growing smaller and losing its diversity" (1969: 16).
3 It is my sense that there is also more sheer enthusiasm expressed for Stead than for White, in particular: many practicing novelists and poets have praised Stead with a warmth and sensitivity that indicate genuine passion. The list includes Hilary Bailey, Saul Bellow, Angela Carter, Randall Jarrell, Tim Parks, and Rebecca West.

4 Marx 2005: 34. As Stefan Hoesel-Uhlig has noted, "world literature" has carried two distinct meanings from the very beginning. On the one side it refers to the archive of literary expression across all languages – the total literary heritage; on the other to a small canon of transnationally recognized masterworks. See Hoesel-Uhlig 2004.

5 The classic account of the emergence of Paris as bohemia's world capital is to be found in Clark 1973: 24.

6 The book which is usually understood to introduce the concept was Thibaudet's *L'Histoire de la littérature française de 1789 à nos jours* (1936).

7 See, for instance, Kuhn 2007: 205–06. For Blake on Grossman's economics see Blake 1939: 513–14.

8 Christina Stead, "The Writers Take Sides," *Left Review* 11 (August 1935): 456.

9 See, for instance, the citation from Dorothy Green's obituary in the *Sydney Morning Herald* as cited in Rowley 1994: 130.

10 The relationship between type and individual was at the core, in particular, of Ralph Fox's *The Novel and the People* (1937) with Fox arguing that for any specific character these could be in conflict, as they are in many of Stead's characters. See Fox 1947: 34.

11 In the 1930s this intersection was an avant-garde interest to which the German communist psychoanalyst Wilhelm Reich was drawing particular attention in his "sex-pol" work in essays and activism of which it is likely Stead and Blake were aware, and which would later lead to the more academically respectable Freudo-Marxism (Erich Fromm, Herbert Marcuse), which, as theory, shadows almost Stead's whole *oeuvre*. For Reich's "sex-pol" work see Sharaf 1983: 131–34.

12 I use the term "noir" here so as to connect her writing with *film noir* and the Popular Front moment from which both emerge. See Davis 1990: 37–38.

13 In a description of the book written in the early 1960s Stead herself called Marpurgo a "satanic type, who coquets with Trotskyism, as part of his showy cleverness" (Geering 1990: 422). This is not quite the character I recognize in the book. For an interpretation closer in spirit to my own, see Brydon 1987: 48–57.

14 One of the rather unusual aspects of Blake's analysis is to place forms of state employment like academic employment under the head of the *rentier*.

15 It is based on her and Blake's experiences at the Travelers' Bank.

16 The history of the novel's reception in traced in detail in Yelin 1999.

17 For a persuasive account of women in the US communism movement in this period, see Foley 1990: 150–69.

18 The novel was reviewed very badly in the *New Masses*: see Williams 1989: 169.

19 The historiography in relation to this election is divided about the causes of the victory: here I am following Looker 1995: 29–30.

20 On Stead's relation to feminism see Sheridan 1988: 1–3. It is interesting to remember that Stead's rejection of feminism and identity politics generally was shared by the Jewish lesbian communist Yvonne Kapp, born the same year as Stead: see Kapp 2003.

21 The republished novels were *The Salzburg Tales*, *The Beauties and the Furies*, *Letty Fox: Her Luck*, *A Little Tea, a Little Chat*, *The People with the Dogs*, *Cotters' England* and a collection of novellas, *The Puzzleheaded Girl*.

22 The fullest account of the emergence of Auslit as a field remains Lawson 1987, to be supplemented by Buckridge 1998.

23 For Burnshaw and the Popular Front, see Pells 1973: 311–12. For Stead's own reminiscence of her friendship with Burnshaw, see Stead 1984.

24 There are several excellent books on lineages of women writers from the British colonies. See for instance Gardiner 1989 and Yelin 1998. My argument is closest to that made in Boehmer 1995: 129. Boehmer mentions Mansfield, Rhys, and Stead as having a commitment to a specific modernist writing practice which comes out of their expatriatism and gender.

25 The literature on these topics is vast, and my argument that Christina Stead is rarely addressed in it is based on some of the more influential texts, namely Baucom 1999, Benstock 1986, Eagleton 1970, Gikandi 1996, and Said 1993.

26 Books on post-war British fiction that don't mention Stead include Allen 1959, Brannigan 2003, Sinfield 1997, Connor 1996, and Laing 1986.

27 She does not appear in Rideout 1966 or Aaron 1992. She's mentioned fleetingly as a friend of Ruth McKenney in Denning 1996, and several times in rosters of communist women writers in Wald 2002.

28 For the Australian book trade at the time see Nile 1990 and Buckridge 1995.

29 Mitchell 1981. Among Mitchell's complaints about Stead's work: it was "muddled," "limited in its emotional range," demonstrates a "persistent melodramatic tendency" which means that it is "more interested in gesture than perception," it "showed an imperfect adjustment between inner and outer realities" and "an interesting misalliance between the novel of manners and the novel of ideas." Boyd was an expatriate writer contemporary with Stead who was sometimes described at the time, rather generously, as an Australian Galsworthy.

30 See Lever 2003 for an excellent account of the communism that informed Stead's own judgments of other writers as well as her own creative writing pedagogy.

31 Denning invents a genre, the "ghetto pastoral," see Denning 1996: 230–31.

32 However, Louise Yelin makes a case that the character of Jules Bertillon in *House of all Nations* does exemplify some of Fox's theories in Yelin 2000: 76.

33 Cauldwell 1970: 99–100. This book was published only posthumously, it was written between 1935 and 1937.

34 My sense of this period owes much to Kynaston 2007 and Hennessy 1994.

35 The month Stead spent in Newcastle researching the book seems to have intensified her dislike of the family as an institution. See a letter she wrote to Blake about the moral blackmail the family. Stead 2005: 243.

36 This was a central debate for leftists in the late 1940s and early 1950s, played out, for instance, in Dwight Macdonald's onetime Trotskyite journal *Politics* with its inclinations towards Simone Weil as well as in Sartre's writings of the period.

37 And also between orthodox Stalinism and those forms of academic and popular Marxism that were the movement's most lively expression in the post-war period, including, for instance, in Britain, the Communist Party Historians Group (1946–56) and, in the States, Blake's friend Leo Huberman's works popularizing left history and economics. This division is indirectly referenced several times so as to bring up to date the critique of the radical Oxford historian Oliver Fenton in *The Beauties and the Furies*. And here the text is ambivalently positioned, since, as we shall see, Nellie's rejection of theory and Marxist knowledge for experience and identity is certainly scorned.

38 The most recent attempt to place Stead into the literary marketplace on those terms was *Letty Fox*'s republication in the *New York Review* Classic Books series with a preface by the English novelist Tim Parks. That edition barely made a splash: as I write it is about 700,000th on the US Amazon sales charts and the 1,800,000th best seller on the British Amazon charts.

39 Although it is possible to suppose that her work might become more relevant to cultural studies, since she is in dialogue with the discipline, given that it, in its originating moment (Richard Hoggart and Raymond Williams) was precisely concerned with the relation between Marxian theory and ordinary life. One way of thinking about her work would be as an Old Left anticipation of the New Left: her Marx, though, is closer to Althusser than to Gramsci.

5 Socialist ends

1 The richest account of the period and topic I am concerned with here is to be found in Dworkin 1997. See also Gilbert 2008: 11–41.

2 See Easthope 1988 for an alternative sense of how to proceed with a history of theory which deals with some of the same topics as mine here.

3 There is no good scholarly history of this branch of theory. But Cusset 2003 is useful.

4 The year 1956 is usually said to mark the beginning of the first New Left, since that was the year that the British Communist Party (CPGB) suffered heavy defections (including E. P. Thompson) after the Russians invaded Hungary; when British imperialist claims floundered with the invasion of Egypt after Nasser claimed back the Suez Canal, and when the manifesto for Labour "revisionism," Tony Crosland's *The Future of Socialism*, provided a detailed and coherent set of policies for an egalitarianism that could be absorbed within capitalism. The term itself derived from the French *la nouvelle gauche* associated with the movement, intellectually led by the Christian Socialist Claude Bourdet, that attempted to reorganize the left outside of either Socialist Party (SFIO) or Communist Party (PCF) structures, particularly after the 1956 election, won by Mollet and the SFIO, which then proceeded further to betray the socialist legacy. See Bourdet 1957.

5 See, for these citations, Murdoch 1958.

6 See Stuart Hall's acknowledgment of Cole in Hall 1989: 15.

7 See Taylor 1968: 181 for one such call.

8 See Kenny 1995: 34 ff. and Anderson1980: 136 ff. for good discussions of the situation at the *New Left Review* at the time. There are two excellent books dedicated to Anderson's intellectual career, Blackledge 2004 and Elliott 1998.

9 Stuart Hall's *Steps Towards Peace* was a manifesto for the CND.

10 The first New Left involvement with structured social sites can partly be regarded as an attempt to replicate communist sociabilities. Blackledge 2004: 167 notes that the movement was in the "political reverberations" of "The Anglo-French invasion of Egypt, the Russian invasion of Hungary, and Khrushchev's secret speech" (exposing Stalin's crimes). The period's nostalgia for the party can be found in Lessing's *The Golden Notebook* and Samuel 2006.

11 See Williams 1977: 2–3 for Williams's own account of his relation to the New Left and the development of his interest in Western Marxism.

12 My sense of the British progressivist tradition owes much to Blaazer 1992.

13 The decline of the first New Left is often said to be linked to the defeat of the left by the right at the 1961 Labour Party conference over the issue of whether Britain should unilaterally disarm its nuclear weapons. See Sedgwick 1976: 134.

14 In relation to Wilson it is not as though New Left intellectuals repudiated him immediately. Perry Anderson himself was an ambivalent Wilsonian around 1963 on the grounds that Wilson's modernizing project had some chance of breaking down the crippling hegemony of gentlemanly culture. See Blackledge 2004: 25–28. This indeed turned out to be the case but the beneficiary was neo-liberalism, not socialism. See also Williams 1979: 365 ff.

15 Anderson also established a book publishing business that introduced the major Western Marxist theorists to Britain, and he supported the translation and publication (by Penguin) of the young Marx's writings.

16 For E. P. Thompson's definition of the New Left, see Thompson 1959. For G. D. H. Cole, see the essay cited above. It would be interesting to analyze with some care the relation between Isaac Deutscher's interventions in British Marxism and the Anderson/Nairn project. One good place to begin would be by reading Deutscher's posthumous collection of essays and talks, which includes (critical) remarks on the New Left (Deutscher 1971). Certainly Deutscher (as a Trotskyite) insisted on internationalism; he was powerfully anti-Stalinist,

and rather skeptical of the New Left and the peace movement; he insisted on the role of the proletariat in leading towards revolution.

17 Perry Anderson like others of his generation became increasingly radicalized in the period after 1964, dissociating himself from the Labour Party in 1965. See Blackledge 2004: 44. For Labourism, see Nairn 1965a: 159.

18 In particular it was not infected by what Tony Crosland had called the "anti-American neurosis" of the British left (which persists to this day) and helps explain the first New Left's critical focus on communications and mass culture. See Crosland 1956: 142. After Vietnam, intellectual flows from the US left to the British left seem almost to have ceased: all theory imports came from the Continent. This meant that much important anglophone Marxist, feminist, postcolonial analysis was not discussed in Britain. For an interesting and informative account of relations between the American left and what he calls "British New Left cultural studies," see Pfister 2006: 49–80.

19 See Nairn 1965b for one of the clearest analyses of neo-imperialism in the context, this time, of the Vietnam War.

20 See Sale 1973: 84–85. Sale here reminds us that the university's capacity for radical analysis and organization was under debate in the early days of the US new left.

21 Talcott Parsons' relation to Nazism has been controversial, since there have been claims he helped ex-Nazis obtain work after the war, but basically I follow Uta Gerhardt in her account of his career. See Gerhardt 2002.

22 A full account of the break between the left and the British working class during the 1960s is to be found in Hindess 1971.

23 Simone de Beauvoir's *The Second Sex* had appeared in English translation in 1953, Betty Friedan's *The Feminine Mystique* in 1963, and Doris Lessing's *The Golden Notebook* in 1962, as we have seen. These texts no doubt lie behind Anderson's attention to women's liberation. The first purely feminist document published within the *New Left Review* circles was Juliet Mitchell's article "The Longest Revolution" (note the title), published in 1966.

24 Among a vast literature I have found two late 1980s accounts very useful for this history: Miller 1987 and Isserman 1987.

25 In this context it does not seem accidental that it was in 1962 that Fritz Machlup's *The Production and Distribution of Knowledge in the United States* first tried to quantify the economic value of knowledge, and in the effort effectively invented what would be called the "information society" and showed the degree to which economic growth depended on the production of knowledge.

26 Another appeal for anti-colonialism to be applied to Western radicalism is to be found in Hall 1968: 217–19.

27 Of course the sense that language itself demanded revolutionary revision had long haunted the English radical left, as we see in Murdoch's *Under the Net* or the discussion of Stalin's linguistics in *The Golden Notebook*, where Lessing puts the case that in the contemporary (atomic) era language was "thinning" while experience was becoming more dense (Lessing 1991: 288).

28 I am more on Gregory Elliott's side than on Khilnani's in ascribing Althusser's turn to a certain Maoism. See Khilnani 1993: 107 and Elliott 1998: 209–11.

29 Althusser's relation to Gramsci was much debated in the 1970s. See, for instance, the CCCS volume *On Ideology* (1977), where the topic surfaces more than once. Althusser's late writings on Machiavelli can also be understood as meditations on a certain Gramsci: Althusser's Machiavelli turns into a Gramsci *avant la lettre*.

30 See Gunster 2004:179–88 for an excellent account of Althusser's relation to cultural studies early on.

31 The best critique I know of post-structuralism's anti-statism is to be found in Brennan 2006.

32 He did so in a stenciled paper as well as in Hall 1968.

33 These remarks do not mean that Leninism did not have its appeal for 1960s radicals. See Elbaum 2002: 55–58 for an account of Lenin's appeal in these circles in the United States at the time. And the question of why theory is more a European than a British tradition is treated illuminatingly in Anderson 1968 and, from a very different perspective, in Hunter 2006 and 2007.

6 Completing secularism

1 My understanding of the history of intellectual conservatism owes something to Quinton 1978.
2 For the Tractarians and "ethos" see Nockles 1994: 6.
3 For "political Joachism" see Reeves 1969: 75.
4 To give just one example of the hundreds of texts written on this theme between the wars let me mention Julien Benda's *Discours à la nation européenne* (1933).
5 As John Milbank, leaning on Lyotard, has pointed out, this process of indifferentiation is embedded in capitalism's tendency to view a variety of needs, products, and values as basically the same. Milbank 2006: 194.
6 For a full account of Hegel's relation to the Scottish school in terms rather different from Ritter's but relevant to this chapter, see Dickey 1987: 186–205.
7 This account of, and the quotes from, Schmitt come from Meier 1995: 113.
8 See also Gerassimos Moschanos's argument that what he thinks of as the great transformation of social democracy covers all social domains: Moschanos 2002.
9 These claims clearly require an essay, or rather a library, to themselves. But in justifying them I would draw attention to the following recent work on contemporary capitalism from very different political positions: Harvey 2006, Bobbitt 2008: 44–124. Howard Brick's historicization of twentieth-century "postcapitalism," as he calls it, and his argument that much social thought from both the left and the right in the short twentieth century (ca. 1914–ca. 1970) failed to address capitalism's embeddedness in Western society is also to the point here (Brick 2006).
10 On experience, I have found Oakeshott 1933 especially useful, and, for historical background, Jay 2005.
11 Henry James's preface to *The Princess Casamassima* is a manifesto for the importance of descriptions of self-perceptive consciousness to the art novel.
12 My knowledge of Thatcherism owes much to Green 2006. See also Hall 1988 and Jenkins 1987.

7 Refusing capitalism?

1 At the time of writing Milbank's *The Future of Love: Essays in Political Theology* is forthcoming.
2 One honorable exception to this empty hope for a radically other future in this volume is Julian Murphet's excellent contribution on Badiou, which does indeed recognize the problem, although unfortunately it shares Žižek's misconception that cultural studies and Badiou, however far apart they are, are united in their failure to recognize the centrality of political economy to social and political life.
3 See Boltanski and Chiapello 2005: 37 ff. for a rather different list of the various forms of "indignation" that capitalism has provoked.
4 The historiography on actual relations between workers and radical students in France in May 1968 is divided between those who argue that, at the time, the workers struck for traditional industrial reasons, using the students' riots opportunistically (Seidman 2004), and those who argue that workers' demands were influenced by student radicalism (Horn 2007).

5 See Coates and Topham 1970: 349–442 on the British workers' control movement of the time.
6 *L'Ange* was supposed to be the first volume of a trilogy, of which one further volume was published. That book, *Le Monde*, extends and hardens their ethical turn through an argument which as, Julian Bourg has pithily remarked, attempts to show how "Freud could be used to supplement Kant" (Bourg 2007: 281).
7 Rancière became a member of the Groupe Information de Prisons and Badiou helped establish a tiny ultra-leftist group, see below.
8 For an account of the GP see Le Goff 1998: 151 ff.
9 One suspects that Macciochi was also a target because she had organized *Tel Quel*'s trip to China in 1970, out of which she published a widely read critique of the Cultural Revolution.
10 There's a non-literal sense (which would no doubt be disputed by these theorists themselves) in which Badiou, with his commitment to secular universality, belongs to the tradition of French republicanism, while *L'Ange*, in its ethical theogony, belongs to the tradition of French Catholicism.
11 The *Manifesto* was first published in 1967 and then, in a longer, widely distributed form as a Penguin Special in 1968. In its first form, at least, it was largely written by Williams. See Williams 1979: 373 for an account of its authorship.

Bibliography

Aaron, Daniel. 1992. *Writers on the Left: Episodes in American Literary Communism*, New York: Columbia University Press.

Adair, James. n.d. *Essays on Fashionable Diseases, the Dangerous Effects of Hot and Crouded* [sic] *Rooms, the Cloathing of Invalids, Lady and Gentlemen Doctors, and on Quacks and Quackery*, London: T. P. Bateman.

Adamson, Sylvia. 2008. "Working out the interest: Williams, Empson and Jane Austen," *Critical Quarterly*, 50: 103–19.

Adorno, Theodor. 1974 [1951]. *Minima Moralia: Reflections on a Damaged Life*, New York: Verso.

Agamben, Giorgio. 1999. *The Man without Content*, trans. Georgia Albert, Stanford, CA: Stanford University Press.

——2005. *The Time that Remains: A Commentary on the Letter to the Romans*, trans. Patricia Dailey, Stanford, CA: Stanford University Press.

Alexander, Ken. 1958. "Conviction," *New Reasoner*, 7: 112–13.

Allen, Walter. 1959. *The Novel Today*, London: Longmans Green.

Anderson, Martin. 1992. *Impostors in the Temple: American Intellectuals are Destroying our Universities and Cheating our Students of their Future*, New York: Simon & Schuster.

Anderson, Perry. 1965. "Problems of socialist strategy," in *Towards Socialism*, eds. Perry Anderson and Robin Blackburn, London: Fontana: 221–90.

——1968. "Components of the national culture," *New Left Review*, 50: 3–57.

——1980. *Arguments within English Marxism*, London: Verso.

Arendt, Hannah. 1965. *On Revolution*, New York: Viking Press.

Arnold, Matthew. 1993 [1869]. *Culture and Anarchy and other Writings*, ed. Stefan Collini, Cambridge: Cambridge University Press.

Audier, Serge. 2008. *La Pensée anti-'68: Essai sur les origins d'une restauration intellectuelle*, Paris: Découverte.

Auerbach, Erich. 1969 [1952]. "Philology and *Weltliteratur*," trans. Maire and Edward Said, *Centennial Review*, 13: 3–17.

Badiou, Alain. 1985. *Peut-il penser la politique?* Paris: Seuil.

——2003a. *St Paul: The Foundation of the Universal*, trans. Ray Brassier, Stanford, CA: Stanford University Press.

——2003b. *Infinite Thought: Truth and the Return to Philosophy*, trans. Oliver Feltham and Justin Clemens, London: Continuum.

——2007a. *The Century*, trans. Alberto Tosacano, Cambridge: Polity Press.

——2007b. *De quoi Sarkozy est-il le nom?* Paris: Nouvelles éditions lignes.

Baker, Walter. 1754. *The Affidavits and Proceedings of Walter Baker, Administrator to the late Baron Schwanberg, upon his Petition presented to the King in Council, to vacate the Patent obtained by Dr. Robert James for Schwanberg's Powder, ... with a Copy of the Report, upon the Hearing before the Attorney and Solicitor General, the sixth of December, 1752*, London: printed, and there published, for physicians, surgeons, and apothecaries, and all others whom it may concern.

Balguy, Thomas. 1769. *A Sermon preached at Lambeth Chapel, on the Consecration of the Right. Rev. Jonathan Shipley, D.D. Lord Bishop of Landaff*, London: L. Davis & C. Reymers.

Baucom, Ian. 1999. *Out of Place: Englishness, Empire and the Locations of Identity*, Princeton, NJ: Princeton University Press.

Bennett, G. V. 1975. *The Tory Crisis in Church and State, 1688–1730: The Career of Francis Atterbury, Bishop of Rochester*, Oxford: Clarendon Press.

——1984. "University, society and Church, 1688–1714," in *The History of the University of Oxford*, Vol. V, *The Eighteenth Century*, eds. L. S. Sutherland and L. G. Mitchell, Oxford: Oxford University Press: 359–400.

Benstock, Shari. 1986. *Women of the Left Bank: Paris, 1900–1940*, Austin, TX: University of Texas Press.

Bentham, Jeremy. 1817. *A Table of the Springs of Action, shewing the several Species of Pleasures and Pains, of which Man's Nature is susceptible: together with the several Species of Interests, Desires and Motives, respectively corresponding to them. ...* London: R. & A. Taylor.

——1989 [1830]. *First Principles Preparatory to Constitutional Code*, ed. Philip Schofield, New York: Oxford University Press.

Berlant, Lauren. 1997. *The Queen of America goes to Washington City: Essays on Sex and Public Citizenship*, Chicago: University of Chicago Press.

Blaazer, David. 1992. *The Popular Front and the Progressive Tradition: Socialists, Liberals, and the Quest for Unity, 1884–1939*, Cambridge: Cambridge University Press.

Black, Jeremy.1987. *The English Press in the Eighteenth Century*, London: Croom Helm.

——1998. "Confessional state or elect nation?" in *Protestantism and National Identity: Britain and Ireland, c. 1650–c. 1850*, eds. Tony Claydon and Ian McBride, Cambridge: Cambridge University Press: 53–74.

Blackledge, Paul. 2004. *Perry Anderson, Marxism and the New Left*, London: Merlin Press.

Blake, William J. 1939. *An American Looks at Karl Marx*, New York: Cordon.

Boaden, James. 1825. *Memoirs of the Life of John Philip Kemble, Esq., including a History of the State, from the Time of Garrick to the Present Period*, 2 vols, London: Longman Hurst Rees Orme Brown & Green.

Bobbitt, Philip. 2008. *Terror and Consent: The Wars for the Twenty-first Century*, London: Allen Lane.

Boehmer, Elleke. 1995. *Colonial and Postcolonial Literature*, Oxford: Oxford University Press.

Boltanski, Luc. 1999. *Distant Suffering: Morality, Media and Politics*, Cambridge: Cambridge University Press.

Boltanski, Luc and Eve Chiapello. 2005. *The New Spirit of Capitalism*, trans. Gregory Elliott, London: Verso.

Bonwick, Colin. 1977. *English Radicals and the American Revolution*, Chapel Hill, NC: University of North Carolina Press.

Bosteels, Bruno. 2005. "Post-Maoism: Badiou and politics," *Positions*, 13/3: 575–634.

Boswell, James. 1998 [1791]. *Life of Johnson*, Oxford: Oxford University Press.

Bourdet, Claude. 1957. "The French left," *Universities and Left Review*, 1/1: 13–17.

Bourdieu, Pierre. 1986. *Distinction: A Social Critique of the Judgment of Taste*, trans. Richard Nice, London: Routledge & Kegan Paul.

Bourg, Julian. 2007. *From Revolution to Ethics: May 1968 and Contemporary French Thought*, Montreal: McGill-Queen's University Press.

Bourseiller, Christophe. 2008 [1996]. *Les Maoistes: La folle histoire des Gardes Rouges français*, Paris: Plon.

Bradley, James E. 1989. "The Anglican pulpit, the social order, and the resurgence of Toryism during the American revolution," *Albion* 21: 361–81.

——1990. *Religion, Revolution, and English Radicalism: Nonconformity in Eighteenth Century Politics and Society*, Cambridge: Cambridge University Press.

Branch, Lori. 2006. *Rituals of Spontaneity: Sentiment and Secularism from Free Prayer to Wordsworth*, Waco, TX: Baylor University Press.

Brannigan, John. 2003. *Orwell to the Present: Literature in England, 1945–2000*, London: Palgrave.

Brennan, Timothy. 2006. *Wars of Position: Cultural Politics of Left and Right*, New York: Columbia University Press.

Brick, Howard. 2006. *Transcending Capitalism: Visions of a New Society in Modern American Thought*, Ithaca, NY: Cornell University Press.

Brissenden, R. F. 1974. *Virtue in Distress: Studies in the Novel of Sentiment from Richardson to Sade*, New York: Barnes & Noble.

Brown, John. 1751. *Essays on the Characteristics*, London: C. Davis.

——1763. *A Dissertation on the Rise, Union, and Power, the Progressions, Separations, and Corruptions of Poetry and Music*, London: L. Davis & C. Reymers.

Brydon, Diana. 1987. *Christina Stead*, London: Macmillan.

Buckridge, Patrick. 1995. "'Greatness' and Australian literature in the 1930s and 1940s: novels by Elinor Dark and Barnard Eldershaw," *Australian Literary Studies*, 17: 29–37.

——1998. "Clearing a space for Australian literature, 1940–1965," in *The Oxford Literary History of Australia*, eds. Bruce Bennett and Jennifer Strauss, Melbourne: Oxford University Press: 169–93.

Burke, Edmund. 2003 [1790]. *Reflections on the Revolution in France*, New Haven, CT: Yale University Press.

Burney, Frances. 1988. *The Early Journals and Letters of Fanny Burney*, Vol. I, *1768–1773*, eds. Lars E. Troide and Stewart J. Cooke, Kingston and Montreal: McGill-Queen's University Press.

Burnshaw, Stanley. 1962. "The three revolutions of modern poetry," in *Varieties of Literary Experience: Eighteen Essays in World Literature*, ed. Stanley Burnshaw, New York: New York University Press: 138.

Butler, Joseph. 1860 [1726]. *Fifteen Sermons preached at the Rolls Chapel*, New York: Robert Carter.

Carlson, Carl Lennart. 1938. *The First Magazine: A History of the Gentleman's Magazine*, Providence, RI: Brown University Press.

Casanova, Pascale. 1999. *The World Republic of Letters*, trans. M. B. Debevoise, Cambridge, MA: Harvard University Press.

Cauldwell, Christopher. 1970. *Romance and Realism: A Study in English Bourgeois Realism*, Princeton, NJ: Princeton University Press.

Champion, J. A. I. 1992. *The Pillars of Priestcraft Shaken: The Church of England and its Enemies, 1660–1730*, Cambridge: Cambridge University Press.

Christofferson, Michael Scott. 2004. *French Intellectuals against the Left: The Antitotalitarian Moment of the 1970's*, Oxford: Berghahn Books.

Churchill, Charles. 1956. *The Poetical Works of Charles Churchill*, ed. Douglas Grant, Oxford: Clarendon Press.

Cingolani, Patrick. 2003. *La République, les sociologues et la question politique*, Paris: Dispute.

Clark, J. C. D. 1985. *English Society, 1688–1832: Ideology, Social Structure, and Political Practice during the Ancien Regime*, Cambridge: Cambridge University Press.

——1994a. *The Language of Liberty, 1660–1832: Political Discourse and Social Dynamics in the Anglo-American World*, Cambridge: Cambridge University Press.

——1994b. *Samuel Johnson: Literature, Religion, and English Cultural Politics from the Restoration to Romanticism*, Cambridge: Cambridge University Press.

Clark, T. J. 1973. *Image of the People: Gustave Courbet and the 1848 Revolution*, Princeton, NJ: Princeton University Press.

Coates, Ken and Tony Topham (eds.). 1970. *Workers' Control*, London: Panther.

Cochrane, J. A. 1964. *Dr. Johnson's Printer: The Life of William Strahan*, Cambridge, MA: Harvard University Press.

Cole, G. D. H. 1957. "What is happening to British capitalism?" *University and New Left Review*, 1/1: 24–7.

Connor, Steven. 1996. *The English Novel in History, 1950–1995*, London: Routledge.

Cookson, J. E. 1982. *The Friends of Peace: Anti-war Liberalism in England, 1793–1815*, Cambridge: Cambridge University Press.

Coppard, Kit et al. 1961. "Television supplement," *New Left Review*, 7: 30–47.

Cornwall, Robert. 1993. *Visible and Apostolic: The Constitution of the Church in High Church Anglican and Nonjuror Thought*, Newark, DE: University of Delaware Press.

——2005. "Charles Leslie and the political implications of theology," in *Religious Identities in Britain, 1660–1832*, eds. William Gibson and Robert G. Ingram, London: Ashgate: 28–42.

Cox, Jeffrey N. 1998. *Poetry and Politics in the Cockney School: Keats, Shelley, Hunt and their Circle*, Cambridge: Cambridge University Press.

Crosland, Anthony. 1956. *The Future of Socialism*, London: Jonathan Cape.

Cusset, François. 2003. *French Theory: Foucault, Derrida, Deleuze & cie et les mutations de la vie intellectuelle aux Etats-Unis*, Paris: Decouverte.

Damrosch, David. 2003. *What is World Literature?* Princeton, NJ: Princeton University Press.

Darbishire, Helen (ed.). 1965. *The Early Lives of Milton*, New York: Barnes & Noble.

Davis, Mike. 1990. *City of Quartz: Excavating the Future in Los Angeles*, London: Verso.

Denning, Michael. 1996. *The Cultural Front: The Laboring of American Culture in the Twentieth Century*, London: Verso.

Deutscher, Isaac. 1971. *Marxism in our Time*, San Francisco, CA: Ramparts.

Dickens, Bruce. 1929. "Dr James's powder," *Life and Letters*, 2: 36–47.

Dickey, Laurence. 1987. *Hegel: Religion, Economics and the Politics of Spirit, 1777–1807*, Cambridge: Cambridge University Press.

Disraeli, Isaac. 1849. "Literary anecdotes," in *Curiosities of Literature*, 3 vols, 14th edn, London: E. Moxon, Vol. III: 300–3.

Doherty, F. C. 1992. *A Study in Eighteenth Century Advertising Methods: The Anodyne Necklace*, Lewiston, NY: Edwin Mellen Press.

Draper, John William. 1924. *William Mason: A Study in Eighteenth Century Culture*, New York: New York University Press.

Duitz, James M. 1968. *The Works of John Nichols: An Introduction*, New York: AMS Press.

During, Simon. 2006. "Is cultural studies a discipline? Does it matter?" *Cultural Politics*, 2/2: 265–81.

——2007. "Mimic toil: eighteenth-century preconditions for the modern historical re-enactment," *Rethinking History: a Special Issue on Re-enactment* 11: 313–33.

Dworkin, Dennis. 1997. *Cultural Marxism in Postwar Britain: History, the New Left, and the Origins of Cultural Studies*, Durham, NC: Duke University Press.

Eagleton, Terry. 1970. *Exiles and Emigrés: Studies in Modern Literature*, New York: Shocken Press.

——1976. *Criticism and Ideology: a Study in Marxist Literary Theory*, London: New Left Books.

Easthope, Antony. 1988. *British Post-structuralism since 1968*, London: Routledge.

Eaves, T. C. Duncan and Ben D. Kimpel. 1971. *Samuel Richardson: A Biography*, Oxford: Clarendon Press.

Eddy, Donald D. 1976. "John Brown, 'the Columbus of Keswick'," *Modern Philology*, 73: 74–84.

Eger, Elizabeth (ed.). 2001. *Women, Writing, and the Public Sphere, 1700–1830*, Cambridge: Cambridge University Press.

Elbaum, Max. 2002. *Revolution in the Air: Sixties Radicals turn to Lenin, Mao and Che*, London: Verso.

Elliott, Gregory. 1998. *Perry Anderson: the Merciless Laboratory of History*, Minneapolis, MN: University of Minnesota Press.

Ellison, Julie. 1999. *Cato's Tears and the Making of Anglo-American Emotion*, Chicago: University of Chicago Press.

Engelsing, Rolf. 1974. *Der Bürger als Leser: Lesergeschichte in Deutschland 1500–1800*, Stuttgart: Metzlersche.

Erskine-Hill, Howard. 1982 "Literature and the Jacobite cause: was there a rhetoric of Jacobitism?" in *Ideology and Conspiracy: Aspects of Jacobitism, 1689–1759*, ed. Eveline Cruickshanks, Edinburgh: John Donald: 49–70.

Evans, Arthur William. 1932. *Warburton and the Warburtonians: A Study in some Eighteenth Century Controversies*, London: Oxford University Press.

Feather, John. 1985. *The Provincial Book Trade in Eighteenth Century England*, Cambridge and New York: Cambridge University Press,

Ferdinand, C. Y. 1997. *Benjamin Collins and the Provincial Newspaper Trade in the Eighteenth Century*, Oxford and New York: Oxford University Press.

Fergus, Jan. 2006. *Provincial Readers in Eighteenth Century England*, Oxford: Oxford University Press.

Fergus, Jan and Ruth Portner. 1987. "Provincial bookselling in eighteenth-century England: the case of John Clay reconsidered," *Studies in Bibliography*, 40: 157–63.

Fielding, Henry. 2001 [1742]. *Joseph Andrews*, ed. Paul A. Scanlon, Peterborough, Ontario: Broadview Press.

Folkenflik, Robert. 2000. "The return of the Jacobites and other Johnsonian topics," *Eighteenth Century Studies*, 33/2: 289–99.

Foley, Barbara. 1990. "Women and the left in the 1930s," *American Literary History*, 2/1: 150–69.

Forest, Philippe. 1995. *Histoire de tel quel 1960–1982*, Paris: Seuil.

Fox, Ralph. 1944. *The Novel and the People*, London: Cobbett Press.

Gadamer, Hans Georg. 2006 [1972]. *Truth and Method*, 2nd edn, trans. Joel Weinsheimer and Donald. G. Marshall, New York: Continuum.

Gallagher, Catherine. 1994. *Nobody's Story: the Vanishing Acts of Women Writers in the Marketplace, 1670–1820*, Berkeley, CA: University of California Press.

Gardiner, Judith Kegan. 1989. *Rhys, Stead, Lessing, and the Politics of Empathy*, Bloomington, IN: Indiana University Press.

Gauchet, Marcel. 2007. *L'avènement de la démocratie. La revolution moderne*, Paris: Gallimard.

Geering, R. G. 1990. "From the personal papers of Christina Stead: extracts and commentaries," *Southerly*, 50: 399–455.

Gerhardt, Uta. 2002. *Talcott Parsons: An Intellectual Biography*, New York and Cambridge: Cambridge University Press.

Gerrard, Christine. 1994. *The Patriot Opposition to Walpole: Politics, Poetry, and National Myth, 1725–1742*, Oxford: Clarendon Press.

Gibson, William. 2001. *The Church of England, 1688–1832: Unity and Discord*, London: Routledge.

Gikandi, Simon. 1996. *Maps of Englishness: Writing Identity in the Culture of Colonialism*, New York: Columbia University Press.

Gilbert, Jeremy. 2008. *Anticapitalism and Culture: Radical Theory and Popular Politics*, Oxford: Berg.

Glendon, Mary Ann. 1991. *Rights Talk: The Impoverishment of Political Discourse*, New York: Free Press.

Godwin, William. 1985 [1793]. *Enquiry concerning Political Justice, and its Influence on Modern Morals and Happiness*, Harmondsworth and New York: Penguin.

Goldmann, Lucien. 1964. *The Hidden God: a Study of the Tragic Vision in the Pensées of Pascal and the Tragedies of Racine*, trans. Philip Thody, London: Routledge & Kegan Paul.

Goldsmith, Oliver. 1904. *The Miscellaneous Works of Oliver Goldsmith*, ed. David Masson, London: Macmillan.

——1974 [1766]. *The Vicar of Wakefield: A Tale supposed to be written by Himself*, ed. Arthur Friedman, London: Oxford University Press.

Green, E. H. H. 2006. *Thatcher*, London: Hodder Arnold.

Green, H. M. 1971. *A History of Australian Literature*, Vol. II, *1923–1955*, Sydney: Angus & Robertson.

Greene, Donald. 1977. "Latitudinarianism and sensibility: the genealogy of the 'man of feeling' reconsidered," *Modern Philology*, 75: 159–83

Gregory, Jeremy. 1991. "Anglicanism and the arts: religion, culture and politics in the eighteenth century," in *Culture, Politics and Society in Britain, 1660–1800*, eds. Jeremy Black and Jeremy Gregory, Manchester: Manchester University Press: 82–109.

——2000. *Restoration, Reformation, and Reform, 1660–1828: Archbishops of Canterbury and their Diocese*, Oxford: Oxford University Press.

Gruel, Louis. 2004. *La Rébellion de '68: une relecture sociologique*, Rennes: Presses Universitaires de Rennes.

Gunster, Shane. 2004. *Capitalizing on Culture: Critical Theory for Cultural Studies*. Toronto: University of Toronto Press.

Guest, Harriet. 1989. *A Form of Sound Words: the Religious Poetry of Christopher Smart*, Oxford: Clarendon Press.

Habermas, Jürgen. 2007. "The secular liberal state and religion," in *Political Theologies: Public Religions in a Post-secular World*, eds. Hent de Vries and Lawrence E. Sullivan, New York: Fordham University Press: 251–61.

Haksar, Vinit. 1979. *Equality, Liberty and Perfectionism*, Oxford: Oxford University Press.

Hall, Gary and Birchall, Claire (eds.). 2007. *New Cultural Studies: Adventures in Theory*, Edinburgh: Edinburgh University Press.

Hall, Stuart. 1968. "The new revolutionaries," in *From Culture to Revolution: The Slant Symposium, 1967*, eds. Terry Eagleton and Brian Wicker, London: Sheed & Ward: 182–222.

——1972. "The determinations of news photographs," *Working Papers in Cultural Studies*, 3: 53–89.

——1979. "Culture, the media and the 'ideological effect'," in *Mass Communication and Society*, ed. James Curran, Michael Gurevitch and Janet Woollacott, London: Sage: 315–48.

——1980. "Cultural studies and the centre: some problematics and problems," in *Culture, Media, Language: Working Papers in Cultural Studies, 1972–1979*, eds. Stuart Hall et al., London: Hutchinson: 15–47.

——1988. *The Hard Road to Renewal: Thatcherism and the Crisis of the Left*, London: Verso.

——1989. "The 'first' New Left: life and times," in *Out of Apathy: Voices of the New Left Thirty Years On*, ed. Robin Archer et al., London: Verso: 11–38.

Hall, Stuart, Charles Chritcher, Tony Jefferson, John Clarke and Brian Roberts. 1978. *Policing the Crisis: Mugging, the State and Law and Order*, London: Palgrave Macmillan.

Hallward, Peter. 2003. *Badiou: a Subject to Truth*, Minneapolis, MN: University of Minnesota Press.

Hambridge, Roger A. 1982. "'Empiricomany, an infatuation in favour of empiricism or quackery': The Socio-Economics of Eighteenth-Century Quackery," in *Literature and Science and Medicine: Papers Read at the Clark Library Summer Seminar, 1981*, Los Angeles: William Andrews Clark Memorial Library: 47–102.

Hamon, Hervé and Patrick Rotman. 1987. *Génération 1. Les années de rêve. Récit*, Paris: Seuil.

——1988. *Génération 2. Les années de poudre. Récit*, Paris: Seuil.

Hargreaves, A. S. 1997. "Some later seventeenth-century book trade activities," *Quadrat* 6: 3–6.

Harris, Michael. 1981. "Periodicals and the book trade," in *Development of the English Book Trade, 1700–1899*, Oxford: Oxford Polytechnic Press: 71–92.

Hartley, David. 1759. *Observations on Man, his Frame, his Duty, and his Expectations in Two Parts*, London and Bath: printed by S. Richardson for James Leake and Wm. Frederick in Bath and sold by Charles Hitch and Stephen Austin, Booksellers in London.

Hartman, Geoffrey. 1997. *The Fateful Question of Culture*, New York: Columbia University Press.

Harvey, David, 2006. *Spaces of Global Capitalism: Towards a Theory of Uneven Geographical Development*, London: Verso.

Hazlitt, William. 1902 [1850]. *Winterslow: Essays and Characters Written There*, London: Grant Richards.

Heidegger, Martin. 1978 [1926]. *Being and Time*, trans. John Macquarrie and Edward Robinson, Oxford: Blackwell.

Helvétius, Claude Adrian. 1777. *On Man: his Intellectual Faculties and his Education*, trans. W. Hooper, London: B. Law & G. Robinson.

Hennessy, Peter. 1994. *Never Again: Britain, 1945–1951*, New York: Pantheon.

Hernland, Patricia. 1994. "Three bankruptcies in the London book trade, 1746–1761: Rivington, Knapton and Osborn," in *Writers, Books, and Trade: An Eighteenth Century English Miscellany for Willam B. Todd*, ed. O. M. Brack, Jr, New York: AMS Press: 77–123.

Higgins, Ian. 1991. *Swift's Politics: the Propertied Englishman*, Cambridge: Cambridge University Press.

Hindess, Barry. 1971. *The Decline of Working Class Politics*, London: Paladin.

Hirschman, Albert. O. 1970. *Exit, Voice, and Loyalty: Responses to Decline in Firms, Organizations, and States*, Cambridge, MA: Harvard University Press.

——1977. *The Passions and the Interests: Political Arguments for Capitalism before its Triumph*, Princeton, NJ: Princeton University Press.

Hirst, Paul Q. (ed.). 1989. *Pluralist Theory of the State: Selected Writing of G. D. H. Cole, J. N. Figgis and H. J. Laski*, London: Routledge.

Hoadly, Benjamin. 1773. *The Works of Benjamin Hoadly*, 3 vols, ed. John Hoadly, London: printed by W. Bowyer and J. Nichols and sold by R. Horsfield.

Hoesel-Uhlig, Stefan. 2004. "Changing fields: the directions of Goethe's *Weltliteratur*," in *Debating World Literature*, ed. Christopher Prendergast. London: Verso: 26–53.

Hoggart, Richard. 1958. "Speaking for ourselves," in *Conviction*, ed. Norman Mackenzie, London: MacGibbon & Kee: 121–38.

Hollinghurst, Alan. 2004. *The Line of Beauty*, London: Picador.

Holmes, Geoffrey S. 1982. *Augustan England: Professions, State and Society, 1680–1730*, London: Allen & Unwin, 1982.

Horn, Gerd-Rainer. 2007. *The Spirit of '68: Rebellion in Western Europe and North America, 1956–1976*, New York: Oxford University Press.

Hunter, Ian. 2006. "The history of theory," *Critical Inquiry*, 33: 78–112.

——2007. "The time of theory," *Postcolonial Studies*, 2007: 5–22.

Hurd, Richard. 1811. *The Works of Richard Hurd, D.D., Lord Bishop of Worcester*, 8 vols, London: T. Cadell & W. Davies.

——1995. *The Early Letters of Bishop Richard Hurd, 1739–1762*, ed. Sarah Brewer, Rochester: Boydell & Brewer.

Husserl, Edmund. 1965 [1935]. *Phenomenology and the Crisis of Philosophy*, trans. Quentin Lauer, New York: Harper & Row.

Ingram, Robert G. 2005. "William Warburton, divine action, and enlightened Christianity," in *Religious Identities in Britain, 1660–1832*, eds. William Gibson and Robert. G. Ingram, London: Ashgate: 97–117.

Isaac, Peter 1998. "Charles Elliot and Spilsbury's Antiscorbutic Drops," in *The Reach of Print: Making, Selling, and Using Books*, eds. Peter Isaac and Barry McKay, Delaware: Oak Knoll Press: 157–74.

Isserman, Maurice. 1987. *If I had a Hammer. … the Death of the Old Left and the birth of the New Left*, New York: Basic Books.

Jackson, Timothy P. 1999. *Love Disconsoled: Meditations on Christian Charity*, Cambridge: Cambridge University Press.

Jacob, W. M. 1996. *Lay People and Religion in the early Eighteenth Century*, Cambridge: Cambridge University Press.

Jambet, Christian and Guy Lardreau. 1975. *L'Ange: Ontology de la revolution* 1, *Pour une cynégétique du semblant*, Paris: Bernard Grasset.

James, Henry. 1977 [1886]. *The Princess Casamassima*, Harmondsworth: Penguin.

Jarrell, Randall. 1975. "An unread book," in Christina Stead, *The Man Who Loved Children*, Harmondsworth: Penguin Books: 1–42.

Jay, Martin. 2005. *Songs of Experience: Modern American and European Variations on a Universal Theme*, Berkeley, CA: University of California Press.

Jenkins, Peter. 1987. *Mrs Thatcher's Revolution: The Ending of the Socialist Era*, London: Jonathan Cape.

Johnson, Samuel. 1952 [1781]. *Lives of the Poets*, ed. and intro. Arthur Waugh, 2 vols, Oxford: Oxford University Press.

Jones, Chris. 1993. *Radical Sensibility: Literature and Ideas in the 1790s*, London: Routledge.

Jordens, Ann-Mari. 1979. *The Stenhouse Circle: Literary Life in mid-Nineteenth Century Sydney*, Carlton, Vic.: Melbourne University Press.

Justice, George. 2002. *The Manufacturers of Literature: Writing and the Literary Marketplace in Eighteenth-Century England*, Newark, DE: University of Delaware Press.

Kapp, Yvonne. 2003. *Time will Tell: Memoirs*, eds. Charmain Brinson and Betty Lewis, London: Verso.

Keen, Paul. 1999. *The Crisis of Literature in the 1790s: Print Culture and the Public Sphere*, Cambridge: Cambridge University Press.

Kenny, Michael. 1995. *The First New Left: British Intellectuals after Stalin*, London: Lawrence & Wishart.

Khilnani, Sunil. 1993. *Arguing Revolution: The Intellectual Left in Postwar France*, New Haven, CT: Yale University Press.

Knapp, Lewis Mansfield. 1949. *Tobias Smollett, Doctor of Men and Manners*, Princeton, NJ: Princeton University Press.

Kojève, Alexandre. 1969 [1934]. *Introduction to the Reading of Hegel: Lectures on the Phenomenology of Spirit*, trans. James. H. Nichols, Jr. New York: Basic Books.

Kuhn, Rick. 2007. *Henryk Grossman and the Recovery of Marxism*, Urbana, IL: University of Illinois Press.

Kynaston, David. 2007. *Austerity Britain*, London: Bloomsbury.

Ladreau, Guy. 1973. *Le Singe d'or*, Paris: Mercure de France.

Laing, Stuart. 1986. *Representations of Working-class Life, 1957–1964*, London: Macmillan.

Langford, Paul. 1991. *Public Life and the Propertied Englishman, 1689–1798*, Oxford: Clarendon Press.

——1998. *A Polite and Commercial People: England, 1727–1783*, Oxford: Oxford University Press.

Lawson, Alan. 1987. "The Recognition of National Literatures: the Canadian and Australian Examples," PhD thesis, St Lucia: University of Queensland.

Le Goff, Jean-Pierre. 1998. *Mai '68: L'héritage impossible*, Paris: Découverte.

Lenin, V. I. 1932. *On Britain*, Moscow: Foreign Languages Publishing House.

Lessing, Doris, 1991. *The Golden Notebook*, New York: Harper.

Lever, Susan. 2003. "Christina Stead's workship in the novel: how to write a 'novel of strife'," *Journal of the Association for the Study of Australian Literature*, 2: 81–91.

Levine, Joseph M. 1991. *The Battle of the Books: History and Literature in the Augustan Age*, Ithaca, NY: Cornell University Press.

Linhart, Robert. 1981. *The Assembly Line*, trans. Margaret Crosland, Amherst, MA: University of Massachusetts Press.

Looker, Robert. 1995. "A golden past? The Labour Party and the working class, 1945," in *Labour's Promised Land? Culture and Society in Labour's Britain, 1945–1951*, ed. Jim Fyrth, London: Lawrence & Wishhart: 28–42.

Lukács, Georg 1971 [1923]. *History and Class Consciousness*, trans. David Livingstone, London: Merlin Press.

Mackenzie, Henry. 1967 [1771]. *The Man of Feeling*, ed. Brian Vickers, Oxford: Oxford University Press.

——1785. *The Lounger*, 20, url: www.english.upenn.edu.\~mgamer/Etexts/mackenzie.html.

McKitterick, David. 1992–2004. *A History of Cambridge University Press*, 3 vols, Cambridge: Cambridge University Press.

Mandeville, Bernard. 1988 [1705]. *The Fable of the Bees, or, Private Vices, Publick Benefits*, 2 vols, Indianapolis, IN: Liberty Classics.

Marcuse, Herbert. 1964. *One-dimensional Man: Studies in the Ideology of Advanced Industrial Society*, Boston, MA: Beacon Press.

——1988 [1968]. *Negations: Essays in Critical Theory*, trans. Jeremy J. Shapiro, London: Free Association Books.

Marr, David and Wilkinson, Marian. 2003. *Dark Victory: The Tampa and the Military Campaign to Re-elect the Prime Minister*, Sydney: Allen & Unwin.

Marx, Karl. 2005 [1848]. *The Communist Manifesto*, New York: Digireads.com.

Maslen, K. I. D. 1993. *An Early London Printing House at Work: Studies in the Bowyer Ledgers*, New York: Bibliographical Society of America.

——1994. "Slaves or freemen? The case of William Bowyer, father and son, printers, of London, 1699–1777," in *Writers, Books, and Trade: An Eighteenth Century English Miscellany for Willam B. Todd*, ed. O. M. Brack, Jr, New York: AMS Press: 145–55.

Mather, F. C. 1992. *High Church Prophet: Bishop Samuel Horsley. 1733–1806, and the Caroline Tradition in the later Georgian Church*, Oxford: Clarendon Press.

Mayhew, Robert. 2000. "William Gilpin and the latitudinarian picturesque," *Eighteenth Century Studies*, 33: 349–66.

McDowell, Paula. 1998. *The Women of Grub Street: Press, Politics, and Gender in the London Literary Marketplace, 1678–1730*, Oxford: Oxford University Press.

——2002. "Enlightenment enthusiasms and the spectacular failure of the Philadelphian Society," *Eighteenth Century Studies*, 35: 515–33.

Meier, Heinrich. 1995. *Carl Schmitt and Leo Strauss: their Hidden Dialogue*, trans. J. Harvey Lomax, Chicago: University of Chicago Press.

Mikhail, E. H. 1993. (ed.). *Goldsmith: Interviews and Recollections*, Basingstoke and New York: Macmillan.

Milbank, John. 2006. *Theology and Social Theory*, 2nd edn, Oxford: Blackwell.

——2007. "The return of mediation, or, The ambivalence of Alain Badiou," *Angelaki: Journal of the Theoretical Humanities*, 12/1: 127–43.

——2008. "Red Toryism is the best hope of a new progressive politics," *Guardian*, Thursday May 22.

Miliband, Ralph. 1958. "The transition to the transition," *New Reasoner*, 6: 35–48.

Miller, James. 1987. *"Democracy is in the Streets": From Port Huron to the Siege of Chicago*, New York: Simon & Schuster.

Miller, Peter N. 2001. "The 'antiquarianization' of biblical scholarship and the London Polyglot Bible, 1653–1657," *Journal of the History of Ideas*, 62: 463–82.

Mitchell, Adrian. 1981. "Fiction," in *The Oxford History of Australian Literature*, ed. Leonie Kramer, Oxford: Oxford University Press: 132–38.

Monro, Donald. 1788. *A Treatise on Medical and Pharmaceutical Chymistry, and the Materia Medica*, 3 vols, London: T. Cadell.

Moschanos, Gerassimos. 2002. *In the Name of Social Democracy*, trans. Gregory Elliott, London: Verso.

Mui, Hoh-cheung and Mui, Lorna. 1989. *Shops and Shopkeeping in Eighteenth-Century England*, Kingston, Ont.: McGill-Queen's University Press; London: Routledge.

Mullan, John. 1988. *Sentiment and Sociability: The Language of Feeling in the Eighteenth Century*, Oxford: Oxford University Press.

Murdoch, Iris. 1958. "The house of theory," in *Conviction*, ed. Norman Mackenzie, London: MacGibbon & Kee: 298–315.

Murray, Nicholas. 1997. *A Life of Matthew Arnold*, New York: St Martin's Press.

Nairn, Tom. 1965a. "The nature of the Labour Party," in *Towards Socialism*, eds. Perry Anderson and Robin Blackburn, London: Fontana: 159–217.

——1965b. "Labour imperialism," *New Left Review*, 32: 3–16.

Nichol, Donald W. 1992. *Pope's Literary Legacy: The Book Trade Correspondence of William Warburton and John Knapton, with other Letters and Documents, 1744–1780*, Oxford: Oxford Bibliographical Society.

Nichols, John. 1812. *Literary Anecdotes of the Eighteenth Century; Comprizing Biographical Memoirs of William Bowyer, Printer, F.S.A., and Many of his Learned Friends; an Incidental View of the Progress and Advancement of Literature in this Kingdom during the last Century; and Biographical Anecdotes of a Considerable Number of Eminent Writers and Ingenious Artists; with a very copious Index*, 6 vols, London: printed for the author, by Nichols Son & Bentley.

Nietzsche, Friedrich Wilhelm. 1986 [1878]. *Human, All Too Human: A Book for Free Spirits*, trans. R. J. Hollingdale, Cambridge: Cambridge University Press.

Nile, Richard. 1990. "Cartels, capitalism and the Australian book trade," *Continuum*, 4/1: 71–91.

Nockles, Peter. 1994. *The Oxford Movement in Context: Anglican Highchurchmanship, 1760–1857*, Cambridge: Cambridge University Press.

North, Michael. 2004. "World War II: the city in ruins," in *The Cambridge History of Twentieth-Century Literature*, ed. Laura Marcus and Peter Nicholls, Cambridge: Cambridge University Press: 436–52.

Nussbaum, Martha C. 1995. *Poetic Justice: The Literary Imagination and Public Life*, Boston, MA: Beacon Press.

Nygren, Anders. 1953. *Agape and Eros*, trans. Philip S. Watson, London: SPCK.

Oakeshott, Michael. 1933. *Experience and its Modes*, Cambridge: Cambridge University Press.

Page, Anthony. 2003. *John Jebb and the Enlightenment: Origins of British Radicalism*, Westport, CT: Praeger.

Paine, Thomas. 1969 [1792]. *The Rights of Man*, ed. Henry Collins, London: Penguin.

Peacock, Thomas Love. 1947 [1861]. *Gryll Grange*, Harmondsworth: Penguin.

Pells, Richard. 1973. *Radical Visions and American Dreams: Culture and Social Thought in the Depression Years*, Middletown, CT: Wesleyan University Press.

Pender, Anne. 2002. *Christina Stead, Satirist*, Altona, Vic: Common Ground.

Pfister, Joel. 2006. *Critique for What? Cultural Studies, American Studies, Left Studies*, Boulder, CO: Paradigm Publishers.

Philip, André. 1967. *Les Socialistes*, Paris: Seuil.

Piozzi, Hester Lynch. 1794. *British Synonymy, or, An Attempt at Regulating the Choice of Words in Familiar Conversation*, 2 vols, London: G. G. & J. Robinson.

Pocock, J. G. A. 1980. "Post-puritan England and the problem of Enlightenment," in *Culture and Politics from Puritanism to the Enlightenment*, ed. Perez Sagorin, Berkeley, CA: University of California Press.

——1985a. *Virtue, Commerce and History*, Cambridge: Cambridge University Press.

——1985b. "Clergy and commerce: the conservative Enlightenment in England," in *L'età dei lumi: Studi storici sul settecento europeo in onore di Franco Venturi*, ed. Raffaele Ajello *et al.*, 2 vols, Naples: Jovene, 1: 523–62.

Porter, Roy. 2000. *Quacks: Fakers and Charlatans in English Medicine*, Stroud: Tempus.

Pottle, Frederick. 1925. "James's powder," *Notes and Queries*, 149: 11–12.

Priestley, Joseph. 1769. *Considerations on Church Authority, Occasioned by Dr. Balguy's Sermon on that Subject; Preached at Lambeth Chapel, and Published by Order of the Archbishop*, London: J. Johnson & J. Payne.

Putnam, Samuel. 1947. *Paris was our Mistress*, New York: Viking.

Quinton, Anthony. 1978. *The Politics of Imperfection: The Religious and Secular Traditions of Conservative Thought in England from Hooker to Oakeshott*, London: Faber & Faber.

Radner, Gerald. 1959. *The Idea of Reform*, Cambridge: Cambridge University Press.

Ralph, James. 1762. *The Case of Authors by Profession or Trade, Stated; with Regard to Booksellers, the Stage and the Public*, London: R. Griffiths.

Raven, James. 1987. *British Fiction, 1750–1770*, Newark, DE: University of Delaware Press.

——2001. *Judging New Wealth: Popular Publishing and Responses to Commerce, 1750–1800*, Oxford: Oxford University Press.

Reeves, Margaret. 1969. *The Influence of Prophecy on the Later Middle Ages*, London: Oxford University Press.

Richards, Thomas, 1990. *The Commodity Culture of Victorian England: Advertising and Spectacle, 1851–1914*, Stanford, CA: Stanford University Press.

Richardson, Samuel. 1753–54. *Sir Charles Grandison, in a series of letters published by the editor of Pamela and Clarissa*, 7 vols, London: S. Richardson & J. Rivington.

Rideout, Walter. 1966. *The Radical Novel in the United States, 1900–1954*, Cambridge, MA: Harvard University Press.

Ritter, Joachim. 1982 [1957]. *Hegel and the French Revolution: Essays on the Philosophy of Right*, trans. Richard Dien Winfield, Cambridge, MA: MIT Press.

Robbins, Bruce. 1999. *Feeling Global: Internationalism in Distress*, New York: New York University Press.

Roberts, William. 1996. *A Dawn of Imaginative Feeling: The Contribution of John Brown, 1715–1766, to Eighteenth Century Thought and Literature*, Carlisle: Northern Academic Press.

Roscoe, S. 1973. *John Newbery and his Successors, 1740–1814: A Bibliography*, Wormley: Five Owls Press.

Ross, Kristin. 2002. *May '68 and its Afterlives*, Chicago, IL: University of Chicago Press.

Rousseau, Jean-Jacques, 1968 [1758]. *Politics and the Arts: Letter to M. D'Alembert on the Theatre*, trans. Allan Bloom. Ithaca, NY: Cornell University Press.

Rowley, Hazel. 1994. *Christina Stead: A Biography*, New York: Holt.

Rubin, Joan Shelley. 1992. *The Making of Middlebrow Culture*, Chapel Hill, NC: University of North Carolina Press.

Sack, James J. 1993. *From Jacobite to Conservative: Reaction and Orthodoxy in Britain, c. 1760–1832*, Cambridge: Cambridge University Press.

Said, Edward. 1994. *Culture and Imperialism*, New York: Knopf.

Sale, Kirkpatrick. 1973. *SDS*, New York: Random House.

Samuel, Raphael. 2006. *The Lost World of British Communism*, London: Verso.

Sanna, Guglielmo. 2005. "How heterodox was Benjamin Hoadly?" in *Religious Identities in Britain, 1660–1832*, eds. William Gibson and Robert. G. Ingram, London: Ashgate: 61–80.

Sedgwick, Peter. 1976. "The two new lefts," in David Widgery, ed., *The Left in Britain*, Harmondsworth: Penguin.

Seidman, Michael. 2004. *The Imaginary Revolution: Parisian Students and Workers in 1968*, Oxford: Berghahn Books.

Sharaf, Myron. 1983. *Fury on Earth: A Biography of Wilhelm Reich*, New York: St Martin's Press.

Shawcross, John T. (ed.). 1972. *Milton: The Critical Heritage, 1732–1801*, London: Routledge & Kegan Paul.

Sherbo, Arthur. 1967. *Christopher Smart, Scholar of the University*, East Lansing, MI: Michigan State University Press.

——1997. *Letters to Mr. Urban of the Gentleman's Magazine, 1751–1811*, Lewiston, NY: Edwin Mellen Press.

Sheridan, Susan. 1988. *Christina Stead*, Bloomington, IN: Indiana University Press.

Sheriff, John K. 1982. *The Good-natured Man: The Evolution of a Moral Ideal, 1660–1800*, University, AL: University of Alabama Press.

Shuttleworth, Alan. 1967. *Two Working Papers in Cultural Studies*, Birmingham: University of Birmingham Centre for Contemporary Cultural Studies.

Sinfield, Alan. 1997. *Literature, Politics and Culture in Postwar Britain*, London: Athlone Press.

Siskin, Clifford. 1998. *The Work of Writing: Literature and Social Change in Britain, 1700–1830*, Baltimore, MD: Johns Hopkins University Press.

Smart, Christopher. 1991. *The Annotated Letters of Christopher Smart*, eds. Betty Rizzo and Robert Mahony. Carbondale, IL: Southern Illinois University Press.

——1990. *Selected Poems*, eds. Karina Williamson and Marcus Walsh, London: Penguin Books.

St Clair, William. 2004. *The Reading Nation in the Romantic Period*, Cambridge: Cambridge University Press: 103–22.

Stanhope, Philip. 1777. *Miscellaneous Works of the late Philip Dormer Stanhope, Earl of Chesterfield: consisting of Letters to his Friends, never before Printed, and various other Articles. To which are prefixed, Memoirs of his Life*, ed. M. Maty, 3 vols, Dublin: W. Watson et al.

Stead, Christina. 1935. "The writers take sides", *Left Review*, 11: 455–57.

——1966. *Cotters' England*, London: Secker & Warburg.

——1981 [1934]. *Seven Poor Men of Sydney*, Sydney: Sirius Paperbacks.

——1982 [1936]. *The Beauties and the Furies*, London: Virago.

——1984. "Some deep spell: a view of Stanley Burnshaw," *Agenda*, 21/22: 125–39.

——1995. "Why I left," *Independent Monthly*, January: 42–43.

——2001. [1948] *Letty Fox: Her Luck*, New York: New York Review of Books.

——2005. *Dearest Munx: The Letters of Christina Stead and William J. Blake*, ed. Margaret Harris, Melbourne: Melbourne University Press.

Stephen, Leslie. 1962 [1876]. *History of English Thought in the Eighteenth Century*, 2 vols, New York: Harcourt Brace.

Sterne, Laurence 1987 [1768]. *A Sentimental Journey through France and Italy*, London: Penguin Books.

Stott, Anne. 2003. *Hannah More: the First Victorian*, Oxford: Oxford University Press.

Sutherland, Kathryn. 2000. "Writings on education and conduct: arguments for female improvement," in *Women and Literature in Britain, 1700–1800*, ed. Vivien Jones, Cambridge: Cambridge University Press: 25–46.

Taylor, Barbara. 2003. *Mary Wollstonecraft and the Feminist Imagination*, Cambridge: Cambridge University Press.

Taylor, Charles. 1968. "From Marxism to the dialogue society," in *From Culture to Revolution: The Slant Symposium, 1967*, eds. Terry Eagleton and Brian Wicker, London: Sheed & Ward: 148–81.

——1975. *Hegel*, Cambridge: Cambridge University Press.

——2007. *A Secular Age*, Cambridge, MA: Harvard University Press.

Thompson, E. P. 1959. "The New Left," *New Reasoner*, 9: 1–17.

——1968. *The Making of the English Working Class*, Harmondsworth: Penguin Books.

——1974. "Patrician society, plebeian culture," *Journal of Social History*, 7: 382–405.

Thompson, George. 1946 [1794]. *Slavery and Famine: Punishments for Sedition, or, An Account of the Miseries and Starvation at Botany Bay, by George Thompson, who sailed in the Royal Admiral, May, 1792, with some Preliminary Remarks by George Dyer, B.A., late of Emmanuel College Cambridge; Author of "Complaints of the Poor"* ed. George Mackaness, Sydney, privately printed.

Townsend, John Rowe. 1994. *John Newbery and his Books: Trade and Plumb Cake for Ever, Huzza!* Metuchen, NJ: Scarecrow Press.

Townsend, Joseph. 1971 [1786]. *A Dissertation on the Poor Laws by a Well-wisher to Mankind*, ed. Ashley Montagu, Berkeley, CA: University of California Press.

Turner, Catherine. 2003. *Marketing Modernism between the two World Wars*, Amherst, MA: University of Massachusetts Press.

Turner, Cheryl. 1992. *Living by the Pen: Women Writers in the Eighteenth Century*, New York: Routledge.

Wald, Alan M. 2002. *Exiles from a Future Time: The Forging of the mid-Twentieth Century Literary Left*, Chapel Hill, NC: University of North Carolina Press.

Walsh, John, Haydon, Colin and Taylor, Stephen (eds.). 1993. *The Church of England, c. 1689–c. 1833: From Toleration to Tractarianism*, Cambridge: Cambridge University Press.

Warburton, William. 1808. *Letters from a late eminent Prelate to one of his Friends*, Kidderminster: George Gower for T. Cadell & W. Davies.

Wardle, Ralph M. 1957. *Oliver Goldsmith*, Lawrence, KS: University of Kansas Press.

Warner, Rex. 1946. "The cult of power," in *The Cult of Power: Essays by Rex Warner*, London: John Lane: 7–21.

Watt, Ian. 2001 [1957]. *The Rise of the Novel: Studies in Defoe, Richardson and Fielding*, Berkeley, CA: University of California Press.

Watts, Carol. 2007. *The Cultural Work of Empire: The Seven Years' War and the Imagining of the Shandean State*, Edinburgh: Edinburgh University Press.

Weil, Simone. 2006 [1955]. *Oppression and Liberty*, trans. Arthur Wills and John Petrie, London: Routledge.

Welsh, Charles. 1885, *A Bookseller of the last Century, being some Account of the Life of John Newbery, and of the Books he published: with a Notice of the later Newberys*, London: Griffith, Farran, Okeden & Welsh.

Williams, Chris. 1989. *Christina Stead: A Life of Letters*, Melbourne: McPhee Gribble.

Williams, Raymond. 1958. *Culture and Society, 1780–1950*, London: Chatto & Windus.

——1961. *The Long Revolution*, Harmondsworth: Penguin Books.

——1976. *Keywords: A Vocabulary of Culture and Society*, London: Fontana.

——1977. *Marxism and Literature*, Oxford: Oxford University Press.

——1979. *Politics and Letters: Interviews with New Left Review*, London: New Left Books.

Williams, Raymond, Stuart Hall and E. P. Thompson. 1968. *May Day Manifesto*, Harmondsworth: Penguin Books.

Wimsatt, William K. 1965. *The Portraits of Alexander Pope*, New Haven, CT: Yale University Press.

Wolin, Sheldon. 2004. *Politics and Vision: Continuity and Innovation in Western Political Thought*, 2nd edn, Princeton, NJ: Princeton University Press.

Wollsterstorff, Nicholas. 2008. *Justice: Rights and Wrongs*, Princeton, NJ: Princeton University Press.

Woodard, Helen. 1999. *African-British Writings in the Eighteenth Century: The Politics of Race and Reason*, Westport, CT: Greenwood Press.

Woodring, Carl Ray. 1952. *Victorian Samplers: William and Mary Howitt*, Lawrence, KS: University of Kansas Press.

Wordsworth, William. 2000. *The Major Works, including the Prelude*, ed. Stephen Gill, Oxford: Oxford University Press.

Yadav, Alok. 2004. *Before the Empire of English: Literature, Provinciality and Nationalism in Eighteenth Century Britain*, London: Palgrave.

Yelin, Louise. 1998. *From the Margins of Empire: Christina Stead, Doris Lessing, Nadine Gordimer*, Ithaca, NY: Cornell University Press.

——1999. "Fifty years of reading: a reception study of *The Man Who Loved Children*," *Contemporary Literature*, 31/4: 472–98.

——2000. "Representing the 1930s: capitalism, phallocracy and the politics of the Popular Front in *The House of all Nations*," in *The Magic Phrase: Critical Essays on Christina Stead*, ed. Margaret Harris, Brisbane: University of Queensland Press: 70–88.

Yglesias, Jose. 1966. "Marking off a chunk of England," *The Nation*, October 24: 420–21.

Young, B. W. 1998. *Religion and Enlightenment in Eighteenth-Century England: Theological Debate from Locke to Burke*, Oxford: Clarendon Press.

Zachs, William, 1998. *The First John Murray and the late Eighteenth-Century London Book Trade, with a Checklist of his Publications*, Oxford: Oxford University Press.

Žižek, Slavoj, 2000. *The Fragile Absolute, or, Why is the Christian Legacy Worth Fighting for?* London: Verso.

Index